ALSO BY CHRIS WHIPPLE

The Spymasters:
How the CIA Directors Shape History and the Future

The Gatekeepers:
How the White House Chiefs of Staff Define Every Presidency

THE FIGHT OF HIS LIFE

INSIDE JOE BIDEN'S WHITE HOUSE

CHRIS WHIPPLE

SCRIBNER

New York   London   Toronto   Sydney   New Delhi

Scribner
An Imprint of Simon & Schuster, Inc.
1230 Avenue of the Americas
New York, NY 10020

First Scribner hardcover edition January 2023

SCRIBNER and design are registered trademarks of The Gale Group, Inc., used under license by Simon & Schuster, Inc., the publisher of this work.

For information about special discounts for bulk purchases, please contact Simon & Schuster Special Sales at 1-866-506-1949 or business@simonandschuster.com.

The Simon & Schuster Speakers Bureau can bring authors to your live event. For more information, or to book an event, contact the Simon & Schuster Speakers Bureau at 1-866-248-3049 or visit our website at www.simonspeakers.com.

Interior design by Davina Mock Maniscalco

Manufactured in the United States of America

10   9   8   7   6   5   4   3   2   1

Library of Congress Cataloging-in-Publication Data has been applied for.

ISBN 978-1-9821-0643-0
ISBN 978-1-9821-0645-4 (ebook)

To Cary

CONTENTS

CONTENTS

CAST OF CHARACTERS

FIRST FAMILY

Joseph R. Biden, president

Jill Biden, First Lady

Jimmy Biden, the president's brother

Valerie Biden Owens, the president's sister

SECOND FAMILY

Kamala Harris, vice president

Douglas Emhoff, Second Gentleman

THE TRANSITION

Bob Bauer, senior legal counsel, Biden campaign

Pat Cipollone, Trump White House counsel

Mary Gibert, federal transition coordinator at the General Services
Administration

Ted Kaufman, Biden transition chairman

Jared Kushner, Trump senior adviser

Christopher Liddell, Trump deputy chief of staff

David Marchick, director of the Center for Presidential Transition at the Partnership for Public Service

Mark Meadows, Trump chief of staff

Robert O'Brien, Trump national security adviser

Matt Pottinger, Trump deputy national security adviser

THE WHITE HOUSE

Kate Bedingfield, communications director

Brian Deese, director, National Economic Council

Mike Donilon, senior adviser

Anita Dunn, senior adviser

Ron Klain, chief of staff

Jennifer O'Malley Dillon, deputy chief of staff

Jen Psaki, press secretary

Bruce Reed, deputy chief of staff

Dana Remus, White House counsel

Steve Ricchetti, senior adviser

Susan Rice, director of the Domestic Policy Council

Cedric Richmond, senior adviser

Andy Slavitt, senior adviser to the coronavirus response coordinator

Louisa Terrell, director of Office of Legislative Affairs

Annie Tomasini, director of Oval Office operations

Jeffrey Zients, coronavirus response coordinator

VICE PRESIDENT'S OFFICE

Tina Flournoy, chief of staff

Philip Gordon, national security adviser

FIRST LADY'S OFFICE

Elizabeth Alexander, communications director

Anthony Bernal, senior adviser

Michael LaRosa, press secretary

NATIONAL SECURITY COUNCIL

Jake Sullivan, national security adviser

Yohannes Abraham, chief of staff

CENTRAL INTELLIGENCE AGENCY

William Burns, director

OFFICE OF THE DIRECTOR OF NATIONAL INTELLIGENCE

Avril Haines, director

STATE DEPARTMENT

Antony Blinken, secretary of state

Karen Donfried, assistant secretary of state for European and Eurasian affairs

Wendy Sherman, deputy secretary of state

Tom Sullivan, deputy chief of staff for policy

CLIMATE

John Kerry, Special Presidential Envoy for Climate

Gina McCarthy, White House national climate adviser

Jonathan Pershing, Deputy Special Envoy for Climate

Todd Stern, climate envoy to Barack Obama

PENTAGON

General Lloyd Austin, secretary of defense

General Mark Milley, chairman of the Joint Chiefs of Staff

CABINET

Marty Walsh, secretary of labor

CONGRESS

Cory Booker, senator (D-NJ)

Liz Cheney, representative (R-WY)

James Clyburn, representative (D-SC)

Christopher Dodd, former senator (D-CT)

Pramila Jayapal, representative (D-WA)

Joe Manchin, senator (D-WV)

Chuck Schumer, senator (D-NY) and Majority Leader

Kyrsten Sinema, senator (D-AZ)

FORMER WHITE HOUSE CHIEFS OF STAFF

James Jones (Lyndon Johnson)

Dick Cheney (Gerald Ford)

Jack Watson (Jimmy Carter)

James A. Baker III (Ronald Reagan)

Kenneth Duberstein (Ronald Reagan)

John Sununu (George H. W. Bush)

Samuel Skinner (George H. W. Bush)

Thomas F. "Mack" McLarty (Bill Clinton)

Leon Panetta (Bill Clinton)

Erskine Bowles (Bill Clinton)

John Podesta (Bill Clinton)

Andrew Card (George W. Bush)

Joshua Bolten (George W. Bush)

Rahm Emanuel (Barack Obama)

Pete Rouse (Barack Obama)

Bill Daley (Barack Obama)

Jack Lew (Barack Obama)

Denis McDonough (Barack Obama)

Reince Priebus (Donald Trump)

John Kelly (Donald Trump)

Mick Mulvaney (Donald Trump)

Mark Meadows (Donald Trump)

FORMER NATIONAL SECURITY OFFICIALS

Richard Armitage, deputy to Secretary of State Colin Powell

Jeremy Bash, former chief of staff, CIA and Pentagon

James Clapper, former Director of National Intelligence

Richard Clarke, counterterrorism adviser to Bill Clinton and George W. Bush

Anthony "Tony" Lake, national security adviser to Bill Clinton

John Negroponte, former Director of National Intelligence

Ronald Neumann, former U.S. ambassador to Afghanistan

Admiral James Stavridis, former NATO Supreme Allied Commander

MAYORS

Eric Adams, New York City

AFGHANISTAN

Ashraf Ghani, president

Sami Sadat, general

CHINA

Xi Jinping, president

Xie Zhenhua, climate envoy

EUROPE

Mario Draghi, prime minister of Italy

Andrzej Duda, president of Poland

Eduard Heger, prime minister of Slovakia

Boris Johnson, prime minister of Great Britain

Emmanuel Macron, president of France

Angela Merkel, outgoing chancellor of Germany

Olaf Scholz, chancellor of Germany

RUSSIA

Vladimir Putin, president

Alexander Bortnikov, head of the Federal Security Service

Valery Gerasimov, head of Russian General Staff

Sergey Lavrov, foreign minister

Nikolai Patrushev, secretary of the Security Council

Sergei Shoigu, defense minister

UKRAINE

Volodymyr Zelensky, president

Olena Zelenska, First Lady

THE FIGHT
OF HIS LIFE

INTRODUCTION

Joe Biden was worried. It was early November 2021 and he and his national security team were gathered in the Oval Office. For months, they'd watched with alarm as Vladimir Putin's troops amassed on the borders of Ukraine. Satellite photos showed tanks and armored columns poised to invade—from Belarus, Russia's vassal state in the north, to the Black Sea in the south. The drumbeat of intelligence had been constant. The President's Daily Brief, or PDB, included a set of indicators tracking how likely Russia was to invade; every week another indicator would be checked. Biden's private warnings to his NATO allies—France's Emmanuel Macron, Germany's Angela Merkel, her successor Olaf Scholz, and others—had been met with incredulity. It was all an audacious bluff, they insisted. Putin would never launch an unprovoked war against a democracy in the heart of Europe. Or would he?

Biden was awaiting the arrival of a man who might know the answer: his CIA director, William Burns. Outside of the Russian president's inner circle, no one knew Putin better. One of the most accomplished American diplomats of the last half century, Burns had served two stints in Moscow, the first when Putin was just coming into power, the second as ambassador from 2005 to 2008; he joked that his hair had turned white from years of trying to fathom the Russian leader. Two days earlier, Biden had sent his CIA director on a trip to Moscow with a message for Putin and his inner circle. Burns had just returned from that visit, a last-ditch effort to prevent war.

The U.S. intelligence agencies had cracked the code of Putin's invasion plan. Through a combination of signals intelligence (SIGINT), human intelligence (HUMINT), and satellite photography, the CIA had pieced together the puzzle. It wasn't a single "red lights flashing" moment but a steady accumulation of evidence that pointed to one thing: a full-scale Russian blitzkrieg. Putin's forces planned to encircle the capital city of Kyiv and, within forty-eight to seventy-two hours, decapitate the regime of President Volodymyr Zelensky. The CIA's pilfering of Putin's plan was an extraordinary intelligence coup—almost as remarkable as the agency's sleuthing during the 1962 Cuban Missile Crisis. Back then, purloined blueprints of Soviet missile sites, supplied by a turncoat Soviet intelligence officer named Oleg Penkovsky, along with aerial photographs from U-2 spy planes, had confirmed John F. Kennedy's worst fear: Offensive ballistic missiles had been installed on America's doorstep. The discovery put the world on the brink of nuclear war.

Putin's invasion of Ukraine, if it came, could be just as dangerous. Ninety thousand U.S. troops were stationed in NATO countries a stone's throw from Ukraine, and thousands more would soon be joining them. An errant missile or wayward bomb—or worse, a deliberate advance by Putin's troops across a NATO border—could trigger war between the U.S. and Russia, the world's dominant nuclear superpowers. An attack on one NATO member would be considered an attack on all, requiring a full U.S. military response.

Waiting for Burns with the president in the Oval Office were Jake Sullivan, the national security adviser; Antony Blinken, the secretary of state; Ron Klain, the White House chief of staff; and Avril Haines, the Director of National Intelligence (DNI).

The CIA director began his brief. Upon arriving at the Kremlin, he'd met first with Nikolai Patrushev, secretary of the Russian Security Council. To Burns's surprise, Patrushev was taken aback when he heard the details of Moscow's invasion plan; evidently Putin had kept this close adviser in the dark. Afterward Burns had met separately with three other members of Putin's inner circle. They blustered about the perfidy of the West and Russian military prowess; none bothered to deny that an invasion was in the works. Finally, Burns spoke with the Russian autocrat himself.

Isolated amid a resurgence of the COVID pandemic, Putin would speak with Burns only by telephone. The intelligence chief presented him with what the U.S. knew about his invasion plan and outlined severe sanctions that would result if he went ahead. When Burns had finished, the Russian leader replied in what Burns described as his "edgy, measured way." He was utterly dismissive of Zelensky, the former comic turned president of the largest democracy in Europe. Ukraine wasn't even a country and wouldn't fight, Putin said. He recounted a familiar list of grievances about Ukraine and U.S. policy over the years.

Burns told Biden that an invasion was all but inevitable. Putin was clearly and defiantly leaning in the direction of an irreversible decision to invade, he told the president. Strategically, Putin had convinced himself that his window was closing for shaping Ukraine's orientation. That's how Putin thought about it; this winter offered a favorable landscape. He didn't fear economic reprisals and believed he'd sanction-proofed his economy over the years. He thought the West was divided, the French preoccupied with an upcoming election, and the Germans with a political transition. Putin's sense of personal destiny was wrapped up intimately with his sense of Russia and Russia's purpose. He was fed up and ready to settle scores.

For Joe Biden, this was both an unexpected crisis and a test he'd been preparing for his entire career. As a senator during the Cold War and chairman of the Senate Foreign Relations Committee, he'd spent decades honing his national security credentials and taking the measure of the Kremlin's leaders; he'd been shaped by the decades-long, Manichaean struggle between the U.S. and the Soviet Union, mortal enemies poised on the edge of nuclear war. Now, thirty years after the Cold War's end, the showdown had resumed.

"If Moscow is allowed to get away with this, what will stop it from invading another country?" Biden posed the question to me in an interview I conducted with him almost a year later, in September 2022. "What will stop any country from invading a neighbor because it doesn't like their democracy, or believes it's somehow entitled to their territory? We can't let these things happen. The consequences would be catastrophic for the world."

It was a fight between good and evil. When Biden thought of Putin, he was reminded of the reason he'd run for president in the first place. In August 2017, white supremacists and neo-Nazis carrying torches had paraded in Charlottesville, Virginia, chanting, "Blood and Soil." Afterward the president of the United States had declared that there were "very fine people on both sides." Until that moment Biden had been undecided about entering the presidential race. But Donald Trump's declaration of moral equivalence had clinched his decision to run.

Presidents had said terrible things before, but Charlottesville was new territory. Biden felt Trump was giving evil a safe harbor. "This was dangerous," said Mike Donilon, one of Biden's closest advisers. "A door was opening that Biden needed to move fast to close." This was why he called his campaign a "battle for the soul of the nation." Every pollster told him to drop the phrase, but Biden didn't care; it was why he was running. Now evil forces like the ones he'd seen in Charlottesville were threatening the heart of Europe.

President now for just under a year, Biden had been focused on urgent domestic crises: a devastating pandemic, a crippled economy, and a homegrown insurrection. Over the longer run, Biden believed, the fate of civilization would hinge on the contest between democracy and autocracy, a twilight struggle that would span the twenty-first century. But, suddenly, here it was. The battle was about to be joined—with the survival of Europe and the West at stake, and even the risk of nuclear war.

Long before Russia threatened Ukraine, Joe Biden's life and career had been a fight—against adversity, tragedy, and bad luck. He'd lost his wife and infant daughter in a car crash; his son Beau to a brain tumor; two campaigns for the presidential nomination. "Get up!" his father had repeatedly told him—and he did, winning the presidency at last.

But this would truly be the fight of his life.

To understand it, you had to go back almost two years.

ONE

WHAT WILL YOU DO IF HE LOSES?

Joe Biden was restless. It was late April 2020, nearly seven months before the presidential election. Biden hadn't even won the Democratic nomination yet; only a few months earlier, after dismal showings in the Iowa Caucus and New Hampshire primary, pundits had declared his candidacy dead. But after a stunning victory in the South Carolina primary and a string of primary wins across the South, Biden was almost sure to be his party's nominee against Donald Trump. At his home in Wilmington, Delaware, Biden called up an old friend, Ted Kaufman, his next-door neighbor. "Want to go for a walk?" he asked.

Contrary to popular belief, presidential transitions don't begin upon the election of a new president; they start almost a year before. That is when the incumbent and the front-runner for the opposing party's nomination begin preparing for a transfer of power. On this spring morning, as he walked around a nearby schoolyard with his best friend, Kaufman, Joe Biden's transition had begun.

Kaufman, eighty-one, was Biden's confidant and alter ego. Lanky and slightly disheveled, with a twinkle in his eye, he resembled an older version of the actor John Lithgow. An engineer by training, Kaufman was like family; he'd been at Joe's side during his first successful race

THE FIGHT OF HIS LIFE

for councilman in New Castle, Delaware, in 1970. He'd been Biden's chief of staff on the Senate Foreign Relations Committee and was appointed to his Delaware Senate seat when Biden joined Barack Obama's ticket in 2008. For decades, Kaufman and Biden had sat together on Amtrak while commuting between Wilmington, Delaware, and Washington, D.C. "We were back and forth on the train for 4,000,827 hours," said Kaufman. "So we talked about *everything*."

Presidential transitions are herculean exercises. That's why Biden's team needed to start so early. More than 200 members of the incoming White House staff needed to be picked and readied to govern; 1,200 officials chosen and prepped for confirmation by the Senate; another 1,100, who don't require confirmation, recruited, vetted, and hired; executive orders written, tabletop crisis exercises conducted. Kaufman explained: "If you went to a corporate CEO and said, 'We're going to take away the very top managers in your organization. And then we're going to bring in a whole new team that has to go through an incredibly complicated selection process. Now let's make it the most complex organization in the history of the world. And then let's say that every one of your enemies around the world knows you're at your most vulnerable when you're turning it over.' Are you kidding? They'd *laugh* at you."

Often, as transitions go, so do presidencies; seamless cooperation with George W. Bush's team, beginning early in 2008, gave Barack Obama a running start when he took office in 2009. By contrast, the bobbled handoff from Bill Clinton to George W. Bush, delayed by legal battles during the tumultuous 2000 recount, was cited by the 9/11 Commission as having left Bush's national security team unprepared for the Al Qaeda attacks on September 11.

But the 2020 presidential transition was unique. It was the most contentious and dangerous since the Civil War. In his effort to remain in power, Trump tried to decapitate the Justice Department, threatened state election officials, pressured state legislators, terrorized local poll workers, and concocted slates of fake electors. When these measures failed, he incited a violent mob to attack the Capitol on January 6, 2021.

All of this happened in plain sight. Beneath the surface, another remarkable drama was playing out.

———

Donald Trump wanted no part of a presidential transition. In 2016, running against Hillary Clinton, when asked if he'd respect the results of the election, Trump had said he'd keep people "in suspense." By early 2020 there was no suspense; Trump would acknowledge only his own victory. How could a transition begin with a president unwilling to give up his office? The task would fall to a little-known White House staffer who worked steps away from the Oval Office. His success would depend on doing everything out of Donald Trump's sight.

Christopher Liddell was one of several assistants to the president—first in the so-called Office of American Innovation, then as deputy chief of staff for policy coordination. A New Zealand citizen, he'd come to the U.S. in 2001 to work for an Auckland-based paper company. He then jumped to the American sector, where he worked his way up to a position as chief financial officer of Microsoft and, later, vice chairman of General Motors.

Liddell, sixty-one, still spoke with a Kiwi accent, called everyone mate, and drove a bright red vintage 1960 Corvette convertible that stood out like a Christmas ornament among the limos and SUVs in the West Wing parking lot. But unlike other wealthy members of

Trump's team—Betsy DeVos, Wilbur Ross, Steve Mnuchin—Liddell kept a low profile; his passion was for *process*: organizing, managing, hitting targets. In 2012, he'd run Republican nominee Mitt Romney's transition team so competently that it was called "the most beautiful ark that never sailed." In a West Wing full of sycophants and conspiracy theorists, Liddell was one of the few rational people in the place.

Why was he working for Trump? Liddell was a fiscally conservative but socially moderate Republican. He didn't like Trump's incendiary rhetoric but thought the presidency would change him. Unfortunately, events showed that to be a fantasy. Liddell was in denial. But, oddly, his blinders served him well—because the less he knew about what Trump was doing, the better he would be at his job.

The 2020 presidential transition became a sub rosa operation, carried out under Trump's nose. The president, publicly and privately, raged about a rigged election and threw up roadblocks, but the wheels of the transition kept turning. Ted Kaufman, Biden's transition chairman, was amazed. "I thought they'd never cooperate with us on anything," he told me. "And that's not the way it worked out." An obscure White House staffer who'd only recently become an American citizen helped make the transfer of power possible.

Yet Liddell was an unlikely leader of a plot to save democracy. One morning in January 2020, a full year before Biden's inauguration, he'd invited two guests to breakfast in the White House Mess: Joshua Bolten, George W. Bush's former White House chief of staff; and David Marchick, director for the Center for Presidential Transition at the Partnership for Public Service, a nonprofit devoted to effective transitions. Marchick had no formal role in the transfer of power, but he would play a vital part in the events to come. Bolten had run the transition between Bush and Obama, which, despite taking place during two wars and a financial crisis, was considered a model.

Over breakfast, Liddell told his guests that he was planning for a second Trump term. Bolten then asked, "Okay. Now what are your plans if he loses?" Liddell stared at his empty plate. "Well, I guess we've got to figure that out," he replied. Liddell was depressed by the prospect of a defeated but defiant Trump. Throughout 2020, every time the president railed about a rigged election, Liddell considered resigning—and Bolten and Marchick talked him off the ledge. They thought of themselves as support therapists—and air traffic controllers. "He would call us and we'd say, 'Hey, you need to land this plane. You can't quit,'" said Marchick. Landing the plane would become the go-to metaphor for the turbulent transition.

By the spring of 2020, Biden's team, led by Kaufman, was anxious to get started. "We had a plan—a very, very complicated plan—and we had excellent people executing it," he said. Kaufman's first hire was Jeffrey Zients, a managerial wizard who, when Barack Obama's health care website crashed upon its debut in 2013, reconfigured the site and got it up and running. For that, he was known as "Biden's BFD," or "Big Fucking Deal"—after the vice president's famous off-mic remark at the signing of the Affordable Care Act (ACA). Other key players in the transition were Ron Klain, Biden's longtime aide and vice-presidential chief of staff; Anita Dunn, a public relations expert and member of both the Obama and Biden inner circles; Yohannes Abraham, a former Obama national security staffer; former Louisiana congressman Cedric Richmond; and New Mexico governor Lujan Grisham.

The fate of Biden's agenda would depend on the preparations they made now, in the spring of 2020. There was no time to waste.

Thousands of Americans were dying of COVID-19 every day. The economy had cratered. Cities were besieged by protesters demanding an end to police killings of unarmed Black men. The dangers posed by climate change were coming to a head. And then there was the war in Afghanistan, where 8,600 American troops were bogged down in a seemingly endless conflict. Trump had pledged to withdraw those forces by May 1, 2021. Biden's incoming national security team would have to prepare a range of options, all problematic, for resolving America's twenty-year quagmire.

The most urgent challenge was COVID-19. Biden ordered his transition team to bring him the news, good and bad, and to fight the pandemic as a wartime effort. That summer, as he ramped up for the challenge, Zients, who would become Biden's coronavirus response coordinator, worked in an office with the television on mute. "But every channel had the number of people who were diagnosed, the number of hospitalizations, the number of deaths," he recalled. "Our team was asked to resolve the greatest public health crisis in a hundred years, which had cost hundreds of thousands of lives and was critical to his presidency. Was that sobering? Was that a little frightening? Absolutely."

Zients and his team worked around the clock. "It was routine to have emails flying back and forth at all hours of the night, to have meetings at three a.m.," said a senior adviser. Ted Kaufman recalled thinking, *I'm too old for this*, when he began getting emails at 5:30 a.m. The intense preparation was aimed at not wasting a moment after noon on Inauguration Day.

Biden's team needed answers to basic questions: What was the status of the vaccine development program, Operation Warp Speed? What was the plan for getting vaccine shots into people's arms?

The first step in taming the pandemic would be climbing out of the hole that Trump and his team had dug. It was a hole that seemed to have no bottom.

————

From the moment the virus arrived on U.S. soil, Trump had denied that there *was* a pandemic. Then he tried to wish it away, insisting that fifteen cases would go down to zero. But while he was publicly calling the coronavirus a hoax, Trump was privately telling the author Bob Woodward that it was "deadly stuff."

There was plenty of blame to go around for the tragically inept pandemic response. Health and Human Services (HHS) and the Food and Drug Administration (FDA) were slow to recognize the threat, and the Centers for Disease Control and Prevention (CDC) botched the early testing. But Trump made it exponentially worse. Obama's team had prepared a sixty-nine-page blueprint, "Playbook for Early Response to High-Consequence Emerging Infectious Disease Threats and Biological Incidents," also known as the pandemic playbook. But Trump's team had ignored it, along with other transition materials.

From neglecting warnings about the virus to pretending it would magically disappear, to failing to mobilize a federal response, to staging super-spreader campaign rallies, to ignoring safety protocols in the West Wing, Trump thoroughly fumbled the pandemic, empowering quack scientists who handicapped the nation's response.

There was still hope that professionals at HHS and the CDC would rise to the challenge. The trouble was, few senior officials in the Trump administration knew how to make the bureaucracy work. Most had come to destroy government, not to mobilize it.

Trust in government had been the first casualty. Competence was the second. In March 2020, Vice President Mike Pence asked the president's son-in-law, Jared Kushner, if he could help with the COVID response. Kushner knew nothing about epidemiology or public health but was undaunted; he cleared his calendar for thirty days. Kushner started calling his friends, mostly private equity entrepreneurs in their twenties and thirties. The "slim suit crowd," as they were dubbed, worked out of the West Wing basement and at the Federal Emergency Management Agency (FEMA), emailing *their* friends. There were no government laptops, so they used their smartphones.

They started cold-calling CEOs in search of testing swabs, personal protective equipment (PPEs), masks, and ventilators. When they found what they were looking for, they'd try to buy it, only to discover that the federal contracting system didn't work that way. One day one of the slim suits came into Kushner's office. "I ordered six hundred million masks," he told Kushner. "Oh, that's amazing," Jared replied. "Where are they?" "The first order comes in June," the young man said. "Are you fucking crazy?" said Kushner. "You know, it's war. We're going to be dead in June." Kushner realized he had a big problem.

Testing had been a disaster. So Kushner started calling his corporate friends. At a briefing in the Rose Garden on March 13, clutching a cardboard chart, Dr. Deborah Birx announced that Google was constructing a website for a testing network. The trouble was, Google wasn't. Someone from Verily, a division of Google's parent company, Alphabet, had told Kushner that engineers were on the case. In fact, the pilot testing program was only for the San Francisco Bay Area, and it was in its early stages.

On a more positive note, Operation Warp Speed, a public-private partnership to develop a vaccine, was off to a promising start. But in every other respect, the U.S. was failing catastrophically to contain the worst public health crisis in a century.

Biden's team couldn't afford to wait until January. "We had to be ready on Day One to set DOD [the Department of Defense] in motion, activating military troops to help in the fight against the pandemic," said Zients. "We had to order FEMA to stand up a whole-of-country emergency response." But there was no one to talk to: Trump's DOD would not cooperate with Biden's team. Neither would the Office of Management and Budget (OMB) or the United States Trade Representative (USTR).

No one knew who was in charge of Trump's pandemic response team. Was it Vice President Mike Pence? Dr. Scott Atlas, Trump's COVID-19 adviser? Kushner? A Yale epidemiology professor who'd joined Biden's transition team, Dr. Marcella Nunez-Smith, recalled: "Warp Speed would say, 'Talk to CDC.' And CDC would say, 'Talk to Warp Speed.' I mean, the silence was deafening." And even if someone *were* in charge, no one dared run the risk of getting caught by Trump talking to Zients and his team.

In April 2020, the number of COVID-19 cases had exceeded one million, with sixty-three thousand lives lost, more than the country suffered during the entire Vietnam War. But Kushner was upbeat: "I think you will see by June, a lot of the country should be back to normal, and the hope is that by July the country is really rocking again."

July came and went. More than a thousand Americans were dying every day. And Donald Trump continued to rail that the upcoming election would be rigged.

TWO

YOU NEED TO LAND THIS PLANE

C hris Liddell became the Biden team's secret weapon. Except when he had to be there, Liddell avoided the Oval Office—fearing Trump would ask him what he was doing. "It was kind of like the eye of Sauron," said a senior adviser. "As long as you stayed out of it, you were okay." The West Wing was now home to a *Star Wars* bar cast of characters that included Rudolph Giuliani, Trump's increasingly erratic, often inebriated personal lawyer; Sidney Powell, peddler of an election fraud theory involving software created by a dead Venezuelan dictator; and Mike Lindell, the unhinged MyPillow CEO. Ironically, for Liddell, Trump's obsession with the fiction of a stolen election was a useful distraction—"because then I could just get on with doing my job."

A presidential transition ultimately depends on the goodwill of people on both sides. It's therefore a leap of faith. "It was incredibly complicated, and it could have stopped on a dime if Trump had just said stop," said Kaufman. Biden's transition chairman could scarcely believe they were pulling it off. "The fact that nobody, not even the sycophants who were around Trump, went to him and told him, 'Oh, wait, see what they're doing?' was truly amazing, incredible."

Mark Meadows, Trump's White House chief of staff, functioned less as a gatekeeper than as a glad-handing maître d'. There was no presidential command, no matter how outlandish, that he wouldn't carry out. With Biden's team, the former North Carolina congressman was as genial and feckless as a game show host. His phone calls with Ron Klain followed a pattern: "*Ron!* I heard that you guys were having problems with A, B, C," he'd say. "You know, Mark," Klain would reply, "we're having problems with A, B, C, D, E, F. I'll tell you what, if you just got A done, I'd be superhappy." To which Meadows would say, "Absolutely, positively, no problem." And then nothing would happen.

Meadows, who'd replaced Mick Mulvaney as chief in March 2020, was among the principal enablers of Trump's conspiracy to overturn the election. Later, in January 2021, he would orchestrate Trump's infamous telephone call with Georgia's secretary of state, Brad Raffensperger—a Mafia-style attempt to browbeat the official into finding 11,780 votes that Trump insisted were hiding under rocks Raffensperger had failed to turn over. Not coincidentally, the number was one more than Biden's margin of victory in the state.

And yet, inexplicably, Meadows gave a wink and a nod to Liddell's stealth transition. Meadows and his deputy told Trump as little as possible about it. Liddell explained later, "I said to Mark, 'Let's make sure that we play this by the book, that we make it sound as boring and procedural as possible.' And Mark said, 'Okay, you do what you need to do.'"

Quietly, Liddell reached out to Mary Gibert. An energetic, conscientious student of transitions, Gibert was the federal transition coordinator of the General Services Administration (GSA). A forty-year veteran, she was responsible for ensuring that the law was followed, whether Trump approved or not. Together Gibert and Liddell would plan the transfer of power. "Liddell was our conduit to keep everything moving," she told me, "very quietly, under the radar."

Liddell couldn't risk speaking directly to Biden's camp; it might get back to Trump. "Chris would have been shot," said Marchick, only half joking. So Liddell communicated with the Biden team through Marchick. Inside the White House, Liddell confided in just a few trusted colleagues: Robert O'Brien, the national security adviser; Matt Pottinger, his deputy; and Pat Cipollone, the White House counsel. Unlike the cultists in Trump's inner circle, these were people Liddell could talk to, who cared more about doing their jobs professionally than about keeping Trump in power at any cost. Marchick called them "the responsibility caucus."

Biden's team anticipated obstruction, delays in getting personnel in place, and a concerted effort to impede the transfer of power. And much worse. They prepared for "unconventional challenges," of which there were too many to count. "Just so we didn't get totally discouraged, we stopped at seventy," said Kaufman. To show how varied those scenarios were, he displayed a few of the headings on the voluminous document they produced:

+ *Recession turns into a Depression.*
+ *Election returns uncertain or delayed. Covid-19 gains traction and limits voting.*
+ *Increased hardening of political divides, tribalism, hyper-partisanship.*
+ *Trump blocks Biden transition claiming he won and utilizing a well-funded highly orchestrated campaign against us.*
+ *Increase in the level and intensity of social protesting and government response.*

This last item was the euphemism of the year; "government response" was code for Trump sending troops into the streets, perhaps declaring martial law. No one in the Biden camp would say publicly that they feared Trump might stage a coup. But privately they were taking precautions. "Is it something we were concerned about and thought about, had plans about?" said Kaufman. "Absolutely. We had a bunch of smart people sitting around a table night and day, saying, 'Okay, what are the plans?' One of the key questions was what's going to happen with Trump and the military?".

Trump's tin-pot strongman brand was on full display. On June 1, after protesters were dispersed with pepper spray in front of the White House, the president, flanked by a Praetorian Guard of aides and military personnel, strutted to St. John's Church in Lafayette Square. General Mark Milley, chairman of the Joint Chiefs of Staff, had dressed in his combat fatigues to pay a visit to National Guard troops. But Trump corralled him into joining his march to the church, a walk the general would later regret having taken. Once there, the president preened for the cameras with a Bible, perhaps not noticing he was holding it upside down.

In July, Fox News anchor Chris Wallace asked Trump if he would accept the results of the election. "I'll have to see," the president replied. He added, "I think mail-in voting is going to rig the election." A few months later, from the podium in the East Room of the White House, Trump declared, "There won't be a transfer; frankly, there'll be a continuation." Still, Liddell kept the train on the tracks.

By law the sitting White House chief of staff, Meadows, and Biden's transition chairman, Kaufman, were required to sign a "Memorandum of Understanding." *Fat chance*, thought Kaufman. But he sent a draft to the White House anyway. "I figured *that's* never going to happen," he said. "This is totally against Trump's interests; he'd *kill* people if he found out it happened."

And yet, on September 30, Kaufman was gobsmacked when his fax machine clanked to life and back came the memorandum—signed by Meadows. Trump's chief of staff almost certainly never told his boss. "I have it here as one of my prized possessions," Kaufman, who saved the memo, told me. "I never in a million years thought Meadows would sign it!"

November 3, 2020, election day, seemed remarkable for its lack of drama: Despite the pandemic, predictions of chaos at the polls, and confusion over mail-in ballots, voting had been a model of fairness and efficiency. In a record turnout, Biden won by 306 to 232 in the Electoral College and by more than seven million in the popular vote—a decisive victory. But Trump, defying his campaign advisers, declared himself the winner and the victim of a grand conspiracy. The real drama was yet to come.

Traditionally, the day after a presidential election, the administrator of the GSA anoints the apparent winner. The act, known as ascertainment, not only formally acknowledges the victor; it also makes available to the incoming administration office space, funding, access to federal agencies, intelligence briefings, and other vital governing infrastructure. But, in a startling break with precedent, the GSA administrator, Emily Murphy, perhaps afraid of angering Trump, refused to ascertain Biden's victory.

This was no idle act. "Ascertainment is not a ceremonial process," explained Mary Gibert, the GSA transition coordinator. "It has potential life-and-death implications: Maybe you'd have made the same decision or maybe you'd have made a different decision, but you don't know because you didn't have access to information." The Biden team was aghast, furious about the delay. Between the election and inauguration, they had just seventy-eight days to ramp up their administration. They'd recruited five hundred volunteers to visit every federal agency and report back on who was doing what. Now they were sitting on their hands.

Biden's team had prepared for almost any eventuality. "We had six hundred lawyers working long, long hours, producing thousands of pages of memos for all sorts of stuff," said Bob Bauer, the campaign senior legal adviser. "This was a genuine national security issue: The fact that the president-elect of the United States would be denied access to the tools and the resources for an effective transition was literally, directly, every day, harmful to the country—and in the middle of a public health crisis." Bauer and his team were prepared to sue Murphy and the GSA. But after a spirited debate, the campaign decided to stand down.

A few days later, Liddell called his confidants Marchick and Bolten. "Remember that dinner we had where we talked about the nightmare scenario?" Liddell told them. "That's what we have." The nightmare scenario was Trump losing the election, but not by enough to convince him that he'd lost. Marchick explained: "Clearly, Liddell was in meetings in the White House where Trump said, 'We're going to fight this and we're going to overturn it.'" Marchick feared Liddell was near the end of his rope. "He thought about quitting many times—and we'd say, 'Hey, you can't quit.'"

Eight days after the election, on November 11, Joe Biden announced that his White House chief of staff would be Ron Klain. The choice surprised no one. Thomas F. "Mack" McLarty, who recruited Klain to work in Bill Clinton's White House, recalled his first impression of Biden's future chief, then thirty-two. "You could see the talent, just like an athlete," said Clinton's chief of staff. "He had the proverbial fire in his belly, that was obvious. But it didn't come through in an off-putting way."

Raised in Indiana, Klain had earnest, midwestern charm; *The New York Times* compared him to an overgrown Model U.N. student. His down-to-earth demeanor disguised a razor-sharp intelligence. After graduating from Georgetown summa cum laude, he'd gone to Harvard Law School, where he was magna cum laude and an editor of the *Harvard Law Review*. Afterward he clerked for Supreme Court Justice Byron White.

In the Clinton White House, Klain rose steadily, becoming chief of staff to Vice President Al Gore. But it was with Biden that his career lifted off—as chief counsel on the Senate Judiciary Committee and later vice-presidential chief of staff. As Obama's "Ebola czar," Klain led a successful campaign to contain an outbreak of the lethal disease in Africa. He was a type A personality with a compulsive Twitter habit. But he was also unflappable, rarely raising his voice no matter how much excitement or chaos swirled around him.

Klain and Biden were like an old married couple, going on four decades. They had their ups and downs and their differences, but they clicked. Klain was straight-ahead. He'd say, "Look, we've got to decide A or B, and here are the five arguments for A and the five arguments for B." Biden would reply, "Well, what about C? What about A and a half?" Biden navigated by feel, nuance, what he'd seen before, a person he'd met, a story he'd heard. Klain, the no-nonsense lawyer, complemented him. Though they were friends, Klain didn't regard himself as Biden's equal. He was a staffer. He'd call his boss Mr. President, or sir.

There was just one thing about his chief of staff that drove the president crazy: Klain talked too fast. He always had.

But Klain hadn't been a shoo-in for the chief job; he had a strike against him. And in Biden's world that could be fatal.

Biden has claimed he's the only Irishman who doesn't carry grudges; Anita Dunn said she carried them for him. But that was, as Biden would say, malarkey. In truth, he rarely forgot anyone who crossed him. And he carried a gigantic chip on his shoulder.

An example of that was Biden's still-burning irritation about an encounter back in the late 1970s with W. Averell Harriman, FDR's former ambassador to the Soviet Union and the patrician embodiment of the WASP establishment. Harriman, a railroad magnate and Democratic Party power broker, had summoned the young senator to his Georgetown study and grilled him about foreign policy. "He did it because he thought I didn't know the answers," Biden complained bitterly to a friend more than forty years later. Biden could barely remember Harriman's name, but he was still mad at "that *rich* guy, the *railroad* guy."

In Obama's White House, the vice president had chafed at the condescension, perceived or real, of Ivy Leaguers. "This is a guy who barely graduated from Syracuse Law," said a friend. (Biden graduated seventy-sixth in a class of eighty-five.) But disrespect from anyone could set him off. David Axelrod, Obama's rumpled, outspoken political strategist, rubbed Biden the wrong way. He could sense that Axelrod didn't think he was presidential timber. Biden thought David Plouffe, Obama's aloof 2008 campaign manager, also underestimated him. One of Biden's close friends put it bluntly: "He hates 'the Davids.'"

If he was prickly about people showing him respect, Biden also expected loyalty. And Klain, on at least one occasion, had come up short. In 2015, while Biden agonized over whether to run for the Democratic presidential nomination, Klain had said yes when Hillary Clinton asked him for help with debate preparation. (He'd prepared both Obama and Vice President Biden to face opponents in televised debates.) Up to that point in the nomination contest, Clinton had been a wooden candidate, losing ground to her upstart opponent, Vermont senator Bernie Sanders. But under Klain's tutelage, on October 13 Clinton delivered a bravura performance in the first Democratic debate, making her the clear front-runner. A week later, Joe Biden announced that he wouldn't enter the presidential race. He cited his continuing grief over the recent death of his son Beau from a brain tumor. But Clinton's impressive debate performance was undoubtedly a factor.

Klain's support of someone who was then a rival wounded Biden. And Klain knew it. In an October 2015 email, later revealed by WikiLeaks, Klain admitted to John Podesta, Clinton's campaign chairman: "It's been a little hard for me to play such a role in the Biden demise—and I am definitely dead to them." But Biden let this grudge go. Klain was too valuable to remain persona non grata for long.

————

Klain and his team were, in effect, designing an airplane in mid-flight. Barred by Trump from access to the agencies, they set up a "shadow agency" process, compiling lists of former officials—and tapped their expertise. Senate Majority Leader Mitch McConnell refused to call the Senate back in session—so they interviewed, vetted, and hired officials who didn't require confirmation. "This was the Biden transition's innovation," explained Marchick. "They lined up thousands of people to go into the government in these nonconfirmed positions so they could staff the government on Day One. They did eight thousand interviews in order to place eleven hundred."

Finally, on November 23, GSA administrator Murphy declared Biden the winner. But the foot-dragging had been costly. Every day Biden's team couldn't access information about Trump's vaccination program meant delays in getting vaccines into people's arms. And that meant unnecessary deaths from COVID-19.

There were also risks to national security. Every day Biden's team was denied intelligence briefings meant less time to prepare for foreign crises. On January 20 at noon, all CIA covert operations ordered by Trump would suddenly belong to Biden. Traditionally, the major party nominees receive the PDB after their party conventions. Biden and the vice-president-elect, Kamala Harris, didn't get their first intelligence briefing until November 30.

The delay also affected Biden's planning for Afghanistan. Everyone knew where the president-elect stood. As vice president, Biden had opposed Obama's "surge" of thirty thousand troops; he thought the president had been "jammed" by his generals. Evacuating U.S. troops along with thousands of U.S. citizens and Afghans who'd joined the American war effort would be a Sisyphean challenge. But Biden's team didn't know the half of it.

The Trump administration had stalled the refugee admissions process. This was in keeping with its well-known xenophobia, which had produced the notorious 2017 Muslim ban. Afghans who'd worked with American troops needed Special Immigrant Visas, or SIVs. The program was ill-suited to the evacuation of tens of thousands of people in a combat zone; in the best of times, obtaining an SIV took eighteen months or even years. But in March 2020, Trump made things worse by virtually shutting the program down, creating a backlog of some seventeen thousand applicants.

"This was no accident, by the way," said Representative Jason Crow, a Colorado Democrat. The congressman had visited the U.S. embassy in Kabul in 2019 and found that visas were being processed by a skeletal staff. As Crow told George Packer, a writer for *The Atlantic*, "This was a long-term Stephen Miller project to destroy the SIV program and basically shut it off." Crow was referring to Trump's notoriously anti-immigrant adviser. An old Indochina hand was even more blunt about the motivation behind stalling SIVs: "They felt the country wasn't ready to have a lot of hook-nosed, brown-skinned Muslims, with blood dripping off their fingers, coming into this country. We had enough trouble with the folks coming out of Vietnam."

Meanwhile Trump appeared intent on staging a coup d'etat. He'd replaced Defense Secretary Mark Esper with Christopher Miller, a compliant acolyte, and installed apparatchiks in high places at the CIA. Some worried that Trump would start a war with Iran as a pretext to stay in power. Quietly, Liz Cheney, the newly elected Wyoming congresswoman, had corralled every living former defense secretary, including her father, Dick Cheney, into signing a letter exhorting the military to follow the Constitution. And General Mark Milley, chairman of the Joint Chiefs of Staff, was preparing emergency contingencies. He suspected Trump might stage a domestic crisis to seize power—a favorite ploy of autocrats who want to stay in office by exploiting voters' fears. In the event of an illegal presidential order, Milley and other top Pentagon officials made a secret pact to resign, one after another.

To avoid the appearance of a power grab, Biden's camp didn't speak directly with General Milley. Instead, they communicated through an intermediary, House Speaker Nancy Pelosi. I asked Biden's best friend, Ted Kaufman, if the Speaker kept the president-elect informed of Milley's contingency planning. "Oh, sure," he said. "Absolutely."

Outwardly, the Biden team projected calm. As Klain explained, "Our whole thing was basically a legal strategy to shut this down in the courts—and a political strategy based on the idea that we won, so we were going to act like we won. We played this out a step at a time. To first get the vote confirmed by the media, to build a sense of inevitability around that, to finally get the GSA to certify us. To get going on the transition." An adviser to the Biden transition put it this way: "We don't need to send up fighter jets to force Air Force One down. Let's just let Trump throw his fit, pursue his legal theories. It'll all fail and he'll run short of fuel and come down for a landing."

In the meantime, Klain was getting ready to help his boss govern.

THREE

WE'LL ALWAYS HAVE YOUR BACK

On December 18, 2020, a month before Joe Biden's inauguration, the most exclusive fraternity in Washington gathered to give the president-elect's incoming chief of staff their best advice.

That morning Ron Klain logged on to a Zoom call with nineteen of the twenty-two living former White House chiefs. These private, off-the-record meetings, arranged by the outgoing chief for his incoming successor since 2008, usually took place in person at the White House. But due to COVID safety protocols, this year's gathering would be held virtually. And with Trump refusing to concede the election, Mark Meadows bowed out. So George W. Bush's chief Joshua Bolten and Barack Obama's chief Denis McDonough organized the call.

Democrats and Republicans, the ex-chiefs had served presidents going all the way back to Lyndon Johnson. There was LBJ's James Jones; Gerald Ford's Dick Cheney; Jimmy Carter's Jack Watson; Ronald Reagan's Kenneth Duberstein; George H. W. Bush's John Sununu and Samuel Skinner; Bill Clinton's Thomas H. "Mack" McLarty, Leon Panetta, Erskine Bowles, and John Podesta; George W. Bush's Andrew Card and Joshua Bolten; and Barack Obama's Rahm Emanuel, Pete

Rouse, Bill Daley, Jack Lew, and Denis McDonough. In a surprise, even Trump's John Kelly and Mick Mulvaney joined the call.

The animosities of the Trump era lingered. Back in March 2016, Bolten had quietly tried to get all the Republican former chiefs to declare publicly that Trump was unfit to serve as president. Bolten had been rebuffed by Dick Cheney, who didn't want to jeopardize the political prospects of his daughter Liz, running for Congress from Wyoming. James A. Baker III, Ronald Reagan's first chief, was also gun-shy. "A lot of people said Ronald Reagan was an idiot," Baker told Bolten. "Now I'm not comparing Trump to Ronald Reagan—" Bolten revered Baker, but he cut him short: "You just did. It's a disgraceful comparison, and you know it."

Baker, now ninety, who'd voted twice for Trump, declined to join the call, saying he had a hunting trip. And Reince Priebus, sacked after six months as Trump's first chief but still the president's loyal flatterer, had cold feet. Priebus, forty-eight, sent his regrets. The only other no-show was Ford's ailing ex-chief, Donald Rumsfeld, who would die a few months later at eighty-nine.

Cheney, now eighty, kicked things off. He'd been Ford's thirty-four-year-old chief long before serving as George W. Bush's formidable VP. "Whatever you do," Cheney pronounced, "*control* your vice president." There were scattered laughs—and a few groans. He'd told the same joke twelve years earlier, during Rahm Emanuel's initiation.

Next to speak was eighty-two-year-old Jim Jones. He'd been just twenty-eight when he became Lyndon Johnson's gatekeeper in 1968, the last year of a presidency marked by the triumph of the Great Society and the disaster of the Vietnam War. Jones believed that the crises facing Biden and his team presented a rare opportunity. "This is one of those moments in history—FDR moments or LBJ moments," he said. "In FDR's case, basically everything he did was to deal with the Depression. In LBJ's case, it was using the tragedy of JFK's assassination as a springboard to do everything he wanted to do." Biden now had a chance to use the twin crises of the pandemic and an economic collapse to forge similarly great achievements.

But Jones had a warning. It was about the personal toll of the presidency, and Biden's age. On his last day in office, LBJ, who was sixty years old, looked eighty. Biden was seventy-eight—and it showed. Jones recognized his own frailties in Biden. "I see in him some of the things that I couldn't do a couple of years ago, and I see how it has progressed," he said. "It's his gait. It's his walking ability. The stumbling on the steps on Air Force One. I've become an expert at falling going up the stairs."

Jones also saw it when the president spoke. "I can tell when he's tired, when he's having trouble getting the right word out—or thinking of the right word. I don't think it's noticeable to most people, but being there myself, I recognize it." Jones wasn't saying that Biden couldn't do the job, just cautioning Klain to conserve his energy. Jones had done that for LBJ. "Everyone's going to want Biden to do this, this, and this," he warned Klain. "And he'll *want* to do it. But harness his sleep time. He's got to keep a clear, rested head and body for the next three years."

Among his supporters, this was the oft-unspoken worry about a Biden presidency: He was older than Ronald Reagan, who was seventy-three when he ran for reelection in 1984 against Walter Mondale. The fortieth president's dotage had become a punch line during a debate. "I am not going to exploit, for political purposes, my opponent's youth and inexperience," Reagan had cracked about his fifty-six-year-old Democratic opponent. But the quip had disguised an unfortunate truth: In his second term, Reagan was sometimes non compos mentis;

dementia had begun to set in. Could Biden, almost an octogenarian, handle the rigors of the presidency for one term, much less two? He would be eighty-two if and when he ran for reelection.

Biden's campaign appearances, often streamed from his basement, had been a kind of Rorschach test: Critics thought he was doddering while supporters thought Biden was remarkably focused given his unscripted history. "They said he doesn't have any discipline," remarked Mike Donilon, Biden's wordsmith and political strategist. "Yet he probably had one of the most disciplined message campaigns in history. They said he would never shut up—yet he gave the shortest acceptance speech in history at the convention."

Everybody had a story about the vintage, unfiltered Biden. "You got on an elevator with him and you might be there for a while," said the former CBS News anchor Bob Schieffer, chuckling as he recalled covering the loquacious senator from Delaware. Richard Blumenthal, the Connecticut senator, once got a voice mail from Biden that lasted thirty-five minutes. Biden could also go rogue, veering dramatically out of bounds. Once, spotting his friend Tom Brokaw, the NBC News anchor, across a room at a party, Biden called out: "Brokaw, how are you and Meredith doing with menopause?"

But those were private fouls; Ted Kaufman argued that in public Biden-the-gaffe-machine was a caricature, a media exaggeration. The narrative of Biden as a crazy uncle, blurting out embarrassing things, was just too irresistible—like the image of President Gerald Ford, forever tumbling down the steps of Air Force One. But it was false; just as Ford, a well-coordinated athlete, was unfairly defined by a few televised stumbles, Biden, Kaufman argued, was judged by a few slips of the tongue: "Go back and look at his speeches when he was vice president and you'll find very few gaffes." Moreover, much of Biden's difficulty getting words out stemmed not from incipient dementia, as many right-wing news outlets would have listeners believe, but from the stutter he'd struggled with in childhood.

Friends and aides insisted that on the eve of his inauguration Biden was, mentally and physically, "a young seventy-eight."

———————

On the Zoom call, the ex–chiefs of staff continued giving Klain their advice. "The role of team leader is really important," said Jack Watson, eighty-two, who served as Jimmy Carter's popular and effective chief during his final year. "A White House that keeps secrets has limited cohesion and loyalties. Share as much information with your staff as you can—you're not going to have as many leaks if you do that." Klain understood what Watson meant; you had to manage down as well as up—so that everyone felt invested in the president's success. Indeed, on Klain's watch, leaks, palace intrigue, and turf battles would be rare.

Ken Duberstein, seventy-six, Ronald Reagan's final gatekeeper, was attending his last gathering with his fellow chiefs; he would die of a rare kidney disease in 2022. "Don't forget about the First Lady," he said. "She's the closest person in the world to the president." Nancy Reagan, known as "the personnel director," had infallible radar for staffers who were pushing their own agendas instead of Ronnie's. "He was trust and she was verify," quipped Duberstein, borrowing Reagan's famous phrase. Dr. Jill Biden was an equally ferocious protector of Joe Biden. When the president-elect interviewed job candidates, Jill often sat in. No one needed to tell Klain how important it was to keep her in the loop. He spoke to her regularly.

Next up was John Sununu, eighty-one, George H. W. Bush's first chief. Gruff and cantankerous, Sununu had resigned in disgrace after being caught using government transportation for personal trips. "Don't forget to have fun!" he said, with no trace of irony. Samuel Skinner, eighty-two, Sununu's successor, echoed this advice. Skinner had been overwhelmed by the job. "This is a once-in-a-lifetime experience, so smell the roses," he told Klain. "You're a part of history. Don't fail to appreciate that and relish it."

Bill Clinton's chiefs were proud of Klain, their star pupil. Mack McLarty, seventy-four, who'd given him his first White House job, urged Klain to stay grounded. "Keep your humanity about you," McLarty said. "Staying connected to where you come from and not letting anything go to your head is important. And be prepared to deal with UFOs"—McLarty's acronym for unforeseen occurrences. There would be plenty of those in the months ahead.

Leon Panetta, McLarty's successor, admonished Klain to tell the president hard truths: "You have to be the son of a bitch who tells the president what he doesn't want to hear, because frankly most people tell him what he *wants* to hear." Along with James Baker, Panetta, now eighty-two, was considered the gold standard at the position. But his habit of criticizing sitting chiefs rubbed some the wrong way. If Klain screwed up, chances were he'd hear about it from Panetta on CNN or MSNBC.

Erskine Bowles, a wealthy entrepreneur who followed Panetta as Clinton's chief, was next. "I offered Leon five million dollars to stay in the job," he cracked. Bowles, now seventy-five, had the misfortune of being tapped just as Clinton began his affair with Monica Lewinsky. "Politicians are great at saying yes or maybe," Bowles told Klain. "And the role of the White House chief of staff is to make it clear when the answer is no. Not maybe and not yes, but no."

"I want to tell a story," said John Podesta. The son of immigrants, an Italian father and Greek mother, Podesta, seventy-one, had run the White House like a drill sergeant during Clinton's impeachment and war in the Balkans. But Podesta also had a spiritual side. In the spring of 1999, during the conflict in Kosovo, he and his wife were at church. "A guy came up to me and said that he'd been praying for me," Podesta said. "I never thought of people I didn't know praying for me. So be aware of the honor of being in the position you're in." In the months to come, Biden and Klain would need all the prayers they could get to pass their ambitious infrastructure and Build Back Better (BBB) bills.

Now it was Andy Card's turn. Klain liked George W. Bush's chief and was in awe of his longevity; his five-year stint as chief was a record. But Klain thought Card's cheerleading for Bush was sometimes over-the-top. In a TV appearance, Card, now seventy-three, had said of Bush on 9/11, "That is the day he became president." Klain thought: *More people were dying every day from COVID-19 than on 9/11. Joe Biden would become a wartime president on Day One.*

Card was blunt about Donald Trump. "The institutions of our democracy were greatly tarnished," he told Biden's chief. "Trump didn't know them or respect them. He hurt the institutions of the presidency, Congress, the CIA, national intelligence community, the justice department, the defense department. It's President Biden's job, and your job, to help polish our democracy and our institutions."

Josh Bolten, sixty-six, Card's wonky successor, brought the conversation back to nuts and bolts. "What gets to the president and through what channel is the most important thing that the chief does," he said. "You've got a lot of 'czars' to deal with. Make sure there's clarity right from the outset." Bolten, a process geek, was speaking Klain's language. "Absolutely, understood," Klain replied.

To everyone's surprise, Rahm Emanuel, sixty-one, Barack Obama's famously profane, hard-charging chief, told Klain to go easy on himself. "Every Friday I'd say, 'Thank God, only two more working days until Monday,'" he said. "Take care of your own spirit and your own soul and reserve time for your family." Emanuel, the former mayor of Chicago, would soon become Biden's ambassador to Japan.

Bill Daley, seventy-two, Emanuel's successor as Obama's chief, told Klain that everything depended on his relationship with the president. Daley's strained chemistry with Obama had forced him out after only a year. In this respect, Mick Mulvaney, Trump's fifty-three-year-old former chief, pointed out, Klain had a head start: "It's a huge advantage to know the president so well and to have worked for him, as you have." Mulvaney's subtext seemed to be, "I didn't know Trump well, and that was a problem." Not knowing Biden wouldn't be a problem for Klain.

Denis McDonough, fifty-one, Obama's final chief and Biden's nominee to run the Department of Veterans Affairs, got personal. "You will need people you can let your hair down with and talk with honestly," he told him. Klain took this advice to heart: On Saturday—always a working day for Biden's chief—he'd often spend an hour or two confiding in someone he could trust. In the beginning that person was often Anita Dunn.

The last to speak was Trump's John Kelly. A four-star Marine general, Kelly, now seventy, had brought military discipline to a dysfunctional White House, but he'd failed to tell Trump hard truths. When, after the infamous rally in Charlottesville, Virginia, the president had defended neo-Nazis and white supremacists, Kelly stood by, staring at his shoes. "Speak truth to power," Kelly told Klain. Was the general regretting the occasions he hadn't done so with Trump? "The Constitution and the rule of law should drive everything. And if it's not ethical, moral and legal, it shouldn't be done. Period. End of paragraph."

It had been an extraordinary virtual gathering, a display of genuine civility and goodwill that was almost unimaginable in such polarized times. The chiefs had checked their egos and their partisan identities at the door and given Klain their best counsel. "It was a totally informal, casual, comfortable event," said one chief. "Nobody was preaching. Nobody was trying to hog the spotlight."

Klain made a promise: "We do plan—and hope—to work across party lines. We want to build bridges and be as bipartisan as we can be." The chiefs didn't see eye-to-eye on policy. Indeed, Josh Bolten, head of the Business Roundtable, would vehemently oppose Biden's ambitious spending agenda, starting with the $1.9 trillion American Rescue Plan (ARP). Bolten warned Klain that by going too big the president would squander any hope of future cooperation with Republicans.

For the Democratic chiefs, Klain's cause was their own. "It's now or never," said Jack Watson. "What we're talking about is a twenty-first-century New Deal. What we have to show is that the government, within a capitalistic system, can moderate and alleviate the inequities that result from an uncontrolled capitalism. And we've got so little time. We can't do this in one term. Roosevelt had three and a half terms. But he did it. And that's Biden's challenge."

The real question was: Could Joe Biden and his chief of staff, in the days ahead, expect anything like the bipartisan cooperation that had characterized this call?

The chiefs could all agree on two things: No one had ever been better prepared than Klain to be White House chief of staff. And no one had ever faced a more daunting set of challenges.

Biden's chief invited his predecessors to stay in touch. "If I do something stupid or I'm going down the wrong path, call me," he said. "We'll always have your back," said Ken Duberstein.

But neither Klain nor the ex-chiefs could have known that a plot was under way that would come perilously close to preventing Joe Biden from taking office.

Just a few hours later, at 1:42 a.m. on December 19, Donald Trump tweeted:

Statistically impossible to have lost the 2020 Election. Big protest in D.C. on January 6th. Be there, will be wild!

FOUR

OUR OWN VERSION OF HELL

As far as Chris Liddell knew, January 6, 2021, promised to be a quiet day. Joe Biden's election was to be certified by Vice President Mike Pence in a routine count of electoral votes at the U.S. Capitol. Liddell, who was doing his best to stay under Trump's radar, could hardly wait. "I woke up in the morning in a good mood, thinking: Finally, we're going to get some resolution," he said. "The vote's going to happen." Liddell looked at the president's schedule and noticed a rally on the Washington Ellipse at noon. But he thought little of it. While there'd been reports of possible clashes that day between Trump supporters and counterprotesters, Liddell had been focused on his job.

Bob Bauer, the campaign legal adviser, was on edge. The truth was that democracy hung by a thread. Bauer's team had spent months preparing for this day—and for all the things that could go wrong. Legal scholars agreed that Pence's role in the certification procedure was purely ceremonial. But that didn't mean that the vice president couldn't plunge the country into a constitutional crisis.

One option was for Pence to delay the certification. That was the goal of Trump's lawyer John Eastman, Giuliani, and their coconspirators, as revealed later in a voice mail that Giuliani left for a Republican ally. (He'd inadvertently dialed the wrong person.) A delayed certification could give states an opportunity to try to replace slates of Biden electors with new ones pledged to Trump. Another option was to declare some Biden slates invalid, thereby denying him the minimum 270 votes. This would throw the whole process into the House of Representatives. Under the law, in the House's election of the president, each state delegation had one vote. And since Republicans in the 2021 House were the majority party in twenty-six states, Trump would almost certainly prevail.

If Pence tried to do Trump's extralegal bidding, Bauer and his team were poised to file for an injunction in the District Court. The issue would probably wind up in the Supreme Court, now stacked with three Trump-appointed justices. "If Pence had gone completely rogue, I think we had a very good chance of stopping it," Bauer told me. "I thought Trump and his legal team, such as it was, would be crazy to imagine that the court would somehow save him in these circumstances."

Bauer had thought of everything. Except what happened shortly after Trump began addressing his followers at the Ellipse.

Joe Biden was in the library of his house in Wilmington, Delaware; he and Bruce Reed, his incoming deputy chief of staff, were polishing a speech on small business initiatives scheduled for that afternoon. The television was on, with the sound muted, when they noticed commotion at the Capitol. The MAGA insurrection had begun.

Biden and his team watched as the violent mob pushed forward, storming the ramparts of the Capitol. "We were watching the riot build," Reed told me later, "and it soon became clear that he was going to need to give a different speech."

Trump, who'd tried to join the mob at the Capitol but was forced by his Secret Service detail to return to the White House, was conspicuously silent.

For Biden, the assault was personal, visceral. "To watch an attack on the place he loved and where he spent most of his career was difficult," said Reed. Biden had seen something like this coming. "He'd been saying for quite some time that he just hoped nobody would get hurt and none of this would lead to violence. Not with any expectation about a particular event—he just had a feeling about a fever rising."

To Biden, the rioters—some carrying Confederate flags, one wearing a shirt emblazoned "Camp Auschwitz"—looked all too familiar. He'd seen a mob a lot like this one just a few years earlier, in Charlottesville. They were neo-Nazis and white supremacists, carrying tiki torches and chanting vile, racist slogans.

Ron Klain was conducting a virtual meeting in his hotel room a few blocks away. He and Biden spoke on the phone. First they postponed Biden's scheduled event, then canceled it, then told the networks to expect remarks from the president-elect. A call was organized with Mike Donilon and part-time speechwriter Jon Meacham, the Pulitzer Prize–winning presidential chronicler and MSNBC commentator. "We were really sick at heart," said Klain, "and thinking: What could the president-elect say to the country to try to address this moment?"

The television was on in Chris Liddell's West Wing office. "And the next thing I knew, I was watching the insurrection," he said. Liddell was horrified, incredulous: *Oh my God*, he thought. *These images are being beamed around the world.* And then, *My job—which I thought was going to finally get easier—just became ten times harder.* Heading downstairs, Liddell ran into his colleague Matt Pottinger, the deputy national security adviser, who was equally stunned. They looked at each other. "It was like, 'Holy Hell, how are we going to deal with this? What does this mean? Do we stay or do we go?'"

At 2:24 p.m., Trump threw fuel on the fire, sending out a tweet:

Mike Pence didn't have the courage to do what should have been done, to protect our Country and our Constitution, giving States a chance to certify a corrected set of facts, not the fraudulent or inaccurate ones which they were asked to previously certify. USA demands the truth!

Reading the tweet, Matt Pottinger decided to resign.

———————

At about 3:00 p.m., Jared Kushner's plane touched down at Joint Base Andrews (formerly Andrews Air Force Base), more than an hour after the MAGA attack on the Capitol had begun. Kushner had an uncanny sense, perfected during his father-in-law's tumultuous presidency, for avoiding trouble; he was often nowhere to be found when things went badly. In the election's aftermath this survival instinct had kicked into high gear. Kushner thought the Democrats had benefited from an influx of early, mail-in voting spurred by the COVID crisis. But when it came to Trump's claim of a "stolen election," Kushner knew there was nothing there. Yet, rather than stick around and try to talk sense into his father-in-law, Jared chose to make himself scarce. He got out of town. "With all due respect, I'm not going to like what you're doing, and you're going to be screaming at me," he told the president. Kushner had flown to the Middle East, seven thousand miles away, to work on his peace deals, known as the Abraham Accords.

But now Kushner was back. His Secret Service detail told him it was too dangerous to go to the White House; instead, they took him to his home in Kalorama. Jared was getting into the shower when his phone rang; it was Kevin McCarthy, the House Majority Leader. Things looked really bad, McCarthy told him. Kushner threw on his clothes and headed to the White House.

At 4:05 p.m. Joe Biden appeared on television from The Queen, a historic Wilmington theater that had been converted into his campaign media center. The president-elect was calm, measured. "At this hour, our democracy is under unprecedented assault, unlike anything we've seen in modern times," he said. "What we're seeing are a small number of extremists dedicated to lawlessness. This is not dissent. It's disorder. It's chaos. It borders on sedition. And *it must end now*."

Biden continued, "The words of a president matter, no matter how good or bad that president is. At their best the words of a president can inspire. At their worst, they can incite. Therefore, I call on President Trump to go on national television now to fulfill his oath and defend the Constitution and demand an end to this siege."

Watching the insurrection unfold on television, Bob Bauer was afraid of what might happen next: What if the mob, which vilified Vice President Pence for certifying Biden's election, captured him? And even if the rioters were subdued, what if Congress didn't return that night to complete Biden's certification? It would be the opportunity Trump and his plotters had sought. Anything could happen.

At 4:17 p.m., Trump finally appeared in a minute-long recorded video from the White House. He looked angry, as though speaking at gunpoint, as he addressed his followers.

"I know your pain. I know your hurt. We had an election that was stolen from us. It was a landslide election and everyone knows it. . . .

But you have to go home now. . . . We love you, you're very special. . . .
I know how you feel. But go home and go home in peace."

That night, at home, Liddell's phone lit up. Friends and family
were calling from around the world, including his native New Zealand, urging him to resign. Trump had incited a violent insurrection,
and Liddell wanted no part of it. He already owned it because he was
there, he told himself—but he doubly owned it if he stayed on. Mary
Gibert, the GSA transition coordinator, was in a state of near panic.
"My biggest fear was that Chris Liddell was going to resign," she said.
"I called Dave Marchick and said, 'Dave, Chris is not going to resign,
is he? If he goes, everything will come to a screeching halt.'"

Bolten and Marchick got through to Liddell by phone. He was
weeping. "And he's not a weepy kind of guy," Bolten observed. "But
he was so outraged and despairing about what had happened." They
appealed to Liddell's love of his adopted country. "We said, 'Look, if
you leave, there is no sane person there to throw a flag. And so it's really important that you stick it out.'" If Liddell left, who would ensure
that command and control were transferred from Trump to Biden at
noon on January 20?

At 9:58 p.m., Bolten sent Liddell a text message:

*I have enormous sympathy for your situation. I still think you
should stay if at all possible, mainly because of your important
role. . . . How about going to Meadows, perhaps in some combo
with O'Brien, Pottinger et al., with these talking points, on
which you write a mem-con [memorandum of conversation] for
the file.*

Bolten suggested that he tell Meadows:

I have disagreed with many things the president has done, above all his behavior since the election to propagate the fiction of a fraudulent election. Even after today's horrifying events, I intend to stay at my station, because I think the work of ensuring a smooth transition is essential to national security. I'm telling you this to reassure you about adequate White House staffing during transition, but also so there's no misimpression that I condone the president's behavior. I continue to urge you to do what you can to persuade the president to accept a peaceful transition of power. . . .

Liddell read Bolten's message but was unconvinced. He started batting out a letter of resignation.

————

Early the next morning, in the West Wing, Liddell met with O'Brien and Cipollone. They were having second thoughts about resigning. "The group of us basically said, 'Look, it's even more critical that we stay than it was before. This is going to be tough. Our reputations are at risk if something worse happens. But it's even more important that we stay—and if we go, who the hell will replace us?'"

At 8:18 a.m. Liddell texted Bolten:

I'm going to do what you suggest above. I'm also getting together with Robert O'Brien to try and have a united front. . . .

Liddell relayed his message to Meadows in person. (He decided against writing a memcon, fearing it would come back to bite him.)

He no longer had any illusions about Trump, or the grave threat he represented. "Until that time I thought there would be a lot of noise, but that eventually it would play itself out and we'd just get on with things," he said. "January 6 changed the world for everyone." But Liddell would stay and carry out the transition.

On January 8, General Milley spoke with Speaker Nancy Pelosi by phone. Once again, Pelosi was acting as liaison to the Biden camp. "Milley communicated quite regularly with her," a senior Biden adviser told me, "and we communicated quite regularly with Speaker Pelosi. She would convey to him that she expected he would only obey lawful orders, and he conveyed to her that he would only obey lawful orders." The Speaker minced no words about Trump. "Who knows what he might do?" she snapped at the general. "He's crazy. You know he's crazy. He's been crazy for a long time." The general assured Pelosi that there were safeguards against a president launching nuclear missiles in a deranged fit of pique; but what those safeguards were was unclear. Later that day, General Milley called together his principal deputies to review the procedures for activating the nuclear arsenal.

Pelosi continued, "This is deep, what he did. He traumatized the staff. He assaulted the Capitol. . . . And he's not going to get away with it. He's not going to be empowered to do more." Pelosi grilled the general about Trump's inner circle. "Is there any reason to think that somebody, some voice of reason, could have weighed in with him?" She questioned whether Milley could "prevail in the snake pit of the Oval Office and the crazy family as well."

———

The violence of January 6 was shocking to Jared Kushner. But, of course, it shouldn't have been. At rally after rally, from the early days of Trump's 2016 campaign to his run for reelection, throngs of angry "deplorables," as the campaign proudly called them (adopting a term Hillary Clinton had used to describe many of Trump's supporters in the 2016 campaign), had shouted death threats at Trump's opponents, some waving Confederate flags, and cheered their leader's invitations to violence. ("Knock the crap out of them!" Trump jeered at protesters during a February 2016 rally.) Kushner had seen all this with his own eyes. And yet he and Ivanka lived in a world of wishful thinking in which Trump's followers were harmless "patriots."

Suddenly, after a bloody attempted insurrection, Kushner was wondering, *Who* are *these people?* The president's son-in-law couldn't grasp that they were the mob Trump had summoned. It was as though a gang of drunken hooligans had crashed his board meeting. During five years of Trump rallies, Kushner rationalized, no one had been hurt—not seriously, anyway. And now a bunch of crazy people had gone and done some stupid things.

Since election day, Jared and Ivanka had kept telling themselves that Trump was just a fighter, he'd come around to accept the results, he just needed time to nurse his wounds. Even after the assault on the Capitol, Kushner told friends he still hoped that Trump would invite Biden to the White House on Inauguration Day—that image of both presidents together, he thought, was what America wanted to see. Failing that, Trump could make a farewell tour, touting his accomplishments. Or he could hunker down until Biden's inauguration and then depart.

Yet Kushner worried that it could all end badly. The country needed healing and he wasn't sure he could get Trump there. Jared thought the president's attorneys, Giuliani and Powell, were clowns.

The Crazy Show, he called them. But Kushner wouldn't or couldn't tell Trump to get rid of his lawyers. Even if he'd won that argument, for the rest of his life he'd have to listen to his father-in-law complain that with Rudy and Sidney he could have won.

Still, Jared and the president had had knock-down, drag-out screaming matches. Trump's son-in-law played the family-is-thicker-than-politics card. "Look, when you're out of here, a lot of people will scatter," Kushner yelled at Trump at one point. "I'm with you until you hit the dirt—so you may want to listen to what I'm saying! These other people are taking you on a funky ride."

A few days after the Capitol riot, Trump's mind-set was better, but it wasn't where Kushner wanted it to be. He felt good about the video message to the rioters that Trump had finally released on January 6. *If the president stayed on a good path,* Kushner thought, *the chances of getting convicted in another impeachment trial were zero. But Trump's continued obsession with a stolen election was dangerous. If he kept doing irresponsible things, anything could happen.*

The last four years, Kushner thought, *had been war from the first minute.* A White House colleague had told him that he wished Trump could be the same person he'd been at the beginning—but four years of getting the shit kicked out of him made that impossible. This was a delusion shared by many Trump loyalists: It was all the fault of the liberal mob. Kushner concluded that the job takes a toll on a human being. He just hoped that his father-in-law would be able to find some peace.

Yet Trump never stopped scheming to overturn the election; he'd tried to install a loyalist, an environmental attorney named Jeffrey Clark, as attorney general, and demanded that DOJ, DHS, and DOD seize voting machines in swing states. Repeatedly, in wild Oval Office shouting matches on December 18 and on January 3, White House lawyers and DOJ officials had refused his unconstitutional orders. Somehow, Inauguration Day came without further incident.

Looking back, Bob Bauer thought that two random, unforeseen events had helped avert disaster. On December 14, Mitch McConnell had acknowledged that Biden won the election; that declaration had thrown a wrench into the slow-moving coup attempt. Then, in a phone call in late December, Dan Quayle, George H. W. Bush's former vice president, told Pence that he had no choice but to certify Biden's election. Heretofore Quayle had been best known for an infamous visit to an elementary school, where he changed a student's spelling of "potato" to "potatoe." Bauer was struck by the irony. "For years political pundits have made fun of Dan Quayle," he said. "But Quayle may have played a significant role in averting a constitutional calamity by helping to dissuade his fellow Hoosier from giving in to Trump."

On the morning of the inauguration, after an awkward farewell ceremony on the tarmac at Joint Base Andrews, Air Force One lifted off with Donald Trump aboard, bound for his Florida exile. But Trump's shadow remained. His presidency had changed everything.

Both the White House and the Capitol were cocooned in a ring of steel. Cement barriers topped with concertina wire surrounded walkways; National Guard troops toting weapons lined Pennsylvania Avenue; the inaugural parade had been canceled. Biden's staff parked their cars at staging areas and were ferried to the West Wing under armed guard. With the White House still ground zero for COVID infections, many worked virtually from home. Below the Oval Office, in the Situation Room, it was all-hands-on-deck, as Biden's key national security staff were at their posts, alert to the possibility of an armed attack.

Twelve years earlier, at Barack Obama's inauguration, intelligence reports had warned of a possible bombing on the Washington mall. That threat had come from Somali terrorists. This one came from Americans, fanatical followers of a man who'd lost a free and fair presidential election.

At 12:01, Biden's team would take control of the "football" with the nuclear codes and have authority over the military and National Guard. It was the moment Liddell and Kaufman and their teams had been working to bring about for the last nine months.

Trump's presidency was about to end the way it had begun. Four years earlier, at noon on January 20, 2017, Barack Obama's outgoing White House chief, Denis McDonough, had been at his desk, awaiting the arrival of Trump's incoming chief, Reince Priebus, and his staff. An hour went by, but no one showed. McDonough finally turned out the lights and left. It was a metaphor for the Trump administration. No one was at home.

Now a similar scene was playing out in reverse. Meadows had invited Ron Klain, Biden's White House chief of staff, to meet him at his office at 10:00. Right on time, Klain came through the West Wing reception room and arrived at the corner office. He tried the door, but it was locked. The West Wing was empty, the lights out. Klain heard someone calling his name and went downstairs to the Situation Room. Meadows was on the phone for him, saying he was running late.

A half hour later Trump's outgoing chief rushed in, out of breath. But he couldn't stay; he had to deliver a last-minute commutation to the Department of Justice. By the way, asked Meadows, had Klain been briefed on classified operations? Klain told Meadows yes, he'd been briefed. With that, Trump's chief departed.

Up at the Capitol, under a blue sky, Ted Kaufman had a prime seat as he watched his best friend take the oath of office as the forty-sixth president of the United States. Kaufman was proud. Against all odds, his team had hit its marks: twelve of fifteen cabinet secretaries announced; 1,100 staffers chosen, vetted, and hired (more than Obama and Trump combined on their first day); 206 White House staffers in place; a presidential agenda prepared. After Biden's swearing-in, Kaufman and his wife drove home to Wilmington.

David Marchick watched the inauguration on his television from home. He felt relief. Later, he reflected: "There were just all kinds of efforts going on to usurp the will of the American people. It was bad—and in hindsight it was worse than even we knew."

No one felt better than Mary Gibert. She'd done her job and the transition had succeeded. She knew the ending could have been different. "It's hard to imagine it could get much nastier or worse than it did. The country had never faced a situation like this. We could have had the incumbent president being forcibly removed from the White House. Thankfully that didn't happen."

Josh Bolten believed the country had come perilously close to disaster. And not just on January 6. The hours before noon on Inauguration Day had been a time of maximum vulnerability. "The entire White House staff turns over," he said. "So if something happens, even if somebody recognizes they're in charge, they don't know how to pull the levers to do anything. We wouldn't have survived an episode on January 20 or 21 if Liddell hadn't stuck around—if he'd not been there to make sure that all the proper stuff, the decision-making apparatus, was turned over."

At 11:59 a.m., in the West Wing parking lot, Chris Liddell climbed into his red Corvette convertible. For the first time in months, he was at peace: "We all went through our own version of hell between January 6 and January 20. But I had an unbelievable sense of fulfillment that it was worth it to have stayed. Because we landed the plane safely and nothing bad happened on January 20."

Liddell pulled up to the Southwest Gate of the White House. He said goodbye to the Secret Service agents. Then he tipped his fedora and roared off down Constitution Avenue.

Ron Klain, now ensconced in his West Wing office, looked around and noticed something odd. Since the days of Richard Nixon's chief of staff H. R. Haldeman, a big wooden desk had sat just to the left of the entrance. Now it was gone. The office looked like a conference or recreation room, not a place where any work got done.

On his mental to-do list, Klain made a note: Find a desk.

FIVE

LET'S GET TO WORK

Joe Biden couldn't wait to get to the Oval Office. Just a few hours earlier, he'd been sworn in as the forty-sixth president of the United States on the steps of a U.S. Capitol so heavily barricaded it resembled Baghdad's Green Zone. Now, at the White House, accompanied by his sister, Valerie, and brother Jimmy, Biden walked down the colonnade past the white columns, and through the French door that opens into the Oval Office.

It's hard to overstate how much this moment meant to Joseph R. Biden. He'd been thinking about being president since grade school and had been running for the office for decades. And yet his previous campaigns had ended in humiliation: In 1987 he'd been forced from the race after quoting a British politician without attribution; in 2008 he'd quit before the New Hampshire primary, outmatched by a promising young African American senator. Biden tried to tell himself that it wasn't his candidacy, just his timing, that was at fault. Each failed bid meant that he'd had to dust himself off and try harder next time. Biden admired John F. Kennedy not for his glamor or wealth or Ivy League pedigree but for his ability "to absorb pain and suffering and move on—the resilience." Now, like his fellow Irishman, Joe Biden was president of the United States.

Biden led Val and Jimmy into the small adjoining study. Then he kissed them goodbye and walked back into the Oval Office. As he approached the *Resolute* Desk, Biden suddenly choked up, unable to speak. Ron Klain, who'd known him for thirty-five years, had rarely seen him so emotional.

A few close aides were waiting for him: Klain; Jennifer O'Malley Dillon, his campaign manager and now deputy chief of staff; Annie Tomasini, director of Oval Office operations; Bruce Reed, deputy chief of staff; and Jen Psaki, press secretary. Psaki noticed that Biden was not himself; normally chatting, telling stories, and asking questions, now he was quiet.

Klain sat on the couch, with a stack of executive orders ready for Biden to sign. But first, he said, there was something the president should know. Psaki jumped in. Did the president want to put out a statement about Trump's letter? "Oh, a letter?" Biden asked. There was an envelope they'd found in the desk. No one had opened or even touched it.

Biden walked around the desk. He slid open the drawer and picked up the envelope. Inside were two oversize pages covered in a hand-written scrawl. It was signed *Donald J. Trump.*

Biden sat down and read the letter silently, while his aides looked on. Finally, the president looked up. He shook his head. "That was very gracious and generous," he said. "*Shockingly* gracious."

Psaki asked again: Did he want to share what was in the letter, or put out a statement about it? "No," Biden said. "It's from him to me."

The idea of Trump writing a gracious letter to Biden was almost inconceivable. The twice-impeached ex-president had savaged Biden—

tried to bully the president of Ukraine into smearing him, and demanded that Biden be prosecuted. Trump had incited a violent mob and watched them on television as they ransacked the Capitol and tried to disrupt Biden's certification as president. Trump had never conceded that Biden had won the election—so how could he wish him well?

Could *someone else* have written the letter?

"It just shows he's got many different layers," said Jared Kushner. I thought I heard Trump's son-in-law chuckle as he told me this over the phone. Trump had not only written the letter to Biden but had spent three days composing it, Kushner told me.

Trump's constant parroting of the Big Lie of a stolen election suggested that he genuinely believed it, no matter how many times his top officials had told him it was nonsense. But this letter to Biden posed another possibility: Trump knew full well it was a lie—and had cynically chosen to exploit the myth of widespread election fraud to set the stage for his eventual return to power.

Only two things seemed certain: There was no explaining Trump. And for Joe Biden, there'd be no escaping him.

Biden's presidency would be judged, in part, by whether he could hold back the angry, authoritarian forces that Trump had unleashed. Those forces were gaining strength, not only at home but abroad; they'd been emboldened by Trump's coddling of foreign dictators and weakening of American alliances that had kept the peace for seventy years. Biden would have to work hard to convince allies that the U.S. could be trusted to keep its commitments again.

He believed the battle against Trump and the authoritarianism of the MAGA ("Make America Great Again") crowd had to be fought—and won. "America is at an inflection point," Biden told me, "one of those moments that set the course for everything that's to come." In a wide-ranging interview for this book, conducted by email in September 2022, the president provided detailed answers to my written questions. "We have to decide if we move forward or backwards, if we're a country that builds the future, or obsesses over the past," he said. "This is about more than just our country; it's a global battle between the utility of democracy and autocracy in the twenty-first century. We have to show the world that democracy still works."

———————

Twelve years earlier Joe Biden and Barack Obama had taken office at a time of genuine peril—the world on the brink of another Great Depression; credit, the lifeblood of the global economy, frozen; the auto industry on the verge of collapse; two wars raging with no end in sight. Yet all that paled in comparison to the crises confronting Joe Biden in January 2021.

The COVID-19 pandemic was a once-in-a-century public health catastrophe. Nearly 500,000 American lives had been lost so far. Fundamental inequities affecting entire segments of society—based on race and class and wealth—had been laid bare. The economy had been virtually shut down. Thousands of companies had been shuttered and millions had lost their jobs. Meanwhile, the cruel strangulation of a Black man named George Floyd in May 2020, by a white cop kneeling on his neck, had triggered protests and demands for police reform and racial justice. Blazing forest fires in the West signaled an existential threat to a warming planet. And American troops were still bogged down in a twenty-year-long conflict in Afghanistan. Biden would soon have to decide whether or not to bring them home—and how.

And yet these challenges would be just a warm-up for the defining tests of Joe Biden's presidency. First, there was Vladimir Putin's invasion of Ukraine, more than a year away, which would shake the foundations of the postwar world and raise the prospect of nuclear war. Second, there was Trump's false narrative of a stolen election, which threatened the viability of American democracy. A nationwide MAGA-inspired campaign sought to suppress the votes of minorities and subvert the election process. "We can withstand the assault, and we have to," Biden told me. "But each and every one of us has to step up."

Biden's presidency would test the idea that government could function effectively. Almost seventy-four million Americans had voted for a man who'd taken a wrecking ball to governing. Biden would have to convince them that democratic institutions can deliver results and improve lives. China's President Xi Jinping and his ally Russian president Vladimir Putin were betting that the United States was in terminal decline, unable to compete with authoritarian regimes.

Republicans, and even some moderate Democrats, would oppose Biden at every step. With an evenly split Senate and a narrow majority in the House, how could he possibly achieve major reforms? FDR and LBJ had much bigger majorities yet still struggled to enact New Deal and Great Society legislation. Besides, many argued, Joe Biden, a centrist Democrat, hadn't been elected to remake America's social contract. He'd been elected to lower the temperature, restore dignity to the office, act as the anti-Trump.

Yet Biden was setting his sights much higher. He'd won with eighty-one million votes, a margin of seven million, and had spelled out sweeping, transformative proposals during the campaign. The lethal combination of a pandemic and an economic meltdown, Biden believed, required bold governmental action—rebuilding America from the bottom up and the middle out, as he put it. That was the only way to address income inequality, racial injustice, and the angry resentment of voters who felt the system was rigged, resentment that had helped produce Trump in the first place. The country faced a choice: It could tackle these problems or slide back into Trump's toxic blend of hatred and scapegoating.

"Our democracy isn't perfect; it never has been," Biden told me. "But every generation has opened its doors a little wider. It's our turn now to keep pushing it forward. We simply don't have time for all this division—we have much more to deliver and do. American history tells us that from some of our *darkest moments*, we've made some of our *greatest progress*. It's the test of our time to do that again now."

Biden's opportunity would be fleeting. New presidents often suffered drubbings in the midterm elections, as Bill Clinton, Barack Obama, and Donald Trump had learned. Biden hoped he could avoid that fate by getting vaccines in people's arms and checks into their wallets.

The conventional wisdom was that bipartisanship was dead, the country so divided into warring camps that no president could get anything done. But Biden was confident he could cajole and flatter and arm-twist Republicans into joining with him to solve problems. Never mind that, even in the wake of the failed insurrection on January 6, Trump's grip on the GOP seemed as strong as ever. Against the odds and evidence, Biden believed he could unite the country.

The alternative was frightening to contemplate: the threat of a Trump restoration in 2024. Could a president who'd rejected the rules of democratic governance run for office again and declare himself the winner—with the connivance of Republican election officials willing to ignore the actual vote? "What's happening in our country today is not normal," Biden told me. "MAGA extremists don't respect the Constitution, the rule of law, or free and fair elections; in fact, they're pushing to install cronies as election administrators nationwide. Every day, they're working to drag our country backwards, stripping away the right to vote, to choose, to marry whom you love. And they're fanning the flames of political violence, trying to achieve through force and lies what they can't at the ballot box. Democracy can't survive when one side thinks there are only two outcomes to an election—that either it wins, or was cheated. That's a threat to the soul of our nation."

And what would Trump do if he returned to power? His former campaign manager predicted that if Trump ran in 2024 it wouldn't be for vindication; it would be for vengeance.

The team Biden had assembled was arguably the most qualified—and diverse—in modern history. They'd spent their careers preparing to make government work. Some had served Biden for decades; others were skilled technocrats and managers, from both the public and private sector, who knew how to work the levers of power. They were, like Jack Kennedy's inner circle, the best and the brightest, standouts at Yale and Harvard and Georgetown Law, tested in the Clinton and Obama wars, ready to apply science and organizational know-how to conquer a debilitating coronavirus and revive a crippled economy.

Biden's national security team possessed equally glittering credentials. Antony Blinken, the secretary of state, was a polished diplomat in the mold of Dean Acheson, the architect of the post–World War II international order. Jake Sullivan, the national security adviser, was considered a rare intellect. William Burns, the CIA director, was the most accomplished diplomat in recent memory. "They are the most experienced collective team to walk into their respective jobs since I can remember," said James Stavridis, the former Supreme Allied Commander of NATO.

Yet Kennedy and his advisers, blinded by hubris and overconfidence, were brought low by an ill-conceived war in Vietnam. Would the pandemic, or the war in Afghanistan, or a Russian tyrant—or something as yet unforeseen—be more than Biden and his team could manage?

The president slipped Trump's letter back into the desk drawer. "Let's get to work," he said.

SIX

WHEN IS THIS GOING TO CREST?

Joe Biden's presidency began with a blizzard of executive action. On Inauguration Day, he signed seventeen executive orders, rejoined the Paris Agreement on climate change and the World Health Organization (WHO), and unveiled his $1.9 trillion American Rescue Plan (ARP). The next day Biden introduced his national strategy for the COVID-19 response, a whole-of-government plan to defeat the pandemic. In his first two weeks, Biden issued forty-five executive actions, twenty-eight executive orders, ten presidential memoranda, and five proclamations. The head-spinning flurry of presidential action had been made possible by the groundwork of Ron Klain and his team.

Just below Klain in Biden's hierarchy was Steve Ricchetti. A longtime aide, he'd also served as Biden's vice-presidential chief and had been a contender to become White House gatekeeper. After the election, while Biden was still mulling his choice, Klain had reached out to Ricchetti in a bid to avoid any hard feelings; each agreed to report to the other, no matter who was chosen. But Ricchetti was "tender" when Klain got the nod, according to a friend. "He told me, 'I love Ron like a brother. But I think I'd have been the better choice.'" Ricchetti swallowed his disappointment; he would serve as counselor to the president, his key legislative strategist on Capitol Hill.

Right after Klain and Ricchetti in the lineup of Biden's most trusted advisers came Mike Donilon. The third of four children raised in an Irish-Catholic enclave in working-class South Providence, Rhode Island, Donilon, white-haired and soft-spoken, had the disposition of a parish priest. He'd started out as Biden's pollster but became his wordsmith, the keeper of his message. If you wanted to know what Biden thought about anything, you could just ask Donilon. These three—Klain, Ricchetti, and Donilon—were Biden's troika, a modern version of Ronald Reagan's James Baker, Edwin Meese, and Michael Deaver. Klain played the Baker role as top dog. As Jen Psaki put it, "Ron is his strategic supergenius mind about policy and all sorts of things."

Just below the troika, with regular access to Biden, were Anita Dunn, a senior adviser, public relations expert, and longtime confidant; Jen O'Malley Dillon, his 2020 campaign manager and now deputy chief of operations; Bruce Reed, who'd succeeded Ricchetti as Biden's vice-presidential chief of staff; and Cedric Richmond, the former Louisiana congressman and the only newcomer.

These seven staffers were Biden's inner circle—along with two others: Dr. Jill Biden, the First Lady, and Valerie Biden Owens, the president's sister. Dr. Biden was first among equals. "She's the top adviser to the president," said a senior White House official, "and is also very clear-eyed about the people who helped elect him, the Biden coalition." Jill and Val were family, of course, but also powers to be reckoned with. As a friend of the president put it, "You can make mistakes and Joe Biden will forgive you. But if you get crosswise with Jilly or Val, you're *dead*."

Val wasn't one to forgive or forget anyone who crossed her brother.

During Biden's ill-starred run for president in 1987, John Sasso, the campaign manager for Biden's rival, Massachusetts governor Michael Dukakis, secretly gave media outlets a video juxtaposing Biden's speeches with those of a British politician, Neil Kinnock. The video painted Biden as a plagiarizer and helped sink his campaign. (In fact, Biden *had* attributed the remarks in question to Kinnock in his previous stump speeches; he failed to do so just once—inadvertently, he insisted.) More than thirty years later, Val was having lunch with a friend in a Boston restaurant when Sasso walked by her table. "I wish he'd come over here," Val whispered to her friend. She picked up her steak knife and made a stabbing motion. "Because I'd *kill* him."

Roughly sixty percent of the White House staff were women. "We have more women in the West Wing than anyone before us," said O'Malley Dillon, "and they lead on almost all the things that we do across the board. It's not uncommon for Ron to be the only guy in some of these meetings."

The White House was family friendly, an ethos set by Biden himself. "There's women and men of all stripes here," added O'Malley Dillon, "but a lot of moms and dads with young kids, a lot of moms with older kids who are going into college too. I have three young children and the reason we felt comfortable taking these jobs—Psaki, Kate [Bedingfield], Cedric [Richmond], Vinay [Reddy, director of speechwriting], Susan Rice, myself, and others—is that the president was very clear about the importance of family from the very beginning." Ron Klain took this ethos seriously; when several staffers asked if they could attend early morning meetings by Zoom so that they could see their children off to school, he readily approved. (Psaki tended to stay home on mornings, while O'Malley Dillon favored nights.) Klain, who was proud of his feminist bona fides, bragged that the Biden White House had the only political director, Emmy Ruiz, ever to take maternity leave during the first year.

Biden was comfortable around powerful women. Psaki, the incoming press secretary, an Obama White House veteran, would become one of his close advisers. "He is completely comfortable with women in authority roles," she told me. "He doesn't need to have, like, a 'bro' conversation. I've never experienced that ever with him." With Psaki, forty-three, a newcomer to his team, Biden was old-school chivalrous; he stood and said, "Have a seat, have a seat," whenever she came into the Oval Office. Psaki didn't want Biden to go easy on her. "I was like, 'I want you to feel that if you're frustrated or mad about a story or about how I handled something, that you feel like you can convey that,'" she said. "I said to him multiple times, 'I'll know we have a really good trusting relationship when you yell at me the first time.'" Psaki wouldn't have to wait long.

Biden's female advisers included not only Psaki and Dunn and O'Malley Dillon but also Susan Rice, who'd been Obama's national security adviser and was now director of Biden's U.S. Domestic Policy Council; Kate Bedingfield, his communications director; Annie Tomasini, who ran the Oval Office; Dana Remus, White House counsel; and Gina McCarthy, who advised the president on domestic climate issues.

"There are strong women leaders here who are really driving a huge part of the portfolio," said O'Malley Dillon. "It's an awesome, awesome, awesome thing. We're all partners and friends with bonds deepened by going through this experience together."

And then there was Vice President Kamala Harris. By most accounts, Biden and Harris had a warm rapport; the president insisted that she join his White House meetings and often deferred to her. But as the months passed and the vice president's missteps drew fire from critics, their relationship would become more complicated.

———

From the beginning, Joe Biden felt like a prisoner at the White House. Having an office in the West Wing for eight years wasn't the same. Obama called the White House residence "the bubble." Biden called it "the tomb." His lifeblood was getting out to union halls and gymnasiums, corralling voters and slapping backs. He hated being cooped up; the COVID pandemic, which severely restricted his travel, drove him stir-crazy. A private person, Biden didn't like being waited on by attendants; every Friday night, he couldn't wait to escape to his home in Wilmington or his weekend place in Rehoboth Beach, Delaware.

Still, the president did enjoy taking friends on walks through the residence. These often triggered bouts of nostalgia.

One evening, Biden led a friend into an upstairs bedroom where his grandchildren stayed on sleepovers. He picked up a photograph from the mantel. "That's my dad," he said, holding it tenderly. The president was suddenly emotional. "One day he told me, 'Joey, we're going to a restaurant in Philadelphia tomorrow and I'm going to show you how to deal with a maître d'.'" Then Biden pulled out his wallet and carefully extracted a small black-and-white photo. "That's my deceased daughter," he said. Tears welled up, and he slipped the photo back into his wallet

The ghosts of previous presidencies were everywhere, from the Lincoln Bedroom to the Truman Balcony. Even, alas, the ghost of Donald Trump. Biden rarely mentioned the "former guy" in public. But in private he would let loose. He'd removed the painting of Andrew Jackson that Trump had put in the Oval Office and replaced it with one of Benjamin Franklin. He'd even tried to get rid of Jack Kennedy's

Resolute Desk—because it had also been used by Trump. But Biden's preferred replacement, FDR's desk, couldn't be moved from the Roosevelt estate at Hyde Park, New York. Reminders of Trump were ubiquitous. One upstairs room was still outfitted with an electronic golf video game that the forty-fifth president had installed: a big-screen television that allowed players to pretend they were on famous courses like Pebble Beach. "What a fucking asshole," Biden said, showing the contraption to a guest.

A bigger problem was Biden's discomfort with his Secret Service detail; some of them were MAGA sympathizers. He didn't trust them. As vice president, he'd grown close to the agents who shadowed him around the clock. He believed he could win over anybody with his retail political skills—that "to meet Joe Biden is to know Joe Biden is to love Joe Biden," as one aide put it. But times had changed and so had American politics. The head of his detail during the transition, whom Biden had become quite fond of, had been rotated out.

Biden's presidential detail was much larger. The fact that many agents were MAGA sympathizers shouldn't have been surprising; the Secret Service is full of white ex-cops from the South who tend to be deeply conservative. But there was good reason to wonder about some agents' loyalties. Trump had exploited their allegiance and tried to politicize the agency, installing one of his most loyal agents, Tony Ornato, as his deputy White House chief of staff for operations. Putting a civil servant in such a post was almost unheard of, a baldly political move. Ornato would become a controversial figure in the congressional hearings on the January 6 attack; Mark Meadows's assistant, Cassidy Hutchinson, would testify that Ornato had told her about a wild altercation in the president's SUV; Trump had lunged for the steering wheel, demanding to be driven to the Capitol where he hoped to join the mob he'd set in motion. The notion that the Secret Service functioned as a kind of Trumpian palace guard would come out later in testimony before the House Select Committee to Investigate the January 6 Attack.

But the Secret Service's fondness for Trump reminded Biden of a larger, unpleasant truth. For decades he'd enjoyed overwhelming support from law enforcement groups only to have many desert him for Trump in the 2020 election. This was all the more galling, Biden thought, because Trump had done nothing to improve police pensions, as he had—it was just the culture wars. Surrounded by a new phalanx of strangers, Biden couldn't help but wonder, *Do these people really want me here?*

It didn't help matters when one of Biden's agents got into a scrape with the president's beloved dog Major. Biden's three-year-old German shepherd had been acting up, evidently spooked by his strange new surroundings at the White House. One day in March, Major bit a Secret Service agent. The injury was minor and the agent was treated by the medical office. Nobody disputed that the incident had taken place. But Biden wasn't buying the details—specifically, *where* the biting had supposedly taken place: on the second floor of the White House residence.

Showing a friend around, Biden pointed to the spot of the alleged biting. "Look," the president said, "the Secret Service are *never* up here. It didn't happen." Somebody was lying, Biden thought, about the way the incident had gone down.

The president's strained relationship with his Secret Service detail would only get worse in the months ahead.

———

In the first year of the Biden presidency, one member of Biden's team had arguably the most important assignment of all.

Jeff Zients, the first person hired for the transition back in the spring of 2020, would become the White House coronavirus response coordinator, the driving force behind Biden's most urgent priority. The son of a psychoanalyst, Zients was, according to his colleagues, "ego-free"; but his unassuming manner belied a laser focus. He'd been director of the National Economic Council (NEC), run OMB, and spent twenty years in the private sector in a range of industries. More important, he'd learned from the blunders of a previous White House.

The 2013 crash of the Obamacare website, HealthCare.gov, had dealt a severe blow to the notion that government could do anything right. For Obama's White House chief of staff Denis McDonough, charged with launching the website, it had been a traumatic experience; for months before HealthCare.gov imploded, Obama had pointedly told him that the ACA would be useless unless the website worked. And then it didn't. The fiasco prevented millions of Americans from accessing health care. McDonough still had nightmares about walking into the Oval Office and breaking the bad news to Obama. No one had any earthly idea how to fix it. This would require not only a superb manager but someone who grasped cutting-edge technology. McDonough could think of only one person: Jeffrey Zients.

Zients had left Obama's OMB but agreed to come back and take a look. The problem, he discovered, was that the website had been jerry-built by too many independent parties. "It was like building a house where you had HVAC and plumbing and all the rest, but there wasn't really a general contractor," he explained. Within weeks, Zients had HealthCare.gov up and running. The lesson, he concluded, was that "a lot of time, energy, and creativity go into making policy, whether that's legislation or executive action. But sometimes in government, not enough time and energy and creativity go into execution." Zients didn't intend to make the same mistake with COVID-19.

––––––

Zients's credo was "to act with urgency, focus on execution, enlist private and public sector partners. And really important—lead with science, facts." Biden's marching orders, he recalled, were clear: "We've got to do whatever we can to overwhelm this problem. Let's pull every lever, leave no stone unturned, and do everything we can to fight this pandemic." Zients described it this way: "If you're a runner, you don't run just to the top of the hill, you run beyond the hill."

On the afternoon of January 21, his first full day, Biden pulled Zients aside. "Look," he said, "I know this is going to be hard. Inevitably, there'll be ups and downs, but what I need you to do is bring me the problems, shoot straight with me. Together we can solve it and deal with it." Soon after, Zients hit "send" on an email to DOD, mobilizing the National Guard to help distribute vaccines. He would draw on Klain's expertise as Obama's Ebola czar, cutting through red tape.

"What Jeff brings to the table is what I wanted based on my experience," said Klain. "Which is someone who understands how to make the government work. Someone who understands how to interact with FEMA and the State Department and DOD and outside contractors. And Jeff's experience at OMB and HealthCare.gov was the template for this. As was the case with Ebola, logistics beats epidemics. And the challenge here was to figure out what it would take to actually stick needles in the arms of two hundred and fifty million adults in America."

On January 21, the first full day of his presidency, Biden released his two-hundred-page *National Strategy for the COVID-19 Response and*

Pandemic Preparedness. It was an expansion of Klain's Ebola playbook, with seven priorities: restoring trust; mounting an effective vaccination campaign; mitigating the spread by expanding masking, testing, and treatment; activating the Defense Production Act; safely reopening schools, businesses, and travel; protecting those most at risk; and taking a global approach to future threats. In his first two days Biden issued twelve executive orders aimed at the pandemic.

A priority was "equity"; the pandemic had ravaged communities of color, exposing fault lines of race, class, and wealth. For Biden, addressing these disparities was more than just lip service. Dr. Marcella Nunez-Smith, a Yale professor who chaired his Health Equity Task Force, recalled an early Zoom call with the president-elect, Kamala Harris, Zients, and Jake Sullivan. "We were talking about masking and Biden interrupted and said, 'I want somebody to give me some data on masking in the African American community. Because I'm hearing that some folks have a fear about wearing masks because that poses a risk to them.'" Indeed, many young Black males feared that masks made them look like criminals to police. Dr. Nunez-Smith was struck by the president-elect's grasp of the problem: "Not just, 'Hey, are we seeing anything different in terms of mask wearing in Black communities?' But saying, 'I understand the nuance and what might go into that.'"

One of Zients's first hires was Andy Slavitt, fifty-five, a health care adviser and former administrator of the Centers for Medicare and Medicaid Services. With his tousled dark hair, he resembled the nerdy mathematician played by Jeff Goldblum in the movie *Jurassic Park*. Slavitt had sounded early warnings about a coronavirus variant called Alpha. "We were racing against the variant," he said, "and needed to vaccinate the country more quickly than the variant could spread." When Slavitt arrived at the White House, he was sobered by the challenge ahead. "The entire first week or ten days was terrifying," he said. "Thousands of people were dying. It was an awesome responsibility and we felt the weight of that responsibility."

"Early on we discovered that there really was no plan for COVID," said Zients. "There wasn't enough vaccine supply; there weren't enough vaccinators, and not enough places to get vaccinated." The first priority was ordering vaccines. "The rest of the world was trying to buy them," said Slavitt, "so the fact that they hadn't procured enough was baffling to us." Trump had placed a large order from Johnson & Johnson but almost nothing from Pfizer and Moderna. Ron Klain had a fix for that. "I said, 'We're going to order everything of everything.' Because you just never know what's going to work and what's not. That was the big lesson I learned with Ebola: If you want a hundred gowns, you have to order a thousand because nine hundred of them are never going to show up. And second, be very transparent about what's working, what's not working. We're not trying to hide the ball. You want to build public confidence and trust."

Suddenly, doctors, scientists, and experts who'd been ignored or overruled were everywhere: Dr. Anthony Fauci, director of the National Institute of Allergy and Infectious Diseases (NIAID); Dr. Rochelle Walensky, director of the CDC; Dr. Vivek Murthy, the surgeon general; and Slavitt. They appeared on televised Zoom calls; one-on-one interviews with cable news reporters; and town halls with network anchors.

Back in December, more than a month before taking office, Biden had set a goal of vaccinating 100 million Americans in one hundred days. Zients and his team had exceeded that pace and locked in enough doses for all 300 million Americans. The problem was getting those doses into people's arms.

Trump's team had no blueprint for that. "They were shipping doses and a lot of them were sitting in freezers in states," Zients explained. "We'd talked to the governors and the governors' teams, and we realized that the plan was to 'drop-ship' doses to states, and then leave it to them to figure out the rest." As Slavitt put it, "It wasn't surprising to me at all that more than half of the doses they were sending the states weren't making their way into people's arms. And Trump's team didn't know it; they weren't even tracking the numbers." It became clear to Dr. Nunez-Smith that Biden's team would be starting from scratch. "They [Trump and his health officials] had spent a lot of time thinking about getting vaccines from point A to point B. But there wasn't a vaccination strategy. Vaccines don't save lives; vaccinations do."

There was also a dearth of vaccination sites. So Zients pressed FEMA and the U.S. military into service. Five thousand active-duty troops and another five thousand federal personnel fanned out to support a vaccination surge. Zients made sure the National Guard was fully reimbursed by the government. "It was about ensuring enough supply, and enough places for Americans to go," he said.

They were riding an emotional bungee jump, whipsawed by the metrics. "Our daily rhythm was defined by two reports, one in the early afternoon and one in the late evening," said Slavitt. "The early afternoon report was how many people got vaccinated the prior day. And that was a hold-your-breath number that we'd be waiting for." The second report came out in the late evening. "It was how many cases, hospitalizations, and deaths," he said. "It lagged slightly behind the vaccines. But it was a bigger hold-your-breath moment, because you're vaccinating everybody and you're assuming it's going to have a big impact on the overall numbers." The zigzagging numbers on hospitalizations and deaths kept everyone on edge. "Those numbers had fits and starts, right? We were nervous when they were rising. So you'd look at those things and say, 'When is this going to crest?'"

The slightest glimmer of hope could make Slavitt giddy. One day in March, he went on Twitter and saw a photograph. "There was a woman who posted a picture of herself in a nursing home, seeing her grandmother for the first time, with her new baby that was born during the time when they were isolated. And it was a beautiful picture, just a very simple picture. But you could read everything. You could read everything on those faces."

Slavitt continued, "And you know the feeling you get when you walk outside and it's been rainy and cloudy for like weeks on end? And then you see the sun poking through in some part of the sky? And you see the blue, and you see the sun, and it kind of warms you? I remember closing my eyes and feeling that sensation. Because I felt like this was the dam breaking. And then it started happening in droves: people posting pictures of themselves and what they did after they got vaccinated. I remember sitting in the White House, with tears coming into my eyes, which I couldn't control. I just was thinking of all the people, up all night, moving vaccines, getting people vaccinated. The military out in force. Everybody coordinating. All the hard work."

Getting hundreds of millions of people vaccinated would be costly. A critical part of Biden's pandemic effort was his so-called American Rescue Plan (ARP). First unveiled in December, the $1.9 trillion package would fund the COVID-19 response. "It was a very big deal in every single way," said Klain. "Without it we would have run out of gas." It was also the most far-reaching anti-poverty legislation in a generation, promising a guaranteed income to every poor and middle-class family, reducing child poverty, at least temporarily, by one third. But pushing such a large bill through Congress was a gamble. "There were several gut-check moments," said Klain. "The first came back in the transition when we decided to put this on the table. As we started to add it up, it was clear it was going to be a very, very large number. Could we really do something this big right out of the box?" The answer was, they *couldn't*—not if they wanted any Republican votes.

The ARP's price tag was more than twice the stimulus passed by Obama during the Great Recession of 2009. It was large for a reason. "The president made a choice," said a senior White House adviser. "In previous periods of economic trouble, the country had undershot the problem. And the impact of that was a slower recovery, worse job creation, and a lot more pain for a lot of people." There was a risk of triggering inflation, but Biden's team believed the larger risk was a stalled economy, massive unemployment, and endless food lines. "This sounds like something that Aaron Sorkin would want to write," said the adviser, "but the truth is, this was not a stimulus. This was a rescue plan. And when you're trying to save the economy and you're trying to save lives, because a big piece of this was funding for the vaccines, you had to prepare to go big and stick with it."

Shortly after Biden was sworn in, a gaggle of Republican senators proposed a pared-down, $600 billion package. "There was an off-ramp there where you could have, two weeks into his presidency, netted a significant, albeit not nearly big enough, win," said Klain. The president could have compromised and pocketed a small bipartisan victory. "But Joe Biden chose to go to the wall. He didn't have any doubt about it. I think his failure to blink is greatly to his credit. He had a real feeling for what the moment required."

By the following year, many would be blaming Biden's ARP—fairly or not—for triggering runaway inflation. But in early 2021, few experts were predicting that long-term inflation was a serious risk.

Within a few months, Zients and his team had set up more than eighty thousand vaccination sites across the country. Ninety percent of Americans lived within five miles of a place where they could get the vaccine. But Zients and his team felt responsible not only for things they could control but also for those they couldn't.

"It was very clear that every bit of it we did better would mean people's lives would be saved," said Slavitt. "And every bit of it we did worse would mean lives that we lost. That's a very unusual position to be in. Consequences that are measured in hundreds of thousands of lives." Indeed, a study by the Yale School of Public Health in July 2021 found that the Biden vaccination campaign had saved 279,000 lives and prevented 1.25 million hospitalizations. "But that's a double-edged sword," said Slavitt. "Because you feel like you could never do enough. You know the movie *Schindler's List*, where they tell him he saved all these people and he cries because he could have saved more? That's what we felt like."

On Saturday, March 6, the ARP passed the Senate, on its way to a final vote in the House, through an arcane process called reconciliation. The procedure required only fifty Democratic votes—with the tie broken by Vice President Harris. Klain had rarely seen Joe Biden more ebullient. Joe Manchin, the Democratic senator from West Virginia, had nearly sunk the bill. But when it finally passed, Biden grinned from ear to ear as he made the announcement, flanked by Manchin and his colleagues on the White House driveway. "He was just thrilled," said Klain, "because it had been in rough shape for a while. And we knew how big and historic it was." It was a "BFD," to use Biden's famous phrase. "It has a lot of historic provisions in it that really burnish his legacy already," said Klain. "To be able to deliver historic achievements on day fifty is pretty rare for a president."

So far Zients and his team had seemed equal to one of the most daunting operational challenges in U.S. history. Emboldened, Biden doubled his original vaccination goal. On March 25, he pledged to have 200 million Americans vaccinated in the first hundred days. In the thirty days before Biden took office, roughly ninety thousand Americans had died from COVID; in the last thirty days the death toll had been cut by two thirds, to thirty thousand. Checks of $1,400 had been delivered to 160 million households, eighty-five percent of all Americans.

In March, Biden announced that vaccines would be available to everyone by the end of May and barbecues would be safe by the Fourth of July. Polls showed his approval rate was in the mid-fifties. (Trump had bottomed out at thirty-four percent.) Sixty percent of Americans believed the country was on the right track. Beltway pundits were bullish. "Biden and his advisers have proven that they are adept at what used to be considered, pre-Trump, the rules of politics," wrote Susan B. Glasser in *The New Yorker.* "They have under-promised and over-delivered. They have resumed the presidential traditions of dog ownership and churchgoing." According to a CNN poll, nearly eighty percent of Americans said that the worst of the pandemic was behind them. "There was no . . . ball spiking in Thursday night's speech," wrote Glasser, "and yet there was the inescapable whiff of a political wind changing, a sense that soon—if not soon enough—the pandemic could be over and life might be normal again."

On July Fourth weekend, Biden threw a party at the White House, welcoming military families and essential workers to the South Lawn. Fireworks lit up the sky. "Together, we are beating the virus," the president declared. "Together, we are breathing life into our economy. Together, we will rescue our people from division and despair."

Ron Klain was upbeat. "On July 2 we had a good jobs report and we swore in a bunch of new citizens," he told me. "And we had the LA Dodgers at the White House, our first sports champions. And then on the Fourth we hosted that big event on the South Lawn. That period was really a pivot point for us as we try to move to doing the normal stuff presidents do. We're crowning baseball teams, we're picking cherries in Michigan, we're celebrating July Fourth—all these classically American things presidents do."

But the celebration was premature. A veteran high-ranking official from a previous Democratic White House used a World War II analogy: "It's as if Eisenhower had succeeded on D-Day and was driving towards Paris, and then suddenly said, 'Okay, we can stop now. Let's celebrate. This cooking here in France is pretty good. Let's have fun for a while and then the Germans will start winning and then we'll start attacking again.' And that's what happened with COVID."

The buoyant mood at the White House, and around the country, was about to take a dramatic turn. New and more contagious variants were arriving on U.S. shores from Britain, South Africa, and Brazil. The most worrisome was called the Delta variant. "We were getting data, the most important from Barnstable, on Cape Cod, in July," recalled Zients. "We knew that Delta was more transmissible. What we didn't know was that it was causing breakthrough infections, which was different from Alpha."

After he'd left the White House to return home to California, Slavitt suddenly realized: "It was going to be the fastest-growing respiratory illness of all time, in recorded memory."

And in a war-torn country on the other side of the globe, a crisis was about to test Joe Biden's claim to competence on the world stage.

SEVEN

IT'S GOING TO BE AWFUL TO WATCH

When it came to the war in Afghanistan, Joe Biden had once been all in. During a trip to the country in January 2002, as chairman of the Senate Foreign Relations Committee, he'd been impressed by the determination of the Afghan people. Biden favored American support for the government and armed forces, and he had a soft spot for Afghan women and girls, whose plight had improved immeasurably since a CIA-led U.S. invasion had toppled the Taliban in 2001. Biden's heart was with a girl he met at a school in Kabul. As he wrote in his book *Promises to Keep*:

> . . . *as I stood to leave I told the kids, "I have to go now." "You can't go!" I heard someone say. I looked up and saw a thirteen-year-old girl standing ramrod straight in the middle of the classroom, so brave and so determined. "America can't go," she said. "I must learn to read. I will be a doctor like my mother." I wanted to walk over and hug her. "No. No. No, honey," I said. "America is going to stay."*

And yet Biden came to believe the war was unwinnable. The turning point occurred in 2009, on a trip as vice-president-elect to

Kabul. "When he came back," said Ron Klain, "he reached the conclusion that there was no way to build a nationwide pluralistic democracy based in Kabul. And that we should focus our mission on counterterrorism, finish the job of getting bin Laden and whatever was left of Al Qaeda, and then end it." Biden believed the generals had boxed Obama in—pressured him into approving a "surge" of more troops. Biden was fed up with the corruption, the feuding warlords, the opium trade, and the ill-defined U.S. mission.

Since Biden had left office as vice president, America's longest war was no closer to being resolved. Osama bin Laden was dead. Barack Obama had set 2014 as a deadline for a U.S. withdrawal. And yet the war ground on.

Donald Trump had promised to end the conflict but had no plan. He started peace talks with the Taliban in 2019 but, having announced a U.S. withdrawal, had no leverage. For dealmaker Trump, the Taliban's refusal to break with Al Qaeda wasn't a deal breaker, nor the fact that the Afghan government was cut out of the talks. Still, Trump set an American exit date of May 1, 2021, and privately boasted that he'd dealt with the mullahs personally. "He talked to the head of the Taliban," one of Trump's senior advisers told me. "And he said, 'I know where you live; I know where your family lives. If you harm Afghan women and children or come after Americans, I will do some crazy shit.'"

Biden thought Trump was right to end the war in Afghanistan, but wrong in the ham-handed, half-baked way he tried to go about it.

During the transition, planning for Afghanistan would fall to Jake Sullivan and Antony Blinken, the incoming national security adviser and secretary of state, respectively.

One of five siblings raised in Minneapolis, Minnesota, Sullivan, forty-four, was already a legend. Biden called him a "once-in-a-generation intellect" and Hillary Clinton tagged him a "potential future president." From his undergraduate days at Yale to his stint as a Rhodes Scholar at Oxford to his postgraduate studies at Yale Law School, Sullivan seemed destined for great things. Tali Farhadian Weinstein, a friend since freshman year at Yale, was struck by his analytical firepower. He could break down a problem instantly and had photographic recall; in class she never saw him take any notes—he'd sit with his hands crossed in front of him and just listen. But she was even more impressed by Sullivan's rectitude and "midwestern wholesomeness." He stood out for his unabashed love of country and for "his sense of responsibility even before he had any responsibility."

For Sullivan, it seemed, everything came naturally. At Weinstein's wedding, he delivered an eloquent tribute to the bride and groom. Afterward the author Malcolm Gladwell, one of the guests, critiqued his speech. The problem, he said, was that Sullivan was *too* perfect; he should have looked down at his notes, appeared a little nervous, tripped over a few words.

After law school, Sullivan clerked for Judge Guido Calabresi of the U.S. Court of Appeals for the Second Circuit and was tapped by then secretary of state Hillary Clinton to be her right-hand person. He was almost always the brightest person in the room. (And the palest; his Yale classmates affectionately mocked him as the whitest person they knew.) Richard Holbrooke, Obama's imperious Special Representative for Afghanistan and Pakistan, would often get switched to Sullivan when trying to reach Clinton by phone. After one such call, Holbrooke, who seldom praised anyone, said to a colleague, "That guy could be secretary of state."

Now, along with Blinken, Sullivan was the intellectual architect of Biden's foreign policy.

Antony "Tony" Blinken was a walking résumé for secretary of state; he'd served in senior foreign policy roles under Clinton and Obama and as staff director under Biden in his work with the Senate Foreign Relations Committee. He was a sartorial throwback to the Cold War era. "If Dean Acheson came back to life, he'd be Tony Blinken," said Admiral James Stavridis, "right down to the suits and the ties and the swept-back silver hair." Stavridis, the former Supreme Allied Commander of NATO, was referring to Truman's legendary pinstriped secretary of state. But Blinken, fifty-nine, had a less buttoned-down side; he played lead guitar in a garage rock band called Coalition of the Willing.

Blinken had worked so closely with Biden for so long that their bond was palpable. "You could *feel* that relationship, how close they were," said a senior State Department official. "Joe Biden has a lot of advisers on national security and foreign policy. But Tony Blinken is in a different weight class. They finish each other's sentences. They look at the world through the same set of glasses and the same lens." When Blinken, then Biden's vice-presidential aide, was tapped to become Obama's deputy national security adviser, Biden could barely let him go. "Tony's office had just moved a few feet down the hall and he still saw the vice president every single day, multiple times a day," said this official. Blinken was as close to Joe Biden as Secretary of State James A. Baker III had been to President George H. W. Bush. In theory that bond would translate into clout; no one doubted that Blinken spoke for the president.

But there was another, less sanguine theory about Sullivan and Blinken: They were staffers, who'd spent their careers writing policy papers instead of getting things done in war zones. "Ideas are great, but at the end of the day they're not worth a tinker's damn if they're not put into effect," said Richard Armitage, a former deputy to Secretary of State Colin Powell. It wasn't personal; it was the nature of the working relationship. "Think tankers and Hill staffers frankly don't run things; they run their boss," said Armitage. "They aren't going to tell their principal, 'You've got your head up your ass, boss.' At best they may say, 'Well, sir, you may want to think of doing it *this* way.'"

Richard Clarke, an NSC veteran under both Bill Clinton and George W. Bush, sounded a similar cautionary note. "A principal realizes that he or she is accountable for everything within their writ," he said, "and takes responsibility for it, acts proactively on it, defends his turf. He has enough background that he can stand up to the president and the president cares not to piss him off and have him quit. Whereas a staffer pretty much does as he's told."

One question on the minds of Washington's political class was whether the three had adequately considered all the options for ending America's longest war. Over the summer of 2020, there were few formal meetings, virtual or otherwise, on Afghanistan. The fraught transition, hobbled by Trump's refusal to concede the election, made preparation difficult; neither the DOD nor OMB would talk with the incoming Biden team. General Mark Milley, chairman of the Joint Chiefs, was preoccupied with averting a possible Trump coup d'etat. "With the situation Milley was in," said the adviser, "Afghanistan planning was really much more a January-February thing."

A prominent foreign policy expert, who favored keeping a small U.S. military presence in Afghanistan, thought Biden and his team were in lockstep. "It was amazing the amount of groupthink there was. There was no one saying, 'This could all fall apart quickly.' They assumed the Afghan government would hold long enough to conduct an orderly withdrawal. And the whole reason you have an interagency process, and a national security council, is to have somebody say, 'Well, have you considered the chance that blank or blank will happen? And what will we do then?' I don't think there was any such process here."

In fact, there *was* a process: Biden insisted he wanted a robust review of Afghanistan options. He'd keep an open mind. To that end, Sullivan had convened twenty-five NSC meetings, large and small, ten meetings of department deputies, three cabinet-level meetings, and four meetings in the Situation Room that included the president.

Early on, Biden, Sullivan, and Blinken took part in a videoconference with Admiral Stavridis, who, from 2009 to 2013, had commanded thousands of American troops in Afghanistan. (Stavridis was joined by four other experts—evenly divided between those who said "pull the plug" and "it's such a small investment. Leave them there.") "We have thirty-five thousand troops in North Korea," Stavridis told the president. "We have forty thousand troops in Europe. We have twelve thousand troops in Japan. We didn't pull them out. We don't think that is a forever war. We think of that as an investment in stability in an important region. So the real debate here is, do you think Afghanistan is strategically important or not?"

The admiral continued, "Look at a map and the location of Afghanistan. I think it's strategically important in that regard, and secondly, Mr. President, there is U.S. credibility on the line here, and thirdly, the investment at this point is modest. When I commanded that mission, we had one hundred and fifty thousand troops there. We're down to three thousand troops. Pulling them out is penny-wise and pound-foolish, in my view."

The president listened politely—and then replied, "I respect the views of those on this call who have said keep the troops there, but we've been at it for twenty years. It's time to go home. I don't see another way out."

Within the administration, there were two forceful opponents of a rapid U.S. withdrawal: General Lloyd Austin, Biden's secretary of defense, and General Milley. They argued that a small U.S. force, from three to four thousand troops, could buy time for a political settlement between the Afghan government and the Taliban.

There were few people Biden respected more than Milley and Austin. The president's son Beau had served on General Austin's staff during his deployment to Iraq; the then vice president had instantly bonded with the general during a visit to that war zone. And Biden's admiration for the chairman of the Joint Chiefs was obvious to everyone. "He *loves* Milley," said one of Biden's close friends.

In late May 2022, I paid a visit to General Milley. I'd been told that the Joint Chiefs chairman didn't like to revisit the Afghanistan withdrawal. But in fact, over coffee and pastries in his Pentagon office, the four-star general with a chest full of medals was expansive about the arguments that he and General Austin had made to Joe Biden for resolving America's longest war.

"The president and the decision-making system were very fair in airing all the views," he said. "So we argued a different, alternative course of action than that which was selected. The fundamental issue for the president was he couldn't see an end and we couldn't articulate an end that didn't involve an unending commitment of significant amounts of U.S. troops—twenty-five hundred, three thousand, four thousand, forty-five hundred."

The larger problem was that those troops would be just a stopgap—because although the Taliban had refrained from attacking U.S. forces over the previous eighteen months, that would change after May 1, when Trump had promised that the U.S. would withdraw. Biden would soon set a new withdrawal deadline of August 31. After that, it would be open season on U.S. troops. It was a formula for endless war.

Milley went on: "So if you stayed past August 31, that meant re-opening the war with the Taliban. And the president said he was not willing to do that."

Milley conceded this point to Biden. "You're right," he told the president, the general recalled. "You'd be starting the war again on the first of September."

"But you still thought it was worth staying?" I asked the general.

"I said, 'Look, it's cost, benefit, risk,'" Milley said. "'Are you willing to incur the risk of collapse of the government, horrific outcome, massive amounts of refugees, significant backtracking of twenty years of sacrifice and what's going to happen with women's rights and all these other things? Are you willing to incur that risk?'

"The counterargument from the president," Milley said, "was, if not now, when?"

Total U.S. withdrawal was anathema to most of the foreign policy establishment. This included not only Stavridis but also Ronald Neumann, former ambassador to Kabul. Bruce Riedel, a highly respected former CIA Middle East analyst, who'd conducted a study of Afghanistan options for Obama back in 2009, shared their view: "Biden's right. We can't beat the Taliban. But we'd produced a stalemate and it cost us very little, about three thousand troops on the ground, a small expenditure in terms of economic and military assistance. And we protected the vast bulk of the Afghan population from the kind of medieval theocracy that the Taliban was threatening."

Deciding to end the war was one thing; executing the withdrawal of U.S. troops and the evacuation of American citizens was another. It would be a challenge unrivaled since the Vietnam War: extricating troops in the middle of a civil war; removing Americans from a combat zone; and resettling tens of thousands of Afghans who'd assisted the U.S. war effort. Trump's team had done little to prepare for any of this.

"We came in and found out it was worse than we'd imagined," said a senior Biden NSC official. "There'd been no coordination with other contributing countries. There'd been no consideration of how do you keep an embassy presence going if the only boots on the ground are the Marine security guards? How do you facilitate humanitarian assistance outside of Kabul if you don't have forces outside of Kabul? And then how do you execute a safe drawdown?"

But it was even worse than that—because Trump had dismantled the SIV program back in March 2020. This crippled the U.S. ability to resettle Afghans who'd helped the American war effort—translators and others who would soon be desperate to flee the country. In March 2021, Blinken's team doubled the number of consular officials conducting interviews at the embassy in Kabul. But the process still moved at a glacial pace. It was never designed for an emergency evacuation of tens of thousands of people fleeing an advancing army.

There was another problem. The Afghan armed forces were reliant on the American military. Anthony Lake, a foreign service officer in Saigon who later became Bill Clinton's national security adviser, described that dependency, in both Vietnam and Afghanistan. "The problem is that we train foreign armies on the American plan, reliant on our airpower and artillery," he told me. "And when we start withdrawing it, they feel naked and suddenly have to fight the way their opponents do." The Afghan armed forces were also dependent on a small army of American contractors who kept their planes flying and vehicles running. When those contractors departed, all bets would be off.

Given those challenges, a too-rapid withdrawal could invite disaster. Ronald Neumann, the ex-ambassador, wondered, "Did people like Blinken see that this was a potential loser and argue with the president? Did they not see it? Or did they see it but stayed loyal staffers and didn't push the argument?" Andy Card, Bush's chief of staff, thought Biden needed "a handful of really deep contrarians to say, 'Wait a minute, what are you doing?'"

In fact, Blinken had tried to tap the brakes on the timing of the Afghan withdrawal. On March 23, at a meeting of the NATO foreign ministers in Brussels, Biden's secretary of state briefed his counterparts from Britain, Germany, France, and Italy. The allies argued that the U.S. should delay a withdrawal—and use it as leverage to force the Taliban into a political settlement with the Afghan government. Blinken called the president that night and told him he was hearing "in quadraphonic sound" that the allies wanted to wait for an agreement with the Taliban before withdrawing. "The president took that on board and said, 'Okay, let's give that a shot,'" a senior State Department official told me. But when U.S. negotiators pitched the idea to the Taliban at talks in Doha, Qatar, they balked; a delayed withdrawal would lead to renewed attacks on U.S. and NATO forces, just as Biden had predicted.

Bruce Riedel wasn't buying it. "Biden just wanted to get out and none of his advisers was going to stand in his way," he told me. "Certainly not Tony Blinken, whose whole career revolves around being Joe Biden's guy. Jake Sullivan was way underprepared for the job as national security adviser of the United States. He may be ready for that job in ten years, but he doesn't have the background to do it now."

As April approached, Admiral Stavridis feared that Biden's team was distracted. "They've got huge domestic political battles they're fighting," he said. "And I think the oxygen for international policy debates was kind of squeezed out by COVID. But sooner or later the world has a way of showing that it will have its way with us. The first example may be Afghanistan. As the wheels come off there, it's going to be awful to watch."

EIGHT

THE HARDEST OF HARD DAYS

On April 14, from the White House Treaty Room, Biden gave his first speech on "the way forward in Afghanistan." He got straight to the point. "I have concluded that it's time to end America's longest war. It's time for American troops to come home." Biden pivoted to the manner of the U.S. departure. "We will not conduct a hasty rush to the exit. We'll do it responsibly, deliberately, and safely. And we will do it in full coordination with our allies and partners, who now have more forces in Afghanistan than we do. And the Taliban should know that if they attack us as we draw down, we will defend ourselves and our partners with all the tools at our disposal."

The president added emphatically, "I'm now the fourth United States president to preside over American troop presence in Afghanistan: two Republicans, two Democrats. I will not pass this responsibility on to a fifth."

After the address, Biden picked up his cell phone and called a friend. "How'd I do?" he asked him. "You were fine; you did great," the friend said. "Yeah, but the press is going to kill me," Biden replied. "I'm fucked no matter what I say."

Every president hates the press—in his own way. Obama regarded the media with disdain; after all, they'd treated him as a saint who could do no wrong and upon becoming president suddenly couldn't do anything right. Trump declared war on reporters who regarded him as a clear and present danger to the republic. Biden would never call the media "the enemy of the American people," as Trump had done. But sometimes he thought they treated *him* like the enemy. This seemed surprising because Biden came to the presidency with eyes wide open. "The press corps coverage during the campaign was always shitty," said a senior White House adviser. "They thought he'd never win, counted him dead fifty times, and then he got here." This official couldn't resist a dig at the media's coddling of Obama: "So he doesn't expect to win the Nobel Peace Prize his first year as president."

Biden's peevishness with the press had been obvious; asked by a CNN correspondent what made him "confident" that Vladimir Putin would keep his promises, the president practically took her head off. Often it was the *form* of the question that set him off. "People ask questions like, 'You're in a crisis, right?'" explained a senior White House adviser. "Some of the line of questioning is almost a self-fulfilling prophecy, which I think gets under every president's skin. I think he definitely feels that when he's under fire."

Three months in, Biden had been changed by the presidency. "He feels the loneliness of the office," one of his close friends told me. When I asked Ron Klain about this, he quarreled with the word. "'Loneliness' is not a word I would use with Joe Biden," he said. "He's always very connected to his family, in particular his grandkids, Jill, and Hunter. But I absolutely agree that what he's feeling is the uniqueness of the office. The fact that it's different to be president than vice president. The fact that it's his *decisions*, not his advice, that are being so heavily scrutinized, that have such great consequences. So yes, I think on him it feels less like loneliness and more like a kind of—'responsibility' is the wrong word. 'Burden,' maybe?"

"'Weight'?" I suggested.

"That's a very good way to put it," Klain said. "The weight. The weight of it. I definitely think he feels that."

But Biden hadn't even taken a punch yet. That would come soon enough.

On July 8, the president gave another speech, from the East Room of the White House. "Our military mission in Afghanistan will conclude on August 31," he said. "The drawdown is proceeding in a secure and orderly way, prioritizing the safety of our troops as they depart."

Afterward a reporter asked: "Is a Taliban takeover of Afghanistan now inevitable?"

"No, it is not."

"Why?"

"Because the Afghan troops have three hundred thousand well-equipped—as well-equipped as any army in the world—and an air force against something like seventy-five thousand Taliban. It is not inevitable."

A few minutes later, he was asked: "Mr. President . . . Do you see any parallels between this withdrawal and what happened in Vietnam . . . ?"

"None whatsoever. Zero," Biden replied. "The Taliban is not the North Vietnamese army. They're not remotely comparable in terms of capability. There's going to be no circumstance where you see people being lifted off the roof of an embassy in the—of the United States from Afghanistan. It is not at all comparable."

One White House staffer cringed when he heard this—*that's a dumb thing to say*, he thought, *because we fly helicopters from the embassy every day.*

More important, the president seemed to be saying that there'd be plenty of time for U.S. forces to make an orderly retreat. But where had he gotten that idea?

This would become the subject of intense debate and bitter acrimony in the months ahead, mostly behind closed doors. Depending upon whom you asked, the shambolic U.S. withdrawal from Afghanistan was due to an egregious failure by U.S. intelligence agencies or wishful thinking on the part of the U.S. military about its Afghan allies. Tony Blinken told me that the seeds of the debacle were sown by a stunningly optimistic intelligence assessment, one that turned out to be dead wrong. "The worst-case prediction for the failure of the Afghan government and the security forces, throughout the spring and into the early summer, was eighteen months–plus," he said. "So that was the underlying assumption of everything we did."

But senior CIA officials rejected the notion that the Afghan fiasco was caused by an intelligence failure. President Biden, they insisted, was under no illusions. He understood the fragility of the Afghan military forces and had a clear-eyed view of the weaknesses of the Afghan political leadership.

Afterward, behind the scenes, there'd be plenty of finger-pointing between Foggy Bottom and Langley.

In the summer of 2021, the unraveling of the Afghan regime had already begun. Unmotivated, demoralized, and unfed, Afghan armed forces were ripe targets for Taliban fighters; bribes and promises to spare families were enough to persuade most to surrender without firing a shot. Little had changed since David Martin, a CBS correspondent, had visited U.S. Special Forces near Tora Bora in 2002.

The recruits were all wearing sandals in the snow. "I asked one of the Green Berets why they didn't have better shoes," recalled Martin, "and he showed me a room filled with winter gear supplied by the U.S.—which the local war lord was keeping to sell rather than distribute to his troops. If you were an Afghan soldier treated like that, would you fight?"

The provincial capitals began falling. On August 8, Sar-e-Pul, Kunduz, and Taloqan surrendered to the Taliban. Three days later, the provinces of Badakhshan and Baghlan to the northeast and Farah to the west followed suit. On August 12, Kandahar and Herat fell.

Biden's national security team still held out hope. A senior White House adviser explained: "What the intelligence community and the military advisers told us was that the Taliban would quickly mop up the rural parts of the country, but that ultimately the Afghan security force would fall back to two or three major provincial capitals and Kabul itself. And they would fight a fierce defense of this handful of urban areas—and then there would be a protracted struggle, where the security forces had the upper hand. And the fact that they basically handed over every city in the country without bullets being fired obviously took us by surprise."

As the Afghan forces disintegrated, Joe Biden was stunned. "Obviously he was surprised," said this senior adviser. "And frustrated."

With Kabul on the verge of falling, the U.S. military command activated emergency contingency plans. Special Forces evacuated the American embassy staff to the airport, and the next day Biden ordered five thousand troops moved from the United States to Doha and other staging areas, so that within hours they could take over the Kabul airport. The Taliban continued to advance.

The American military command had been rendered blind. U.S.

commanders had no meaningful presence outside headquarters and no feel for what was happening at the unit level.

But the delusions about the Afghan armed forces started at the top.

On Saturday, August 14, Biden and his national security team gathered in the Situation Room to monitor the deteriorating situation in Kabul. General Milley delivered a pep talk, an impassioned monologue about how well he knew a commander in the southern part of the country. His name was Sami Sadat. Afghan president Ghani had just appointed Sadat to lead the defense of Kabul. Milley raved about his friend Sami's prowess as a fighter and brilliant military leader.

"Just days later Sami Sadat had an op-ed in *The New York Times*, explaining how the U.S. had fucked up its role in Afghanistan," said a senior adviser, incredulous. Sadat fled the country. The Afghan armed forces melted away. This adviser was stunned by Milley's blind faith in Sadat and his fighters.

Only weeks earlier President Ghani had visited the White House, where Biden pressed him to concentrate his troops in defense of Kabul. Ghani had vowed instead to defend every inch of Afghan soil. In a telephone conversation on the evening of August 14, the Afghan president told Secretary of State Blinken: "We're going to fight to the death." But the next day Ghani fled the country, reportedly accompanied by a pile of misappropriated cash. Within forty-eight hours he was in Abu Dhabi.

Meanwhile, ragtag Taliban fighters strolled unopposed into the capital. Kabul had fallen.

I asked General Milley, "Did it shock you when the Afghan armed forces collapsed in eleven days?"

"Yes. Absolutely, totally," he said. "You know, there are some people who argue, 'Oh, you should have known, you could have known—

in some cases you *did* know that this was on the brink.' That's utter nonsense."

What happened, I asked, to his friend Sami Sadat? "I absolutely thought he was going to fight," Milley said. "And he did for a while. But when he saw Ghani go, he bolted."

Milley conceded that the fish rotted from the head. "At some point a really good historian is going to dig into the exact causal effects," he told me. "I think one of the key ones is the abandonment of his own country by its national leader. Ghani and his entire national security apparatus, they bolted. But there are deeper causes than that. This war wasn't lost in eleven days in August. There were strategic decisions made over the course of twenty years—when people chose to go left instead of right."

"It was a failure of twenty years of military-to-military relationships," said a senior White House adviser. "There's just twenty years of believing we had built an army over there, twenty years of believing in the commanders—and there was nothing there."

A former State Department Indochina hand, who'd spent decades in the region, was appalled by the American military's trust in its Afghan counterparts. "I think you have to start with profound misassumptions about the Afghan forces," he said. "Then, when we began to withdraw, we didn't have any eyes. We didn't have anybody left in Herat and Kandahar. We were totally dependent on people like Sami Sadat. And even if Sami Sadat was Jesus Christ, you should have known that these guys were on the ropes."

As millions watched on television and live streams across the globe, the U.S. withdrawal devolved into chaos; throngs of people swarmed onto the tarmac of the Hamid Karzai International Airport (HKIA), as the American forces scrambled to evacuate. As an enormous C-17 plane taxied down the runway, several desperate Afghans climbed into the wheel bed; they were crushed by the landing gear or fell to their deaths. The evacuation had become an operational fiasco.

Leon Panetta, former White House chief of staff, CIA director, and defense secretary, watched the spectacle in stunned disbelief from his home in Carmel Valley, California. "I had the same feeling that I had January 6," he told me, "looking at the U.S. Capitol and not seeing it surrounded by National Guard, to deal with a crazy crowd that everybody knew could attack the capital of the United States. I had the same reaction when I saw what was happening in Kabul." Panetta went on CNN and compared Biden's handling of the crisis to John Kennedy's disastrous Bay of Pigs.

Scrambling to meet the withdrawal deadline of August 31, U.S. troops tried to secure HKIA as crowds of desperate Afghans pressed against the gates. On August 15, the commander of the U.S. Central Command, General Kenneth McKenzie, went to Doha to meet with the Taliban; he intended to present them with a map of Kabul, showing a zone around the airport that they must stay away from or be attacked. By the time he got there the Taliban were already entering the city; the best McKenzie could do was warn them not to interfere with the evacuation. The American military—and the U.S. civilians and Afghans who depended on them for their safety—were now at the mercy of the Taliban, which controlled Kabul. They'd have to negotiate for permission to depart in one piece.

On August 23, at Joe Biden's direction, CIA Director Burns met with Taliban leaders at the palace recently vacated by Afghan president Ghani. They were angry; frustrated that in their moment of triumph, U.S. troops were occupying their airport. Burns echoed McKenzie's warning not to interfere with the American evacuation, and the Taliban agreed—as long as the U.S. didn't stay beyond the August 31 deadline.

The evacuation was challenging enough, but it was made more difficult by a feud that developed between the U.S. military and the CIA, which hasn't been reported before.

As military commanders at HKIA rushed to get desperate Afghans onto C-17 transport planes, they noticed that no matter how many people they evacuated, the crowds at the gates kept growing. The manifests didn't add up. Finally, the commanders realized why: Unbeknownst to the Pentagon, the CIA was bringing in its own evacuees by helicopter from a nearby secret base and dumping them on the tarmac at HKIA. They then clambered aboard the C-17s.

A senior Pentagon official explained: "We were trying to run a plane out of there every forty-eight minutes at the height of this thing. And we were just jamming people on these C-17s as much as we could. And there were days when we couldn't get more people through the gates because the CIA kept pushing people of their own. They wanted them out. We wanted to do what we could to help, but it threw us back. And there were days when we couldn't let others in the gate because we were helping them."

The DOD couldn't get answers from the CIA about its evacuees. Defense Secretary Austin was furious and vented his frustration with White House advisers.

And things were about to get a lot worse—because of a threat from the terrorist group known as ISIS-Khorasan, or ISIS-K.

U.S. intelligence had been monitoring a constant stream of chatter about an imminent suicide bombing. Director Burns had rarely seen anything like it. "The threat streams were as intense as anything I've seen, not just in this job but in my previous incarnations," the veteran diplomat told me. And yet the intelligence was maddeningly imprecise. U.S. commanders knew something was coming but could do nothing to prevent it. At HKIA, thousands of Afghans and the American service members who were trying to help them were sitting ducks. "Sadly, it was a question of when, not if, something was going to happen," said Burns.

"We held our breath every day about whether or not we'd lose any of the six thousand people he sent to Kabul," said Klain. "If you look at what happened in the evacuation of Saigon, hundreds of people died as planes were shot down. And other accidents happened. This was very much on Joe Biden's mind when he agreed to authorize the evacuation mission. We always knew it was a risk. Particularly as the threats from ISIS-K and the specific terror threat rose, we knew the odds of something happening were higher."

While U.S. troops were on the ground, one of Biden's close friends told me, the president barely slept. "You're watching intel and holding your breath, really just praying that nothing will happen to your people," said a senior NSC adviser. "The sound of my phone ringing at any point of the day brought . . . I was terrified that something had happened to our men or women in the country. Just completely terrified." On August 25, before departing Kabul, Bill Burns had gone out to HKIA to check on the situation there and paid a visit to Abbey Gate. "That day the crowds weren't quite as numerous as they would be the next day," he recalled.

On August 26, Biden's national security team filed into the Situation Room. Burns, who'd just returned from Kabul, joined them. General McKenzie was on a video screen from Afghanistan, and the group watched as an aide pushed a piece of paper to him. McKenzie read it and looked up. "We just got a report that there was an explosion," he said. At that moment Joe Biden walked into the Situation Room and took his seat.

Jake Sullivan brought the president up to speed, and then McKenzie was slipped another piece of paper: "Four service members have died," he announced. "Some others were injured. Some likely fatally." The reality slowly sank in: A suicide bomber had blown himself up at Abbey Gate. The death toll was sure to climb. Joe Biden looked down at his feet. He sat in silence for several minutes that seemed like an eternity. Then the president looked up. "The worst that can happen has happened," he said.

Over the next hour, updates trickled in from commanders in Doha and Kabul—five, six, seven, ten, and finally thirteen service members killed in action. And dozens of Afghan civilians were also dead. "It was awful," said Burns. "And you could just see the enormity of this for the president."

Biden's team digested the news in silence. "You know how the military gives briefings; they give things in very direct and matter-of-fact updates," recalled Jen Psaki, who was present. "It wasn't that people were crying in the room. It was more that people were very somber." Vice President Kamala Harris was listening in from Air Force Two, somewhere over the Pacific, on her way home from a trip to Southeast Asia.

Even for General Milley, with nearly five decades of military service, this was a blow. "I've had some horrible days over the last forty-three years," he told me. "I've been blown up and shot at—minefields and firefights and this, that, and the other thing many, many times. I've buried the dead and comforted the wounded, been there with the families—and I've had a lot of bad days. That was certainly one of them."

As word of the bombing spread, a massive thunderstorm swept over the White House grounds. Lightning bolts struck both the North and South Lawns; the Marine guard outside the West Wing reception room slowly turned and marched inside. Booming thunder suited the dark mood. "You could just feel the weight of everything," said Psaki.

The weight felt heavier because they'd known an attack was coming. Jake Sullivan was beating himself up over it. The wunderkind who'd had a sense of responsibility before he had any actual responsibility was second-guessing his decisions. "We were getting very good intelligence about the type of plotting and potential attacks that ISIS-K was attempting to do right around that time," said a senior State Department official who knows Sullivan well. "And to not be able to prevent it from happening . . . Jake certainly did take it hard. The secretary took it hard. All of us took it hard."

A few days later, in an email, I asked Klain how he and the White House staff were doing.

He replied:

Tough week but we are executing on important work and find purpose and solidarity in that.

Just over a year later, Joe Biden described that terrible day to me with the unique perspective that comes with being president. "There are a lot of hard days on this job," he said. "Nineteen beautiful, innocent, little children massacred at school in Uvalde, Texas. Grandmothers and churchgoers gunned down while grocery shopping in Buffalo, New York. You look survivors in the eye, and you just feel the black hole in their chest that's sucking them in. You try to give them some hope. You try to change things, so these disasters stop happening and all that pain isn't for nothing."

But for Biden the bombing at HKIA was different; he'd put the service members in harm's way. "August 26 was one of the hardest of the hard days," he said. "There's no question. Those thirteen proud, patriotic American service members were beloved sons and daughters, brothers and sisters. They came from all over our country, each with a unique story and the dreams of loved ones who'd nurtured them, united by a common call to serve something greater than themselves. They were ultimate heroes, and each saved countless other lives as part of the largest airlift evacuation operation in our history."

On August 29, a U.S. military drone launched a lethal strike on a vehicle thought to be carrying explosives intended for a suicide attack on the Kabul airport. Ten people were incinerated, killed instantly by a U.S. Hellfire missile. But the identity of the target was immediately questioned by witnesses. A few days later, *The New York Times* published an investigation, concluding that the casualties were innocent civilians, including seven children. At first, General Milley adamantly defended the strike, calling it "righteous." But an official investigation by the U.S. military's Central Command soon confirmed the *Times*'s account: It had been a deadly mistake. In October, the Pentagon announced that it would provide condolence payments to the victims' relatives and help to settle them in the U.S.

Another hard day came on Sunday, August 29. That morning the president and the First Lady traveled to Dover Air Force Base for a ceremony honoring the thirteen fallen U.S. service members. Before the "dignified transfer" of the flag-draped coffins from an Air Force C-17 to waiting hearses, Biden met with grieving relatives. In a spare room furnished with chairs and couches, the president moved from one family to the next. He spoke of his late son, Beau, who'd served in Iraq and then died of a brain tumor six years before. The time would come, he promised, when the memory of their loved one would bring a smile instead of a tear. Biden had given this heartfelt message to suffering families countless times before.

Widows, mothers and fathers, sisters and brothers of the fallen service members exchanged handshakes and hugs with the president. But three of the families were angry, enraged. Some had wanted to meet not with Biden but with Donald Trump. A sister of Jiennah McCollum, the pregnant widow of Marine Corps Lance Corporal Rylee McCollum, snapped at a reporter. "You cannot kneel on our flag and pretend you care about our troops," she said, referring to Biden. "You can't fuck up as bad as he did and say you're sorry. This didn't need to happen, and every life is on his hands."

As the families boarded buses to depart, one woman screamed across the tarmac: "I hope you burn in hell! That was my brother!"

Nothing had prepared Biden for this moment. "Over the next couple of days he just felt a deep, misunderstood sadness, you know?" said Jen Psaki. It was not only that a few of the families blamed him; it was that invoking Beau somehow made things worse. "Some of the criticism was about him praising his son," Psaki said. "And to him, and to a lot of people he's helped through grief, that had been something that helped. That's deeply personal."

Biden had been masterful at dealing with others' grief, but this was something else. "It's just a very different thing," his friend said.

Afterward Joe Biden told a senior White House aide: "This is what being president is."

NINE

ELEVEN DAYS IN AUGUST

After twenty years of fighting and $2 trillion dollars of American aid, the Afghan government had collapsed in less than two weeks. When I spoke with Ron Klain a few weeks later, he sounded weary. Did it have to end that way? "There are no 'have-tos' in the world, I guess," he said. "We were genuinely surprised that the Afghan army didn't last at all. Ghani didn't even negotiate a political settlement; he just fled the country. No one thought that the gap between the first provincial capital falling and Kabul falling would be eleven days. And so the suddenness of it was certainly a surprise, and the lack of any effort to defend Kabul."

But not everyone was surprised. Back in May, on a visit to the country, Ronald Neumann, the ex-ambassador, had written on the Atlantic Council website: "If multiple cities fall the game may be over, and a rapid unraveling of the Afghan army and the Kabul leadership becomes a possibility. . . ." Richard Armitage, who'd helped evacuate Saigon during the Vietnam War, said, "Everyone knew it was going to happen fast, whether it was eleven days or a month and a half. Anybody involved in a meaningful way knew it was over."

Leon Panetta argued that Biden could have bought time with

a careful drawdown of forces. "I think we could have maintained a presence in order to develop a withdrawal plan," he said. "And then reinforced that plan with military assistance and counterterrorism operations and with a close relationship with our allies. I mean, Jesus, we had NATO fighting with us. I think we could have had our NATO allies playing a bigger role in maintaining some semblance of stability there. I refuse to believe that we couldn't have done this in a better way."

Bruce Riedel, the former CIA analyst, agreed. "The status quo of April, May 2021 was evidently sustainable," he said. "It had to be done in a way in which the contractors that supplied the Afghan army with vehicles and the Afghan air force with planes could be kept there. The contractors would've stayed if they hadn't been told they had to leave. And in that sense, we self-destructed our ally." Moreover, Riedel argued, the U.S. should have waited to withdraw until November or December, when the fighting season ended. "You start a drawdown when you know that for the next five months they're snowed in, nobody can move. Instead, they rolled the dice and the result is catastrophe. For twenty years, rightly or wrongly, we've been telling the Afghan people, particularly Afghan women, 'We're not going to desert you.' And we've abandoned them."

Still, for better or worse, the decision to withdraw was Biden's to make. The real question was why the evacuation had been so tragically flawed. And in particular, why did American forces depart precipitously, before American diplomats and embassy staff and their families had been safely evacuated?

Having lost the argument to keep a larger U.S. force, Milley and Austin were following orders to expedite the American withdrawal. They were doing so with a limited force of seven hundred U.S. troops.

"We began pulling out the troops and of course subsequent decisions were made to go to zero and we did that," said Milley. "We executed those decisions." I asked him why the American contractors were pulled out. "The contractors weren't going to stay if there weren't going to be American troops to protect them," he replied. "It's that simple. And the seven-hundred-troop limit, the cap limit, was simply to protect the embassy. That's all."

But the seven-hundred-troop limit was based on the assumption that the Afghan government would stay in power long enough to get the Americans and Afghan allies out; it wouldn't be nearly enough to secure their evacuation in a city overrun by the Taliban.

Richard Clarke, the NSC veteran, had a theory: "As best I can tell, Milley and Austin fought hard. And I think they said, 'Okay. We did our best. You want us out? We're going to get out.' I think they felt, 'Okay, we fulfilled our responsibility. We told him this was stupid. He said no, slapped us down.' That's the point at which the national security adviser and secretary of state step in and say, 'Ah, no, wait a minute.' The real question is to what extent did Jake and Tony try to push back on the decision or the timing."

Clarke continued, "I think they could have walked into the Oval Office and said, 'We understand you're the boss. We understand you get to say no. We know you wanted to get out as soon as possible. And we'll do that, but we have a responsibility to not have things go terribly bad and hurt your reputation and the reputation of the United States. And the idea of pulling the military out first and then the women and children is probably not the smartest thing we could do.'"

Leon Panetta observed: "You just wonder whether people were telling the president what he wanted to hear. And whether or not there was that contrarian in the room, saying 'you're about to take one of the biggest gambles in your presidency and you'd better damn well be prepared for any contingency.'"

When I repeated Panetta's comments to him, Klain shot back. "*Joe Biden* didn't pay a trillion dollars to these people to be trained to be the army. He wasn't out there saying for years, as Leon was, that we had built a viable fighting force. Leon favored the war. Leon oversaw the training of the Afghan army. He was CIA director and defense secretary when many of the Afghan troops were trained. If this was Biden's Bay of Pigs, it was Leon's army that lost the fight."

Klain went on: "What Joe Biden was being told by the military commanders was that the Taliban was a bunch of guys in pickup trucks with AK-47s and we'd trained the Afghan military for twenty years with a trillion dollars. And the rural parts of the country would fall, but there would be a valiant defense of Kabul. That defense never showed up."

———

Biden's vaunted national security team had been knocked off stride. Blinken, grilled by Congress and on cable news shows, looked shell-shocked. As *Washington Post* columnist David Ignatius put it on MSNBC's *Morning Joe*, "These are people who've never gotten a bad grade in school." A State Department veteran couldn't understand how Biden's best and brightest had become the gang that couldn't shoot straight. "They're all so damned able," he said. "Joe Biden's an able man—and decent. It just doesn't add up. It's one plus one plus one equals zero."

For six months, Biden's team had been remarkably free of internal strife. But in the aftermath of the bungled Afghan withdrawal, the knives came out.

At Foggy Bottom, Secretary Blinken's defenders insisted he wasn't to blame; the intelligence had been fatally flawed.

But of course, the other obvious fall guy was Jake Sullivan.

Sullivan was an easy target. Some believed he was too green to be national security adviser, a job thought better suited to old warriors like George H. W. Bush's Brent Scowcroft and Bill Clinton's Tony Lake. (Scowcroft was an Air Force lieutenant general; Lake, a foreign service officer in Vietnam.) Sullivan, according to this theory, was better suited to the halls of academe than the corridors of power.

Sullivan was well-liked, but even that made him a target. "That Sullivan may be too nice a guy," Armitage complained to me. Indeed, Biden's national security adviser was a rarity in Washington, D.C.: grounded, with a strong attachment to his roots in Minnesota; close friends; and few enemies. Friends knew that he'd agonized over the tragic loss of lives on his watch. "This definitely weighed on Jake very heavily," said Ron Klain. "Did he give the right advice? Did he push back on the military enough? What were the choices and so on and so forth? So what I see in Jake is sadness, not anger."

A New York Times piece on Sullivan was titled "A Figure of Fascination and Schadenfreude." This struck a former State Department colleague as unfair: "Schadenfreude? Who doesn't like Jake? Who thinks Jake should fall or suffer? He's not an arrogant person. He's a decent, kind person. And you want people like that in these jobs, even if they don't do everything perfectly."

Others thought Biden should fire General Milley or Defense Secretary Austin; after all, they'd executed the bungled withdrawal.

Joe Biden felt let down by his briefers. His longtime colleagues Blinken and Sullivan blamed the intelligence community for the debacle. A senior White House adviser minced no words: "There's no question that the intelligence was wrong. I mean one hundred percent."

On April 7, eight months after the U.S. withdrawal, I went to see CIA director Bill Burns in his seventh-floor office at CIA headquarters. We sat around a coffee table high above the agency's wooded campus in Langley, Virginia. Draping his lanky frame over a chair, the director was soft-spoken and disarming; it was hard to imagine him being flustered by anyone.

"There are people who say this was an intelligence failure," I said. "Was it?"

Burns replied, "I don't believe it was. I think we and the intelligence community did an honest, straightforward job of pointing out the frailties—of the Afghan political leadership, especially, but also the Afghan military and the increasing momentum of the Taliban."

How long the Afghan armed forces could survive, Burns said, depended on when you asked. Of all the U.S. intelligence agencies, he insisted, the CIA had been the most pessimistic about the Afghan government's odds for survival. "It was a pretty sober analysis of what would happen to the Afghan military when you pulled out several legs of the stool. Not just the U.S. military presence but also the contractors who kept their air force up in the air. If you pulled those legs out, it was a prescription for things unraveling pretty quickly," said Burns. All of this, he said, was communicated to Joe Biden.

A senior White House aide retorted: "Bill can point to things that said 'it's possible that X will happen,' right? In a twenty-page document, 'it's possible that X will happen' in one line. But the overwhelming weight of the material provided to the president was that the Taliban would take these rural areas quickly, and it would be a long time before they would launch an assault on major cities, let alone on Kabul itself."

When I spoke with him in April 2022, Tony Blinken was blunt: "Throughout this whole process there was an intelligence assessment that proved to be wrong: that the Afghan government and security forces would remain in place and hold on to the major cities well into the following year." The worst-case prediction, Blinken reiterated, was "eighteen months–plus."

But that wasn't the way General Milley recalled it. "The intelligence I saw predicted months," he told me. "So we leave the country in August—and in a reasonable, worst-case scenario it's a Thanksgiving, Christmas, January time frame when things fall apart. I think the intelligence was very, very good. The one exception was that no one predicted eleven days."

The truth was that the Afghanistan withdrawal was a whole-of-government failure; everyone got nearly everything wrong. "It's hard to look back at this and not realize that we missed an awful lot," confessed a senior Pentagon official. "We missed a general understanding of the Afghans' will to fight and their ability to fight without us. We didn't realize the depth of corruption in the officer ranks and the lack of unit cohesion they had in the field. We didn't appreciate how much they depended on us for intelligence surveillance, reconnaissance, command and control support, and air strikes. We failed to realize the effect of the Doha agreement that Trump put in place. That was the beginning of the end of the Afghan national security forces and the beginning of the end of the Ghani government. And we didn't see the degree to which the Taliban were executing a very long-term, strategic strategy of slowly accumulating power inside the country."

This official concluded: "We all missed it. And it wasn't just the

United States. The Brits, the Canadians, the French, the Germans—nobody saw this coming."

Joe Biden had decided it was time to leave Afghanistan. A different intelligence estimate wouldn't have dissuaded him. Nor would arguments that the Afghan military just needed more time to stand on its feet. And he wasn't going to fire anyone either. Both the decision to withdraw and its flawed execution belonged to him.

From the beginning, hubris was the midwife of the American mission in Afghanistan. The U.S. military tried to mold the Afghan army in its own image so that it relied on intelligence, logistics, and airpower. When those things were gone, Afghan troops were on their own, knowing no help was coming and wondering if they'd get paid or fed. A veteran Indochina hand explained: "We didn't understand that Afghans don't just slaughter each other till the last man; they watch to see where the wind is blowing."

It was obvious to the Afghans which way the wind was blowing. Over three administrations, the U.S. had telegraphed its intentions. First, Obama had set a departure date of 2014; then Kabul's government was dealt out of the negotiations with the Taliban in Doha; and Trump summarily announced the U.S. would withdraw by May 1. Biden set a deadline of September 11, a date that many thought had more to do with politics than strategy. He finally settled on August 31.

Biden was responsible for what followed. The U.S. had promised to support the Afghan armed forces—but effectively pulled the rug out, sending most of its troops and all the American contractors home while U.S. diplomats, American citizens, and Afghan allies were still on the ground.

"The larger point is this," Secretary Blinken told me. "The idea that we pulled the rug out from underneath the Afghans after twenty years and billions and billions and billions of dollars of investment in them and their security forces through training and equipment— if people believe that despite all of that the whole enterprise would collapse within weeks, well, that also speaks volumes to what was done over the last twenty years and whether we got a lot of things wrong for a long time."

It wasn't the first time a U.S. ally had imploded. The Afghans drew the same conclusion that the South Vietnamese had drawn at the Paris Peace Talks a half century before: They'd been sold out. And so the Afghans vanished or joined up with the Taliban.

John Negroponte, a veteran diplomat and ex-DNI, had seen it all before as a young foreign service officer in Saigon. "There's a lack of appreciation in Washington for the real fragility of these third-world governments," he told me. "When their confidence starts to unravel, there's no telling how quickly everything will fall apart."

———

Yet lost amid the narrative of the bungled exit was a remarkable success story: The evacuation had been an astounding logistical feat. Over seventeen days, under fire, exposed to suicide bombings and rocket attacks, the U.S. military had evacuated 124,000 people. The operation involved 387 sorties, carrying 7,000 passengers a day on U.S. military aircraft and civilian airliners; almost overnight, the U.S. military had constructed a network of "lily pads," bases in nearby countries from which refugees were leapfrogged to safety. Every flight departed without a hitch. As an operational success, it ranked with the Berlin airlift or the rescue of British troops from advancing Nazis at Dunkirk.

Still, the Afghan withdrawal gave Biden a black eye. In public, he'd been oddly defensive, reluctantly owning the mistakes with a belated declaration: "The buck stops with me." Until this point of his presidency, even in the face of a crippling pandemic, Biden had been nearly pitch-perfect. Suddenly he was tone-deaf. Anybody could see that the operation had been botched even as Biden called it "an extraordinary success." His reputation for honesty and empathy was tarnished.

But there was another casualty. Until mid-August 2021, Biden and his White House team had been regarded as avatars of competence. They were ruthlessly executing ambitious plans to tame a lethal pandemic and revive a crippled economy. These domestic enemies had begun to yield, slowly but surely, to science and organizational know-how.

The Afghan fiasco had punctured Biden's aura of competence. The president's approval rating reflected that, tumbling from fifty-two to forty-three percent.

The reality was that America had blundered into a country it didn't understand. Admiral Stavridis reluctantly concluded that, as with Vietnam and Iraq, the U.S. effort had been doomed from the start. "The central failure of Afghanistan was our certainty that we could create a modern, democratic, centralized government with a strong national army," he said. "We always knew it would be 'Mission: Very, Very Hard.' History should have taught us it was in fact 'Mission: Impossible.'"

Ron Klain believed the price of the ill-fated withdrawal was worth paying. "The president could have basically done what his predecessors did and fought the war out," he said. "He could have escalated and added troops just to hold our own, and watched more Americans perish in a losing fight. And he just wasn't going to do that. And he knows he's paid a political price for it. But he believes he made a decision that was in the best interest of the country, and one that his successors will be glad he made."

Along with his late son Beau's rosary, Biden still carried in his pocket a card denoting American casualties in Afghanistan over twenty years: 2,461 dead; 20,744 wounded. "It's the clearest and most painful reminder," he told me, "that there's nothing low-cost or low-grade about war."

Still, some warned that the United States' retreat from the graveyard of empires would embolden America's adversaries. Joe Biden's next foreign policy crisis, a showdown with Russian president Vladimir Putin, would make the withdrawal from Afghanistan look tame.

TEN

A WORK IN PROGRESS

I n the beginning, Joe Biden liked having Kamala Harris around. He made it clear that he wanted the vice president to be with him not only for the PDB but for meetings on almost *everything*: from COVID-19 to the economy to voting rights. Since the inauguration, Biden and Harris had been almost inseparable, at the president's insistence. "If he doesn't see her, it means there's a reason she's not there," said a senior adviser. Usually, it meant that Harris was traveling, or casting a vote on the Senate floor.

During meetings the president often deferred to Harris. Part of it was that Biden valued her life experience, so diametrically opposed to his own. "He trusts the different point of view that she brings to issues," said Anita Dunn, "and the different background and experience that she has had in her life." During the summer of 2020, Biden had leaned on Harris for advice on how to respond to police killings of unarmed Black men; during the federal trial for the death of George Floyd he wanted to know how the African American community would react if the jury failed to convict Derek Chauvin, the cop charged with his murder.

COVID-19 safety protocols, which drastically curtailed their official travel, meant that the president and vice president spent hours together every day. "That led to a deepening of the relationship," said Tina Flournoy, Harris's chief of staff. A longtime Democratic operative who'd been Bill Clinton's chief during his post-presidency, Flournoy, who is African American, was struck by the way Biden and Harris interacted in meetings. When the president asks the staff questions, she explained, "the VP always lets this unfold a little bit. But then, in an almost Socratic way, she starts asking questions. And her goal is to provide the president with additional information and potentially different views. And you can see the president's brain sort of churning and churning on this information and looking at this as it unfolds. And it helps him arrive at a decision. And I've seen this time after time after time after time."

During a meeting with Biden and Harris and civil rights leaders in the Roosevelt Room, Dr. Johnnetta Cole, president of the National Council of Negro Women, was moved by what she called "the synergy between the president and the vice president of my country." Klain insisted that Biden and Harris had a genuine bond. "There's a real sense that she has his back and he trusts her to deal with difficult problems. It always surprises me when people are surprised because I see it every day."

But the relationship between Harris and the White House was about to get much more complicated.

———

Harris had been a bold choice as Biden's vice president. Not only because no Black woman had ever been chosen for the job but also because of a potentially disqualifying episode during their battle for the nomination. On June 27, 2019, during the last televised Democratic debate, Harris had launched an attack on Biden over the ancient but contentious issue of forced busing. In the late 1970s, Biden had opposed the controversial compulsory busing of students from predominantly white public schools to achieve integration. Fifty years later, given his dependence on Black voters, this issue was a hand grenade waiting to explode. And sure enough, standing on the debate stage, with Senator Bernie Sanders between them, Harris pulled the pin. After criticizing Biden for speaking warmly of two segregationist senators, she paused and then added:

> *And it was not only that, but you also worked with them to oppose busing. And there was a little girl in California who was part of the second class to integrate her public schools. And she was bused to school every day. And that little girl was me.*

Biden looked as though he'd been punched in the stomach. Harris continued:

> *So I will tell you that on this subject, it cannot be an intellectual debate among Democrats. We have to take it seriously. . . .*

Biden stammered through an answer, and the episode blew over. But Harris's carefully staged ambush had drawn blood. "What Kamala Harris said to him was obnoxious, but she wasn't wrong," said Jonathan Alter, author of *His Very Best*, a biography of Jimmy Carter. "Biden had been a strong opponent of busing. He'd been Carter's first supporter in the Senate, and he went to him and said, 'Busing's this huge problem in Wilmington. You were against busing in Atlanta. I want your support for a bill that prevents judges from ordering busing as a remedy to segregation.' And Carter looks at him and says, 'Joe, that bill would be flatly unconstitutional. I can't do that.' And Biden left really disappointed."

Still, Biden's close supporters considered Harris's attack a cheap stunt. In the eyes of his fiercest protectors, Jill Biden and Val Biden Owens, this could be unforgivable.

But Biden and his team got over it. The California senator had redeeming qualities. Biden needed a person of color on his ticket. He'd made justice for communities of color a central campaign promise. Moreover, Harris was a sharp prosecutor and an effective interrogator who could be counted on to eviscerate Trump's vice president, Mike Pence, in their debate. And there was one other thing: Harris had been close to Beau Biden. As attorneys general for California and Delaware, respectively, Harris and Biden's beloved late son had forged a personal bond while negotiating with banks during the foreclosure crisis in 2011.

By 2020, the vice presidency had come a long way since John Adams called it "the most insignificant office that ever the invention of man contrived." Vice President George H. W. Bush, who attended his share of state funerals, once cracked to a foreign leader: "You die, I'll fly." But since Jimmy Carter's vice president, Walter Mondale, had been given an office in the West Wing and major responsibilities to go along with that valuable real estate, vice presidents had actually done real work.

Before the election, Klain presented Harris with five historical models on how to conduct the job: Mondale (Carter); Dan Quayle (George H. W. Bush); Al Gore (Clinton); Dick Cheney (George W. Bush); and Biden (Obama). The Cheney model, of a domineering vice president under George W. Bush, was not an option. The choice came down to two: Gore and Biden. As Clinton's vice president, Gore had taken on more-or-less permanent assignments: the environment, technology, reinventing government, the US–Russia and –South Africa relationships. Gore was, Klain explained, the quasi-president of those five things. As Obama's vice president, Biden, on the other hand, was more of a generalist. He spent a lot of time with the president and took on tasks that were time limited: the U.S. military mission in Iraq, and the Northern Triangle—alleviating the root causes of immigration from Guatemala, Honduras, and El Salvador.

Harris chose the Biden/Obama model.

It was a template that had served Obama's presidency well; Biden had carried out important responsibilities and mostly stayed in his lane. Still, the Obama-Biden relationship was not without strains. In the first volume of his memoir, *The Promised Land*, Obama professed his love for his vice president. He'd been there for Biden, lending emotional support during the dark days of Beau's terminal cancer. They'd had private weekly lunches. But Biden was never fully convinced that he'd earned Obama's respect.

Part of Biden's insecurity came with the job. "Show me a vice president who hasn't been frustrated," said one of his senior advisers. But some of it stemmed from Obama's aloofness. In his postpresidency, Obama kept a certain distance from his old running mate. In the late summer of 2021, the ex-president told close friends that he approved of Biden's decision to withdraw from Afghanistan. But they were struck by Obama's apparent indifference to the battering Biden was taking for the botched evacuation. "If you ask Biden about Obama, the first thing he'll say is, 'I love the guy,'" one said. "But you never hear Obama saying that about Biden." Of course, First and Second Families are not always social friends; during two terms in the White House, Ronald and Nancy Reagan never invited

George and Barbara Bush up to the residence, a snub that Barbara never forgave.

No one was suggesting that the Obamas were as haughty as the Reagans. But it was true that in the Obama White House the Bidens, like the Bushes, had rarely spent time upstairs.

It remained to be seen just how much Biden would involve Harris in actual governing. During the 2020 campaign, Biden had repeatedly promised that she'd be the last person in the room when he made big decisions. That wasn't really true when Biden was vice president; that role was usually played by Obama's chief of staff. But, at least in the beginning, Biden wanted Harris to be perceived as his full partner.

With an evenly divided Senate, Harris's most important duty would be casting tie-breaking votes for the Biden-Harris legislative agenda. The question was what other assignments she'd take on. Harris had one in mind: voting rights.

She'd been involved in the cause for decades. As California attorney general, Harris filed an amicus brief in the Supreme Court case *Shelby County v. Holder*, opposing the gutting of Section 5 of the Voting Rights Act, allowing states to pass restrictive voting laws. As senator, she'd cosponsored the For the People Act and the John Lewis Voting Rights Advancement Act. And as COVID-19 threatened to derail the 2020 election, Harris wrote another bill, the VoteSafe Act, to make it easier for people to vote during the pandemic. In March 2021, Flournoy, her chief of staff, asked Ron Klain to make voting rights one of Harris's assignments. When she heard nothing back, Harris went to Biden and Klain directly, and they agreed.

Among the Biden administration's priorities, voting rights rivaled

COVID-19, the economy, and global warming; after all, the issue posed an existential threat to American democracy. Would anything else matter if elections were no longer free and fair?

Trump's Big Lie of a stolen election, which he repeated throughout 2021, had stoked a nationwide Republican effort to suppress Democratic votes and subvert the election process. Eighteen states had passed restrictive measures limiting mail-in voting, early voting, and absentee ballots. A Georgia law made it a crime to give water bottles to people standing in line. These measures had nothing to do with voter fraud, for which evidence was negligible, and everything to do with limiting the participation of Blacks, women, and other groups that tended to vote for Democrats. Even more alarming, in several states Republicans were stripping from secretaries of state the authority to certify elections and handing it to partisan officials or state legislatures. The threat was all too real: If Republicans couldn't win legitimately, they'd rig the rules.

On March 25, 2021, Biden held his first, highly awaited press conference. The president announced his goal of administering 200 million vaccines in one hundred days and spent fifteen minutes fielding questions about conditions on the southern border.

Then Biden was asked about voter repression. "What I'm worried about is how un-American this whole initiative is," he said. His indignation rising, the president declared:

> It's sick. It's sick. Deciding in some states that you cannot bring water to people standing in line, waiting to vote; deciding that you're going to end voting at five o'clock when working people are just getting off work; deciding that there will be no absentee ballots under the most rigid circumstances.

Biden leaned into the podium and stared into the camera.

The Republican voters I know find this despicable. Republican voters, the folks out in—outside this White House. I'm not talking about the elected officials; I'm talking about voters. Voters. And so I am convinced that we will be able to stop this because it is the most pernicious thing. This makes Jim Crow look like Jim Eagle. I mean, this is gigantic what they're trying to do and it cannot be sustained. I'm going to do everything in my power, along with my friends in the House and the Senate, to keep that from becoming law.

Few presidents, including John F. Kennedy and Lyndon B. Johnson, had spoken so passionately about civil rights. But what, if anything, would his administration do about it? That was now the responsibility of Kamala Harris.

And Biden had another assignment in mind for his vice president: the so-called Northern Triangle.

During Obama's first term, Biden had taken on the challenge of tackling the root causes of illegal immigration, negotiating with the governments of Guatemala, El Salvador, and Honduras. In his book *Promises to Keep*, he proudly recited his successes in wrangling foreign aid for that effort, combating corruption and eliciting cooperation from those countries' leaders. It was a thankless, low-profile assignment but also a politically harmless one—as long as the southern border stayed relatively quiet.

But for Harris, the Northern Triangle would prove to be radioactive. To be sure, Biden hadn't asked her to solve the immigration crisis, or to fix security at the southern border. The former required congressional action and the latter was the responsibility of the Department of Homeland Security and its director, Alejandro Mayorkas. But few people understood this distinction; the difference between tackling root causes and fixing immediate problems at the border seemed lost on the media and the public.

Meanwhile, illegal immigrants kept arriving. And Biden was furious.

Aides had rarely seen him so angry. From all over the West Wing, you could hear the president cursing, dropping f-bombs (he'd always apologize when women were present). "It was just the frustration of a lack of solutions," said a senior adviser. "It's like, 'how would you feel if you were me and these were the solutions you had?' It's the weight of the presidency, right?" The seemingly insoluble problems at the border crystalized what Obama's chief of staff Rahm Emanuel used to say: In the Oval Office all the choices were between bad and worse.

While Biden groped for solutions, Republicans wrapped the crisis around Harris's neck. "I think there is a definite targeting of the vice president that has nothing to do with her assignment," said a senior adviser. "And it has everything to do with who she is and the desire by some in the right wing to make her gone."

One of Harris's senior advisers, who was also Black, argued that it wasn't just Republicans who were unfair to her. The media couldn't fathom a vice president who was not only female but also Black and South Asian. This adviser called this syndrome "the Unicorn in a glass box." She explained: "Kamala Harris is unique to so many people. They'd never seen anybody like her before. So they don't know how to treat her." As a case in point, the adviser cited an interview Harris had done with a magazine. "And the first question out of the reporter's mouth is, 'Tell me about your experiences with racism.' *What?!*" It wasn't that the question wasn't legitimate; it was the seemingly relentless harping on her race instead of substance. This adviser thought a double standard was at work. Was the press treating Harris more aggressively than it did Biden? On the campaign trail, reporters would ask Biden's staff blunt questions: "Is he too old?" But never to Biden's face. But they didn't hesitate to ask Harris about her experiences with racism.

Still, some of Harris's wounds were self-inflicted. Part of the problem was her seeming inability to find her voice. As confident and effective as she'd been as a senator, skillfully interrogating witnesses in televised hearings, Harris seemed awkward and uncertain as vice president. She laughed inappropriately and chopped the air with her hands, which made her seem condescending.

One unforced error occurred during the vice president's two-day visit to Guatemala and Mexico in June 2021. It didn't help that Guatemala's president, Alejandro Giammattei, publicly disagreed with Harris over the best approach to the migration crisis. "We are not on the same side of the coin. It is obvious," he told CBS News. Things went from bad to worse when Harris sat for an interview with Lester Holt, the anchor of *NBC Nightly News*.

Holt asked her: "Do you have any plans to visit the border?"

"At some point," Harris replied. "This whole thing about the border, we've been to the border. We've been to the border."

"You haven't been to the border."

"And I haven't been to Europe. I don't understand the point that you're making."

Holt's point was that the border crisis was out of control, record numbers of immigrants were arriving, and that Harris, whether she liked or not, would be held responsible. Border Patrol agents were no longer deliberately wrenching children from their parents' arms, as they'd done under Trump, but refugees were languishing in overcrowded warehouses in deplorable conditions.

The reality was that the border problem couldn't be solved without overhauling the immigration system and there was no political will for that in Congress. But Harris's unwillingness to make going to the border a priority had become a symbol of Biden's failure to stem illegal immigration.

Under questioning from Holt, Harris dug the hole deeper. "I'm in Guatemala because my focus is dealing with the root causes of migration," she insisted, defensively. "There may be some who do not think that is important. But it is my firm belief that if we care about what is happening at the border, we'd better care about the root causes and address them." This was true but politically clumsy; it was like saying you were studying the causes of forest fires while towns were burning to the ground.

The vice president had wobbled in her first foray overseas. "The Lester Holt thing was a disaster," said a longtime Washington observer. "The Guatemala trip was a disaster. So I don't know what Biden's brain trust is going to do about that."

Harris's advisers protested that the vice president's successes were ignored. A case in point was a productive trip to Vietnam during the frenzied American evacuation from Afghanistan. "She did backflips walking a tightrope with four books on her head," said an adviser, "and people were like, 'Well, okay, whatever.' It was barely a blip on the screen. But she has a flippant moment in an interview with Lester Holt and somehow she's the worst vice president ever."

In fact, Biden and his team thought highly of Harris. Ron Klain was personally fond of her. He met with the vice president weekly and encouraged her to do more interviews and raise her profile. Harris was reluctant, wary of making mistakes. "This is like baseball," Klain told her. "You have to accept the fact that sometimes you will strike out. We *all* strike out. But you can't score runs if you're sitting in the dugout." Biden's chief was channeling manager Tom Hanks in the film *A League of Their Own.* "Look, no one here is going to get mad at you. We *want* you out there!"

A few weeks after her Guatemala trip, Harris was tripped up by sloppy advance work. A hastily planned visit to El Paso, evidently arranged to show critics she *would* go to the border, left her staff scrambling. The vice president ended up holding a news conference on a busy airport tarmac, trying to be heard over the roar of a plane engine. "This never would have happened," said a friend of Biden, "if Ron Klain had been her chief of staff."

Finally, in the spring, came some good news: Arrivals of unaccompanied children at the border were down thirty percent. Arrivals of families were down forty-four percent. No one could be sure why.

But the respite was short-lived. In July, the U.S. Border Patrol reported nearly 200,000 encounters with migrants, the highest monthly total in twenty-one years. At his first press conference, Biden had ridiculed the idea that immigrants were coming "because they know Biden is a good guy." But he was trying to have it both ways—insisting that the border was closed but promising to treat those who came humanely.

In September, another wave of immigrants arrived. At the Texas border town of Del Rio, a dystopian scene played out: Thousands of ill-clothed, malnourished Haitian refugees milled about in a sprawling tent camp beneath a bridge; border guards on horseback, wielding bridle reins like whips, tried to herd them. It looked like Birmingham,

Alabama, in the 1960s—when Bull Connor, the racist Commissioner of Public Safety, unleashed attack dogs and fire hoses on unarmed Blacks.

Harris issued a statement condemning the use of border agents on horseback. But she was silent on the administration's forced deportation of Haitians back to their island country, a failed state ruled by warring street gangs. The deportations were carried out under Title 42, a controversial HHS health provision, anathema to progressives, that allowed the removal of immigrants to prevent the spread of COVID-19. Meanwhile, desperate Haitians kept heading for the southern border.

Harris had become a political lightning rod. Some of the criticism was undoubtedly due to her race and gender. But Biden's aides pointed out that taking flak also came with the job. "I get the fact that there's a lot of anxiety around her," said a senior White House adviser. "She's the first Black South Asian woman to hold the office. Some of it's racism and sexism. Some of her problems are self-inflicted. But a lot of it's just being vice president. I'm sorry, it's a shitty job."

And more trouble was headed Harris's way.

A week after her visit to El Paso, *Politico* published a long piece portraying the vice president's office as a poisonous snake pit. The vice president's shop, it reported, was suffering from "low morale, porous lines of communication and diminished trust among aides and senior officials." Citing interviews with twenty-two current and former Harris aides, administration officials, and associates, the report described "an abusive environment" where "people are thrown under the bus." It all "starts at the top," said an unnamed administration official. Plummeting office morale was supposedly causing an exodus of personnel. Two top advance staffers had already left, and others were eyeing the exits.

Harris's office was hardly a well-oiled machine. Just before the vice president's trip to El Paso, a staffer for Representative Henry Cuellar, the Democratic congressman for the region, tried to arrange a call with the congressman and vice president to discuss her visit. No one from her office called back.

Now anonymous staffers were describing Harris's office as a den of dysfunction. Months after the *Politico* report, a similarly damning article appeared in *The Washington Post*, with the headline: "A Kamala Harris Staff Exodus Reignites Questions about Her Leadership Role— and Her Future Ambitions."

When I asked her about these reports, Flournoy, Harris's chief, said that turmoil was inevitable in any high-pressure, high-stakes organization. "You're going to have some times where people knock up against one another," she said. "Certainly, that's happened." But Flournoy insisted that the friction was overblown, magnified by the media's intense spotlight; Harris, she pointed out, was the first vice president to be assigned a dedicated traveling pool of reporters. As for the specifics in the *Politico* and *Washington Post* stories, Flournoy said, "I stopped reading those articles, because I live every day with this staff and this team."

Turmoil in the office wasn't a new problem for Harris. It went back to her days as a district attorney in San Francisco.

Gil Duran joined Harris's staff as senior adviser and communications director when she was California's attorney general in 2013.

"There was nothing we seemed to be doing besides dealing with her dysfunction," Duran told me. Harris, he said, failed to do her homework before events, refused to be prepped by her staff—and then blamed them when she was ill prepared. "The amount of stress she created by constantly being impossible to manage and taking out all her stresses on staff—usually women, or people who were not in great positions of authority—was just kind of unbearable." The last straw for Duran was when Harris failed to show up for several scheduled prep meetings, and couldn't be reached by phone, before a televised event in Los Angeles. When the attorney general finally arrived, Duran says she gave him a profane tongue-lashing and reduced a female staffer to tears. After only five months on the job, he resigned.

Duran could be dismissed as a disgruntled aide who'd served Harris only briefly. But he had company. Another staffer who'd worked for her for years, and insisted on anonymity, told me that Harris engaged in "really unnecessary gamesmanship" driven by "deep, deep insecurities." Harris, she said, "refused to do the kind of preparation that you need to do before going public on hard-core policy matters. And then she became incensed and outraged when things wouldn't go the way she thought they were supposed to. There was a lot of magical thinking." This staffer said that current reports of dysfunction from the vice president's office were all too familiar. "Now there's a generation of staff people who simply won't put up with this stuff. They leave. They tweet. They leak."

This former staffer rejected the idea that Harris's critics were racists or misogynists. "When somebody raises an issue about Kamala, everybody's like, 'you don't want to see Black women succeed.' That's completely backward. Everybody who goes to work for Kamala by definition wants to see her succeed. That's why you take these jobs."

Harris's past behavior was relevant, she insisted, because the stakes were higher now that she was vice president. "I think it's helpful for people to know that this is not new, and it will inhibit any administration that she is the leader of."

A senior female adviser to the vice president insisted this portrait didn't add up. "She was a twice-elected district attorney from San Francisco, twice-elected attorney general of California, and a United States senator," this adviser said. "You don't just luck up into those roles." In the accounts of Harris mistreating briefers, she saw an old sexist double standard at work: "I haven't ever read one story about how Joe Biden is a terrible boss to work for or Bernie Sanders is a terrible man—you know what I mean? I've heard it all, and the audacity of Kamala Harris is oftentimes what it boils down to."

Whatever the reason, Harris's staff seemed to be in a state of constant upheaval. Her ill-fated 2020 presidential campaign had dissolved in a storm of acrimony, with operatives blaming one another. "She was leading the race at one point," said a senior White House adviser, with a dose of schadenfreude. "She had a ton of money and as soon as they got in trouble, they blew all the money. The thing just fell apart. And she didn't even make it to Iowa. Her inner circle didn't serve her well in the presidential campaign—and they are ill-serving her now." Harris's campaign staffers were gone, but the dysfunction persisted.

Meanwhile, Harris's approval rating had plunged to twenty-eight percent, lower than Dick Cheney's during the Iraq War. Many Democrats were anxious, imagining her as the party's nominee in 2024 in the event that Biden passed up a second term. Though he insisted he was planning to run for reelection, what if Biden changed his mind—or, at eighty-two, was too frail? Harris would be poised to become the Democratic standard-bearer. "The liberals' fear stems from the assumption

Biden's not going to run," a prominent Democratic strategist told me. "And so they're in a panic—afraid she's going to be the nominee and Trump's going to run and crush her."

As if this Sturm und Drang weren't enough, some of Harris's supporters were complaining that Biden had set her up for failure. Who could possibly solve intractable problems like the Northern Triangle or voting rights? "Her portfolio is trash," said Bakari Sellers, a former South Carolina legislator and staunch Harris ally. Sellers blamed Biden for giving her "a portfolio that's not meant for [her] to succeed."

It wasn't just Democratic operatives who were venting their unhappiness. In fact, word had got back to Biden that someone else was complaining about Harris's portfolio. It was the Second Gentleman, Douglas Emhoff.

Biden was annoyed. He hadn't asked Harris to do anything *he* hadn't done as vice president—and she'd begged him for the voting rights assignment. A few months into the presidency, a close friend asked Joe Biden what he thought of his vice president: "A work in progress," the president said.

ELEVEN

IT'S A WHOLE NEW BALL GAME

By the summer of 2021, Joe Biden had achieved many of his first-term goals: passage of a $1.9 trillion economic rescue plan; sixty-seven million relief checks issued; three million jobs created, more than under Ronald Reagan; childhood poverty on track to be cut by forty percent. On the COVID-19 front, 133 million Americans had been vaccinated; new cases had dropped from 195,000 a day on January 20 to 12,000 on July 4.

It was a track record that any president might envy. As Ron Klain put it, "If I told you, in just a hundred and fifty days, that he will go from fifty thousand jobs a month to six hundred thousand jobs a month; he'll cut the deaths from COVID by ninety percent; he'll cut poverty by thirty percent, and we'll begin sending people monthly checks to help them raise their children—oh, and by the way, he's going to end America's longest war—how's that president going to be regarded by the American people? You'd be telling me, 'Well, historically that person would be beloved.'" If Biden wasn't beloved, according to Klain, it was because during these bitterly polarized times only a tiny percentage of voters was persuadable. No matter how successful a president might be, margins in this politically toxic era were razor thin.

But as summer turned to fall, Biden and his team were grappling with a cascade of crises that would send his popularity into a downward spiral.

A new and virulent strain of the coronavirus had surfaced. Dubbed the Delta variant, it had first been detected in India in late 2020 but was now on American soil and spreading rapidly. "It was a whole new ball game," said Andy Slavitt, who'd left the Biden pandemic response team in July. "And a lot of the assumptions that we believed to be true—that vaccines would not only prevent you from getting seriously ill but from transmitting the virus—were no longer valid. It changed the calculus."

Infection rates were soaring; businesses were shuttering again, hospital ICU units filling beyond capacity. Not only was Delta far more transmissible; it was a breakthrough virus, causing infections among people who were fully vaccinated. Jeff Zients explained: "That's what led to the decision to reinstate mask recommendations even for vaccinated people." Zients and his team knew that asking people to wear masks again would be unpopular. "Sometimes the science and facts are easy and welcome and sometimes they're tougher pills to swallow," he said. "But our belief is that when the science showed us something, we had a responsibility to react and share it with the American people—to be transparent, act quickly." On July 27, the CDC, which in May had said that vaccinated people could forgo masks indoors, did an about-face, advising them to remask.

In hindsight Slavitt thought the president should have hedged his optimistic message back on July 4: "I think if we'd had perfect foresight, he would have said that it's not over. We've got to be vigilant. The ability of this virus to thrive and survive and stay present was very, very impressive. And that wasn't true of the previous mutations."

Back in April, Biden's approval rating for handling COVID-19 had been sixty-four percent; by August it had dropped to fifty-three percent.

More ominously, the Delta variant exposed the Achilles' heel of America's war against the pandemic: the tens of millions of people who refused to be vaccinated. They were like dry tinder in the path of a raging forest fire. Not only were they putting their own lives at risk, but they were also endangering millions of others and jeopardizing the entire U.S. pandemic response. The unvaccinated were overwhelmingly more likely to be hospitalized and die; they were also, even when asymptomatic, spreading the deadly virus to others.

Vaccine resistance was endemic in red, southern states—some with Republican governors who pandered to the notion that vaccines were an infringement on their liberty. Never mind that schoolchildren had been required for decades to be inoculated against measles, mumps, and polio. Or that no one, in a civilized society, is permitted to drive through a red light at an intersection. The Delta variant was now burning through this population; the death toll was rising to levels not seen since 2020.

Nothing baffled Joe Biden more than people refusing vaccines; he couldn't fathom it. Almost every day, he complained to his advisers: "I don't understand it. What more can we do? Is there something we're missing here? What's going on?" Reasoning with anti-vaxxers was like talking to children, Biden thought: "It's like the debate you had with your mother," he told an adviser, "where she'd put some food on your plate and say, 'Eat that. There's someone starving in India. Be grateful to have that.' No country in the world has made it as easy, as convenient, as straightforward, to get vaccinated as we have." The president got calls every day from world leaders begging him to send vaccines.

"They're saying, 'Please, send me five hundred thousand doses. Please send me a million doses,'" said a senior White House adviser. "And yet we literally have millions of doses sitting in drugstores less than five miles from the homes of ninety percent of Americans. And it's free. And you don't need an appointment. The fact that a third of the country won't do it is just not right."

Biden and his team were surprised at how politically toxic vaccines had become. "When we sat there in December 2020, laying out these plans, we understood that *masks* had become very political," said a senior White House aide. "But given that Trump had spent an entire year boasting about Operation Warp Speed and the fact that it was *his* vaccine, we didn't see that *the vaccine* would become so political. And the combination of misinformation, disinformation, and Republicans stirring up vaccine resistance just put us in this box."

Biden was furious about vaccine disinformation and the internet platforms that spread it. Returning from a trip or from church on Sunday in Wilmington, he would vent to his pandemic team. "He would bring these stories back," recalled Zients, "and sometimes they were littered with misinformation that people were getting on the Web or on television, and he'd push us: 'How do we get the truth out to people?'"

It was this torrent of disinformation that ultimately led Biden to embrace vaccine mandates. The president was reluctant at first; he knew that enacting them would be politically costly; it fed the Republican narrative of an overreaching federal government.

In early August, Biden and the pandemic team met on a Zoom call with CEOs, business leaders, and university presidents. Kaiser's CEO, Greg Adams, told the president about an employee who'd recently died of COVID; Adams thought he could have saved that life if the mandate had kicked in earlier. "That was a really important meeting about the power and the effectiveness of vaccine requirements," recalled Zients. The Sunday before Labor Day, Biden called a meeting with his COVID team. "Before we go to broader vaccine requirements, have we done everything we can?" the president asked. "Because I only want to do this if it's the only lever left to pull."

On September 9, the president announced that businesses with more than one hundred employees would have to require vaccinations or weekly testing. "He signed off on vaccination requirements for federal contractors, health care workers, federal employers, the OSHA rule," said Zients. The OSHA rule, imposed by the Occupational Safety and Health Administration, would affect as many as one hundred million Americans—private-sector employees, health care workers, and federal contractors. Speaking at the White House, the president didn't mince words. "We've been patient," he said, his eyes narrowed, gripping the lectern. "But our patience is wearing thin, and your refusal has cost all of us."

"People don't like the mandates," Klain admitted. "But we've tried putting vaccines in everyone's neighborhood and begging them and literally offering people a free beer and giving them a hundred bucks. And we still have sixty-five million people who haven't done it. And so we've gone from carrots to sticks. People don't like sticks. I get it. I'm an adult. I don't like to be told what to do. But if we don't tell people that they have to do it, we're going to be in this mess forever."

Biden's mandates would be challenged in the courts, and they couldn't reach all seventy-five to eighty million people who refused to be vaccinated. Meanwhile, as the Delta variant raged from June to November 2021, an estimated ninety thousand Americans died unnecessarily due to vaccine resistance, according to a Kaiser Family Foundation analysis.

Klain saw the measures as a necessary evil. "The mandates are going to have to drive twenty or thirty million people to get vaccinated," he said. "It's unpleasant. It's divisive. It's definitely part of our political problem. We're paying for it in the polls, no question about it. But as I said to the president, we're at forty-three percent approval. If we didn't do the vaccine mandates, I think we'd be at forty-seven or forty-eight. But we'd have a thousand additional people die a day from COVID for the rest of his presidency. And that would be a tragedy."

In early 2022, Biden's campaign for vaccine mandates would suffer a severe blow. On January 13, the Supreme Court struck down the administration's OSHA mandates for private businesses. The court let stand a mandate for health care workers who worked at facilities receiving federal money. That small victory was little consolation for Biden's pandemic response team.

As if the Delta variant and vaccine resistance weren't enough, Biden faced another emergency in late summer: inflation. Prices were soaring on everything from groceries to high-end sports cars. Republicans were quick to blame Biden's stimulus bill, the ARP. But the causes ranged from bottlenecks in the supply chain to a shortage of silicon chips; more broadly, inflation was inevitable when an economy sputtered back to life from the near-death experience of the pandemic. But the biggest, and most painful, problem was at the gas pump.

Klain understood that high gas prices kill presidents in the polls. Biden's chief of staff knew this history by heart and recited it to the boss: Obama was at forty percent approval when gas was at $3.40. George W. Bush was in the thirties when gas was at $4.00. Klain joked that Biden had the highest approval rating of any president when gas cost $3.40. But there was nothing funny about the political price. "Gas is the only product in America," Klain explained, "where they post the price on a sign that you pass twenty times a day. You see it in consumer confidence. Now I could argue that with a spike of twenty cents a gallon, when you buy like, twelve gallons a week, that's only $2.40. And because the economy's getting better your real wage this month went up twenty bucks!" But Klain knew you couldn't argue with people at the gas pump. "It's a huge psychological thing," he said.

And then there was the crisis at the southern border. Next to vaccine disinformation, this was the thing that made Biden's blood boil. As September approached, illegal immigrants were still coming by the thousands. "It's been vexing and frustrating," said a senior adviser. "Frustrating because we put a lot of energy into fixing parts of it and we get no credit for it. It's definitely a major problem. And it's a problem that hurts us on both sides of the aisle."

No one was congratulating Biden and his team for ending Trump's sadistic policy of separating families from their children. Or the fact that fewer children were being detained. "When we got here there were twenty thousand kids in Customs Border Patrol custody, kids who were sleeping in border control stations," said the adviser. "We cleaned all that up. I get a report every day on the number of kids sleeping in border patrol stations and yesterday, the number was three. No one cares that we solved that problem. They care that we have this other problem—Haitians or whatever."

The forced repatriation of Haitians to their homeland, under Title 42, was angering liberal Democrats. So was the exploding number of illegals at the border. "We're arresting more people at the border than ever—many more than Trump did," said the adviser. "Republicans are using that as a sign that the border's a mess. I could use it as a sign that it's working, like we're catching all these people!"

This official continued, "So we've got liberals who are mad about

Title 42 and the Haitians. We've got independents who are mad that we let anybody in. And so, of all these problems, it's perhaps the most vexing. If we get the price of gas down, by and large everyone in America will be happy. But everything we do at the border pisses off forty percent of the country."

The immigration problem was deep-rooted. As another White House aide put it, "During Trump's last year no one came because we were a shit show of COVID and death and whatnot." Now improving conditions in the U.S. had triggered a stampede of desperate immigrants. "If you live in Ecuador or El Salvador or Guatemala, and you hear there are ten million jobs open in America, and the COVID death rate is down, you're coming. Look, fundamentally, the problem is that America's in very good shape, all things considered. And every country to the south of us is in horrible shape."

Afghanistan, the Delta variant, inflation, supply chains, the border—it had been "the Summer from Hell," as one headline put it. The unraveling had begun with Biden's handling of the chaotic Afghanistan withdrawal. Even months later, in focus groups, it topped the list of complaints among voters who disapproved of Biden. To Josh Bolten, George W. Bush's former chief of staff, the Afghanistan debacle had hurt Biden "in much the way that Hurricane Katrina did Bush." Of course, the bungled federal handling of a hurricane that cost hundreds of American lives was arguably more serious than a flawed military evacuation on the other side of the world. But the political damage done to Biden was similar. His approval rating was underwater.

And now pundits began to complain that the problem was Biden himself—specifically, his "messaging."

What had become of "Scranton Joe," some critics asked, the plain-spoken president who could explain inflation and supply chains to folks around the kitchen table? A close friend of Biden wondered if his inability to cut through the national discord was the staff's fault—in effect, no one was letting Biden be Biden: "Is the White House staff being overly protective of one of the only Democrats on the national stage who actually knows how to talk about things the average American voter talks about in language ordinary people use?"

I asked Biden's friend Chris Dodd, the former senator, about that. "No one is ever really prepared to be president of the United States," he said. "President Biden is, in my opinion, the best prepared person, certainly in my lifetime and maybe in the history of our country. But there is always a danger of overexposure. The goal is not how many times you're on television, but rather being more selective about those appearances."

If Biden was failing to connect with Americans, it wasn't for lack of trying. Before stepping before the cameras, the president always asked his staff, how do we tell the story? This was his strength, the homespun stories about ordinary people—like his father trying to make ends meet. "It's like my dad used to say, 'I just need a little breathing room,'" Biden kept saying, when he talked about helping Americans. But these homegrown chestnuts seemed unequal to the challenge of a crippling pandemic.

Still, it was doubtful if any of Biden's ills could be cured with speeches. People seemed to think, wrote Paul Waldman in *The Washington Post*, that "somewhere out there . . . is a powerful set of words that when uttered will alter this political trajectory. . . . It's nonsense. Yet smart and experienced people continue to believe it."

"Look, we could be better, we should be better," said a senior White House adviser. "But I tend to believe that problems that are often described as messaging problems are just in fact real problems. I don't think it's a messaging problem when someone goes to buy a pound of hamburger and says, 'No, I'm not doing that this week because it's too expensive. I'm buying chicken.'"

Indeed, soothing words couldn't change the stark reality of five-dollar-a-gallon gas. Or one third of the country refusing lifesaving vaccines.

The country's most serious problems stemmed from COVID-19 and its variants. And there was little Biden could do if tens of millions of Americans opted out of a solution. It was becoming, as Biden said, "a pandemic of the unvaccinated." There were many reasons for vaccine resistance, varying from community to community. But it was increasingly clear, as hospitalizations and deaths soared in red states but not blue ones, that the country's health and its economy and well-being were being held hostage by a Republican cult of reality deniers.

Yet Klain believed his team had made progress. "When Delta started we had one hundred million people who were not vaccinated; it went down to sixty-seven million. We fought a giant fight over masking and generally won in many schools. We've accelerated the drop of the Delta variant, even as we've allowed life to get somewhat back to normal. When we got here, forty-nine percent of the schools were open. Today ninety-six percent of the schools are open."

But the challenge ahead was daunting. "To get from where we are to where we need to be," Klain said, "we need there to be more vaccination, and that's largely the resistant adults and the kids. And we have to go from sixty-seven million unvaccinated adults down to forty to fifty million unvaccinated adults. And that's what the mandates are about."

The larger battle would be waged around the world. "It's no longer about Delta," said Slavitt. "It's about preparedness for future waves. It's about the globe."

TWELVE

I'M NOT FEARED

President Lyndon Johnson corralled votes by the force of his outsize personality; when flattery and cajoling didn't work, he'd employ the "Johnson treatment," getting right in senators' faces. Joe Biden was more like Franklin Roosevelt, whose sunny disposition left legislators thinking they'd gotten their way. Like the late Democratic Speaker of the House Tip O'Neill, Biden believed that all politics were not only local but personal.

"For the president it's personal relationships," explained Steve Ricchetti, his legislative strategist. "It's examples of generosity of spirit or concern. It's picking up the phone and saying 'Happy Birthday' to a kid or to a mom. It's doing the little things that express a desire for closeness, generosity of spirit, trustworthiness." It wasn't that Biden couldn't twist arms or hold grudges or use the f-word with legislators behind closed doors. But his modus operandi since his days in the Senate had been carrots, not sticks. "It's who he is," said Ricchetti. "It's who he's been in public life."

Would it be enough to get his way with Congress?

Biden's ARP was as ambitious—and expensive, at $1.9 trillion—as some of LBJ's Great Society programs. But it was only the beginning of his legislative agenda. Biden's top first-term priorities, initially lumped together as an "American Jobs Plan," were the Bipartisan Infrastructure Framework (BIF) and a "human infrastructure" bill known as Build Back Better (BBB).

BIF was the most sweeping infrastructure project since the creation of the interstate highway system under President Dwight Eisenhower in the 1950s. It would provide $550 billion in new spending toward roads, bridges, broadband internet access, clean water, and utility systems. BBB, an even more ambitious package, would rewrite the American social safety net. Its provisions included universal preschool; home care for the elderly; a cap on childcare costs of seven percent of income; paid family and medical leave; a limit on prescription drug costs; health care subsidies; hearing aid benefits and glasses for seniors; and an expanded child tax credit. (First included in the ARP, the tax credit program had cut child poverty by forty percent but was set to expire.) BBB also featured the most sweeping array of measures ever proposed to combat climate change, including tax credits for electric cars, solar panels, and weatherizing homes. It was the centerpiece of Biden's plan to reduce global warming.

In their original form, the bills represented spending of nearly $5 trillion. But unlike Trump's $1.7 trillion tax cut, these programs would be spread out over a decade and, according to the Congressional Budget Office, mostly paid for, partly by raising taxes on the rich. Still, the stratospheric price tag posed a question: Had Joe Biden, the centrist Democrat, become a big-spending socialist?

Six months into his presidency, Republicans were already excoriating Biden, calling his promise of bipartisanship a lie. It wasn't just the Trump cultists who were saying this; even those Republicans who'd grudgingly shown Biden past respect were critical. They cited his ARP, passed without a single Republican vote, as proof that he was embarked on a reckless spending spree. Joshua Bolten, George W. Bush's ex–White House chief of staff, was among the critics. "Having been elected precisely because he was neither Bernie Sanders nor Elizabeth Warren," Bolten told me, "Biden is governing like both of them."

President Biden bore no resemblance to *Senator* Biden, complained Bolten, now head of the Business Roundtable. "The Biden I knew would not have celebrated deficit spending," he said. "He was a working-class populist and always had the vocabulary of workers' rights. Now he has the vocabulary of someone who gives not a fig for the deficit, not a fig for the competitiveness of U.S. business."

Jonathan Alter, author of *The Defining Moment*, on FDR's first hundred days, argued that labeling Biden a socialist was nonsense. In fact, both FDR and Biden were misunderstood. "Franklin Roosevelt was not a Bernie Sanders Democrat," he explained. "There's this complete misunderstanding of him. He wasn't a socialist and he used [Republican president] Herbert Hoover's bank rescue plan. The ardent progressives of his day were saying, 'Take over the banks! Take over the banks!' And FDR was like, 'No. I'm going to leave the banks in private hands. I'm not going to do it the progressive way.'"

Biden, like FDR, believed that government had to tackle the current crisis with bold experimentation. He was an FDR Democrat and always had been. "Joe Biden grew up in a Democratic, Franklin Roosevelt, Harry Truman, John F. Kennedy, Lyndon Johnson household," said Alter. "They were solid Democrats. He was always a lunch-bucket Democrat. Those were the FDR Democrats." Almost a century later, the urgent crisis of the pandemic was Biden's equivalent of the Great Depression, a call to action.

Roosevelt and Biden had something else in common. "Because

Roosevelt had polio, he saw his whole administration in a medical context," said Alter. "First you had to get the patient up and walking again." With his young sons hospitalized after the death of his wife and infant daughter in a car crash, and Beau's protracted struggle with a fatal brain tumor, Biden had experienced plenty of medical tragedy, and he'd needed insurance to get through it. "FDR's providing relief in his first hundred days was a lot like what Biden would later do with COVID relief," said Alter. "And the far-reaching social legislation of the later New Deal was like Build Back Better. The New Deal was an effort to rewrite the American social contract, and BBB, if it's passed, will be the same thing."

I asked Biden's friend Ted Kaufman if Biden's ideology had changed since he became president. "Not a whit," he said emphatically. "I haven't seen Joe Biden change in terms of who he is, and I've known him for forty-nine years."

What about Biden's deficit spending? "You've gotta be kidding me," said Kaufman. "There's a conventional wisdom about Joe in Washington that's just wrong. Look, we're going into the worst economic crisis that we've had since the Depression. And Josh Bolten complains that Joe Biden is for spending a lot of money to get us straight now? We've been living with the idea that the federal government can't do anything right. Let's give it all to the private sector. But the private sector can't do it. And if you're listening to what Joe Biden's saying, there's lots of things the federal government can do better than the private sector can. He's fiscally responsible. But this is the time when you go big."

Mike Donilon, Biden's political strategist, said it all depended on your perspective. "You can look at Build Back Better and say it's an effort to be like FDR, a transformation," he said. "But here's a different way to look at it: Joe Biden was a single father for five years. He looks at what a lot of folks in this country are going through with childcare, daycare, and he's asking the question, how are they going to make it? That's not like some FDR-level transformational question. That's a pretty straightforward question that says, 'You know what? I've lived that experience.' And there's a lot of evidence that if childcare and daycare costs were more reasonable in this country, it would help a lot of families to be in a better position to succeed."

Biden didn't mind being compared to FDR, but the president's friend and confidant Representative James Clyburn rejected the analogy. "I hope nobody elected Joe Biden to be FDR," he told me. "FDR was not that good for people who look like me." Clyburn, the revered eighty-year-old African American congressman, noted that Roosevelt refused to integrate the armed services and barred domestic workers from receiving Social Security. In the Oval Office, Biden had a large oil painting of Roosevelt and a small bust of Harry Truman. Clyburn told his friend it should be the other way around. "I said, 'Look, man. I need to see more Harry Truman in this office!'"

Having passed the ARP with only Democrats, Biden was desperate to show that he could deliver a bipartisan victory. He would begin by trying to do what no president had done in seventy years: repair America's crumbling infrastructure.

The president was his own chief strategist. Ricchetti knew his way around Capitol Hill, but he followed Biden's lead. "It's *his* strategy and his personality," Ricchetti insisted. "He does the initial framework and establishes the parameters and gives the direction on where there might be room to make accommodations. He's intimately involved in every aspect of it. I don't go up to Capitol Hill and freelance."

When I spoke with him in February 2021, Josh Bolten predicted that Biden's legislative charm offensive would fail. Pressed to support an infrastructure bill, "Republicans will now behave like obstructionists, but they will not be viewed as unreasonable because the Biden administration overshot on the ARP."

To the contrary, Ron Klain predicted that Biden's passage of the ARP would enhance the prospects of the rest of his agenda: "In terms of establishing the president's power, his ability to get things done, I think that opens the door for a lot of things to follow."

The trouble was, behind that door were two senators who could stop everything in its tracks, Joe Manchin (D-WV) and Kyrsten Sinema (D-AZ).

Joseph Manchin III, then seventy-four, the senior senator from West Virginia, was in many ways like Joe Biden: a white, Catholic septuagenarian and former football player who was proud of his hard-scrabble, working-class roots. He was a skilled retail politician with a hail-fellow-well-met personality. Stubbornness went along with Manchin's outgoing personality. Maddening as he could be, everyone in the Biden White House had grudging respect for him. "I like Joe," Marty Walsh, Biden's secretary of labor, told me. "You know, he's an old-school pol. He's very principled and you're not going to get his vote by pushing him." Raised in the tiny West Virginia town of Farmington (population 365), Manchin had sold furniture, carpets—and coal—before taking up politics, as first a state legislator, then governor, and finally senator.

A conservative Democrat, Manchin voted with his party on most big issues: He was thumbs-down on Trump's tax cuts and his attempts to repeal Obamacare. But Manchin was mercurial and unpredictable. Trump had carried his state by almost forty points in 2020. During his presidency, Manchin had voted with Trump nearly seventy-five percent of the time. Now, because the Senate was evenly split with fifty Democrats and fifty Republicans, with the tie-breaking vote falling to Vice President Kamala Harris, Manchin could be the difference between success and failure for Biden. Without Manchin, the president couldn't pass anything through the process known as reconciliation. And with Republicans resisting almost all of Biden's agenda, that was practically the only game in town.

Manchin had flexed his political muscle back in March, during the wrangling over Biden's $1.9 trillion ARP, the COVID relief package. He brought the bill to a standstill over a tax break on unemployment payments; Manchin insisted that the break should not apply to households earning more than $150,000. Biden and the Democratic leadership had been forced to rewrite the package. And yet, at the eleventh hour, the president still had to reach out directly to Manchin and plead for his vote. "Joe, if you don't come along, you're really fucking me," Biden told him, in a last-minute call. "I need you on this. Find your way to yes on this." Manchin did, and Biden had his first big legislative victory.

If Manchin was a familiar Capitol Hill creature, Kyrsten Sinema, the forty-five-year-old Democratic senator from Arizona, was sui generis. A former Green Party spokeswoman and the first openly bisexual person elected to the House of Representatives, she had morphed from liberal "bomb thrower," in her own words, to one of the most conservative members of Congress. She thought of herself as a maverick in the mold of her state's late senator John McCain. Yet in some ways she'd broken the mold. In March, while voting against an increase in the minimum wage, Sinema did a half curtsy and made a dramatic thumbs-down. Later she posted a picture of herself on Instagram wearing a bright pink hat and a "Fuck off" ring.

She was an enigma. To succeed with his legislative agenda, Biden would need to decipher both Sinema and Manchin.

———

The bipartisan infrastructure bill began to take shape one night early in 2021. Gathered for dinner at the Washington, D.C., home of Lisa Murkowski (R-AK) were a handful of senators: Mark Warner (D-VA), Jon Tester (D-MT), Mitt Romney (R-UT), Jeanne Shaheen (D-NH), Susan Collins (R-ME), Bill Cassidy (R-LA), and Manchin. They'd come to talk about Biden's COVID relief bill, said Senator Warner. "But then we started thinking, could we do infrastructure?"

Meanwhile Kyrsten Sinema reached out to Rob Portman (R-OH). The two senators hashed out the broad outlines of an infrastructure package. The buttoned-down, white-haired conservative Republican and idiosyncratic Democrat were an odd couple. "Portman is by nature very, very detail focused," said Warner. "He'd run the Office of Management and Budget. He parses every word, and Kyrsten Sinema is the absolute opposite of that. But they're friends and Rob has an ability to get Sinema to do stuff that nobody else could ever get her to do."

Shelley Moore Capito, the Republican senator from West Virginia, had offered to work with the White House on an infrastructure deal. But Capito's proposal, which called for $568 billion in spending, fell far short of what Biden had in mind. After three weeks of negotiations, Capito stepped aside.

Meanwhile, the "Gang of Ten" senators were making progress. There were disagreements about the elements of the package, and the

Republicans and Democrats were $150 billion apart on how much they wanted to spend. Since nothing got done with everyone in the room, Portman negotiated one-on-one with Steve Ricchetti, Biden's chief legislative strategist. "It almost came undone a couple of times in the last two weekends," said a Democratic senator. "And we were getting rolled with all these things—and at one point Manchin was so upset with Sinema it almost fell apart. Everybody lumps them together, but they're not close at all."

According to Marty Walsh, the labor secretary, Joe Biden closed the deal. "The president was able to talk to Sinema and talk to Manchin; he talked to Speaker Pelosi and the Speaker was able to get her team on board to vote for the bill. I mean, honestly, the president was just a master at this one. And I don't think he's gotten the credit he deserves for the political skill he had to get this thing done."

On June 24, Biden and the senators hammered out the final details of the $1.2 trillion BIF bill. But the president wanted an assurance. He went around the room, looking each senator in the eye. "Just so there's no misunderstanding here," he said, "the way this is going to work is we're going to do this, and then we're going to do BBB." The senators just stared back at him. "He did not get a commitment in any way that they would work with him on Build Back Better," said a senior White House adviser.

Afterward Biden led the gaggle of senators out onto the North Portico to a clutch of cameras. "We had a really good meeting, and to answer your direct question, we have a deal," the president said, grinning.

But the battle to turn the BIF bill into law had only just begun. The trouble was, progressive members of the House Democratic caucus had no intention of voting for it—unless the BBB bill was voted on simultaneously. And Republicans who'd agreed to the infrastructure bill were decidedly *not* on board for a multi-trillion-dollar package that would rewrite the social safety net. Neither was Joe Manchin nor Kyrsten Sinema. The contents and the cost of BBB had yet to be thrashed out. In its latest iteration, the price tag was a whopping $3.5 trillion.

Now came a series of actions by Biden and his team that left everyone uncertain about where the president stood and led to months of internecine Democratic warfare. The trouble began right after Biden's meeting with the senators on June 24. Later, taking questions from reporters in the East Room, Biden said that he expected both BIF and BBB to be passed together. "If they don't [both] come, I'm not signing. Real simple," he said.

The Republican backlash was instantaneous. Senator Lindsey Graham (R-SC) called foul on Biden's condition. "No deal by extortion!" he tweeted. "It was never suggested to me during these negotiations that President Biden was holding hostage the bipartisan infrastructure proposal unless a liberal reconciliation package was also passed."

Josh Bolten, who was watching the verbal scuffle on television, shook his head. "That came very close to making the whole infrastructure bill fall apart," he said.

Jen Psaki, the press secretary, walked back Biden's statement linking the two bills. But the president's gaffe foreshadowed a legislative campaign marked by mixed signals from the White House—in which Biden's team tried to appease both moderates and progressives by telling each side what it wanted to hear.

On August 10, the Senate passed the Infrastructure Investment and Jobs Act, recording a vote of sixty-nine votes to thirty, with nineteen GOP senators voting for it. Bolten's prediction that bipartisanship was dead had been dead wrong. Joe Biden was now well on his way to fulfilling one of his most important campaign promises. But the hardest part lay ahead—getting the bill over the finish line in the House.

Most of the progressive Democratic caucus was firm in its demand that BIF and BBB should be passed together. The "hard-core five"—Alexandria Ocasio-Cortez (D-NY), Rashida Tlaib (D-MI), Ilhan Omar (D-MN), Jamaal Bowman (D-NY), and Cori Bush (D-MO)—opposed the infrastructure bill on its merits; they were a solid "no" on passing BIF—with or without BBB. Representative Ayanna Pressley (D-MA), another member of the so-called Squad, was among twenty-five other progressives who would vote against BIF unless BBB passed with it. They were, as Lindsey Graham suggested, holding infrastructure hostage to the bolder, more ambitious "human infrastructure" package. Representative Pressley explained: "I refuse to choose between the livelihoods of the union workers who build our highways and bridges, and the childcare and health care workers who care for our children, elderly, and disabled loved ones."

The House's progressive caucus, led by Pramila Jayapal (D-MN), was a formidable coalition. "You don't want to get on their bad side," explained Peter Baker, chief White House correspondent of *The New York Times*. "They are one hundred votes, right? That's more than the Freedom Caucus ever had in the Republican Party." White House chief of staff Ron Klain now began a delicate dance with Jayapal and her caucus.

In fact, Biden and his team desperately wanted to pass BIF. There was tremendous pressure to notch a political victory—and not only from House moderates. Terry McAuliffe, a Democrat running to regain his old job as governor of Virginia, pleaded with his close friend

Nancy Pelosi and the White House to pass BIF and give him ammunition against his Republican opponent. More important, passing BIF would likely boost the perception of Biden's competence and his anemic approval rating. "We would have taken BIF alone in a heartbeat any time after it passed the Senate on August 10," said a senior White House adviser. "We just never had the votes in the House."

In public, the White House team, led by Klain, seemed to favor passing the bills together. "He saw what that center of energy was, right?" said Peter Baker of Biden's chief of staff. "And he didn't want to alienate the progressives. So Ron's calculation was to make common cause with them. He was sort of willing to let them fight it out without taking overt sides."

The intraparty feud went on for months, as moderates demanded that BIF be passed without delay and progressives insisted that it be linked with BBB. With Klain's blessing, John Podesta, Bill Clinton's former chief of staff and head of the Center for American Progress, sent a letter to all members of Congress, exhorting them to pare down the $3.5 trillion BBB and pass both bills. "To those Democrats who only favor the bipartisan infrastructure bill," Podesta warned, "know this: You are either getting both bills or neither."

It was a political scrum, both sides thrashing against each other to move the ball their way, with the president right in the middle. To Klain, it was exasperating but the inevitable cost of getting bills passed. "All presidencies face this—which is to get stuff done, you have to stick the president into the legislative process. He has to be part of the sausage making in the early phase of the presidency. And yet the sausage making is extremely unattractive to voters and leads to all kinds of horrible political process media coverage, and to this drama of 'what did Joe Manchin have for breakfast and what did Joe Biden feed him and blah, blah.' It's obnoxious and politically harmful. And so you face this choice. Either you decide you're not going to get things done, or you stick the president in the middle of getting the work done. And everyone is like, 'Oh, he looks like a prime minister. He looks so small.'"

Previous administrations had kept the president above the fray; the model was the Reagan White House, where chief James Baker's Legislative Strategy Group (LSG) had done the dirty work in the trenches and brought the president in only when the deal was all but done. But times had changed, Klain argued, and so had circumstances. "Number one, because our majorities are so narrow, the need for the president to personally be interjected into this process is much greater. Number two, one of the things he sold to the country is, 'I'm good at this getting-things-done-in-Congress thing.' People expect him to do it!"

On October 1, the president traveled to Capitol Hill for a meeting with the Democratic caucus. Expectations were high that he'd break the impasse at last by calling for a vote on BIF alone.

The night before, Speaker Pelosi had scheduled a House vote on the bill, but after a day of intense wrangling with her caucus she scrapped it; she didn't have the votes. Now it seemed that Biden might summon all his negotiating skills and presidential prestige to put BIF over the top. "I think the president might be the only person who can bridge both the trust gap and the timing gap," said Representative Dean Phillips (D-MN). "Joe Biden is president, and not Bernie Sanders, for a reason. And I think it's his time to stand up."

Biden huddled behind closed doors with his Democratic caucus. A senior White House adviser explained the dynamic: "The House leadership wanted a vote. And the president's position was really clear, which was, if you have the votes, let's have the vote. If you don't have the votes, let's not have a vote. And their position was, well, if you call a vote, we will get the votes. And his position was, I'm not going to call for a vote until I know you have the votes! Because I'm not going to lose!" Biden emerged from the meeting without a deal. Nancy Pelosi was incensed. Looking chastened, Biden addressed the cameras: "We're going to get this done. It doesn't matter when. It doesn't matter whether it's in six minutes, six days, or six weeks—we're going to get it done."

Some suspected that Klain had talked Biden out of getting it done. A Democratic senator told me, "I think it was political malpractice when the president went to the caucus and didn't call for a vote on BIF. Pelosi was furious because they thought he was going to go up and ask for it and somehow Ron Klain at the last minute convinced Biden not to close the deal. He's tied into the progressive groups. I'm like, 'Holy crap, what are you doing?'"

But Ricchetti insisted that the idea that Klain was doing the progressives' bidding was nonsense. "We just don't operate that way, where one of us owns one ideological group and the other owns another," he told me. There was no daylight between him and Klain. "I know for a fact that Ron talked to as many moderates as I did, and I talked to as many liberals or progressives as he did during that period of time."

Some Republicans groused that Biden's chief wielded too much power. Early on, when Klain was caught shaking his head during a meeting with senators, someone dubbed him "the prime minister." Andy Card thought that understated Klain's clout. "I want Ron to succeed," George W. Bush's former chief told me. "But I do feel that he is playing more the role of president than chief of staff." Card said he'd fielded complaints from Republicans. "When senators would negotiate with Joe Biden in the Oval Office and think they had a deal, an hour later Ron Klain would say, 'No, you don't.' And they'd say, 'Well, the president said it.' And Ron would say, 'No, that's not it.'"

But taking blame for presidents just went with the chief's job. Reagan's James Baker used to say, "The White House chief of staff walks around with a target on his front and on his back." To which Obama's Rahm Emanuel added, "Those aren't the only parts." Klain wasn't shy about arguing his case, but he was an honest broker to the president and made sure everyone's opinion was heard. And passing BIF and BBB together was hardly some scheme cooked up by Klain. Labor Secretary Marty Walsh insisted that Biden approved the strategy: "When he talks about these two bills, he's passionate about both. And it's not like he's more passionate about roads and bridges and Amtrak. He's passionate about childcare. He's passionate about paid family leave. He's passionate about workforce development and the environmental stuff."

Nevertheless, the pressure to pass BIF and notch a legislative victory was mounting. At the end of October, Biden was scheduled to make an overseas trip—to Rome, where he'd visit the pope and attend a meeting of the G20; and to Glasgow, Scotland, where world leaders were gathering for a climate change summit known as COP26 (the twenty-sixth annual U.N. Climate Change Conference of the Parties). Biden had hoped to have BBB, with its sweeping climate provisions, passed and signed to show the world that the U.S. was serious about its commitments. Now he might not even have the more modest BIF. "There was a moment right before Biden left for Europe," said Peter Baker, "where the White House changed tactics, and decided it was time for him to force them to stop squabbling and start getting to some votes. Finally Biden said, 'Okay, enough. Let's just go ahead and get it done.'"

On the evening of October 27, Representative Jim Clyburn (D-SC), the Majority Whip, huddled with Speaker Pelosi and a group of moderates who supported the infrastructure bill but opposed BBB. Clyburn, whose endorsement of Biden before the 2020 South Carolina primary had effectively clinched his nomination, had had enough. "The question," he told me, "was how do you get this done? This debate was going on and on. Nobody could see an end to it, and we were going to have a real bad situation." Clyburn told his colleagues a story. Thomas Edison, he said, couldn't get his lightbulb to work until he sat down with Lewis Latimer, the son of former slaves, who'd invented the filament. "Thomas Edison's lightbulb never worked until he got Lewis Latimer's filament in it," Clyburn told them. "It required that Edison step out of his comfort zone and Latimer step outside of his. But the two of them—one Black, one white, giving up some of their comfort—lit the world." It was time, Clyburn told them, to give up something to get BIF passed.

The next day, Biden paid another visit to the Democratic caucus on Capitol Hill. But once again, the president stopped short of calling for a vote on BIF. Afterward, speaking to cameras outside the caucus room, Biden made a startling admission about the stakes of getting BIF and BBB passed in the days ahead: "I don't think it's hyperbole to say that the House and Senate majorities and my presidency will be determined by what happens in the next week."

It appeared that Biden had twice stepped up to the plate, only to strike out without taking a swing. But Klain insisted that the president got what he wanted: The progressives had agreed to pare down BBB from $3.5 trillion to a more manageable $1.75 trillion. "He went up there that day not to get a vote but actually to sell the progressives on cutting Build Back Better in half," said Biden's chief. "So we considered that an incredibly successful visit because we got Democratic unity be-hind the version of Build Back Better that did indeed eventually pass the House."

Still, as Biden boarded Air Force One for Europe, the fate of his domestic agenda hung by a thread. The president's old friend former senator Chris Dodd, no stranger to Democratic squabbling, thought Biden had missed an opportunity to seize the moment. "I can't recall, in my almost forty years in the Congress, that a sitting president, on his way to major global conferences, was denied a major legislative victory by his own political party," he told me. Months of legislative bloodletting had damaged the Democratic Party and the president. "What we've been watching for the last six months is an internecine battle within the Democratic party," Dodd said. "There is not a mayor or governor in the country that wasn't anxious for the resources that the infrastructure bill could provide."

It was hard to imagine LBJ getting stiffed like this by Congress. But given the bitterly partisan climate of 2021 and his razor-thin ma-jority, how much power did Joe Biden really have?

The president might well have agreed with Dodd. Before flying off to Europe, empty-handed, Biden took a walk around the White House residence with an old friend. Reflecting on his inability to bend Congress to his will, he confessed: "I'm not feared."

THIRTEEN

IT'S FIFTY-FIFTY

With the fate of Joe Biden's legislative agenda in the balance, I went to visit Ron Klain at the White House. It was Saturday, October 30, 2021, and with the president overseas, the West Wing was quiet. The Marine guard who stood outside when Biden was in the Oval Office was gone. Except for the receptionist, I was the only person in the West Wing reception room, with its Chippendale-replica furniture and nineteenth-century oil paintings of Revolutionary War scenes.

Greeting me a few minutes late, Klain apologized; he'd been on the phone with Majority Leader Chuck Schumer. "My first call in the morning and last call at night," he said. Schumer called Klain at least six times a day, including weekends, with updates on the progress of Biden's legislation. We walked past the Oval Office; in the president's absence its doors were locked, with uniformed Secret Service standing guard. As we entered the chief of staff's office, I noticed a big wooden desk just to the left of the entrance; it was the replacement for the one Trump's chiefs had removed.

We stepped outside onto the flagstone patio, enclosed by a trellis, that Ronald Reagan's chief Don Regan had ordered built back in the

1980s. We pulled up chairs to a table and took off our masks. The sky was overcast. Klain looked tired.

I wondered what he thought of Joe Biden's remark that his presidency would be determined by what happened on Capitol Hill in the next few days. "Is this really the week that makes or breaks the presidency?" I asked him.

"I don't think any week makes or breaks the presidency," Klain said. As usual, even after his white-knuckle ride with Congress over the previous forty-eight hours, Klain was even-keeled, philosophical. "Weeks are neither as big on the upside or as bad on the downside as you think."

I asked him why the president hadn't pressed for a vote on the infrastructure bill on his visit to Capitol Hill—when that was clearly Nancy Pelosi's plan. "Yeah, I know," he said. "It wasn't our plan. Our plan was to try to sell the framework of both bills to the left and the center of our party. It was a three-month-long negotiation to get that done. And I think, by and large, knock wood, that has succeeded. We'll see when the vote comes this week."

He went on to analyze BBB: "The challenge here is we took their six-trillion-dollar plan and cut it by seventy-five percent. And then had to sell it to the broader center of the party that has concerns. Sell it to the women's caucus, even though it doesn't include paid family leave. Sell it to the Black caucus, even though it doesn't include the increases they were looking for on Historically Black Colleges and Universities (HBCUs), and housing, and more. But we found a number that Manchin and Sinema will support."

"Are you sure about that?" I asked.

"They've told us that they'll support the number. Obviously, they'll want to see what's in the bill. But I feel like—look, it could still blow up. We're trying to pass something—if you add the two bills together—three times as large as the New Deal in real dollars with a three-vote margin in the House and no-vote margin in the Senate."

Then Klain said something stunningly candid: "Maybe we'll get it done and maybe we won't. I think it's fifty-fifty." He said this almost casually, as though Biden hadn't staked his presidency, and control of the House and Senate in the next year's midterm elections, on passing both bills.

Klain explained what they were up against in the tug-of-war over the final shape of BBB: "Look, any one senator could say no. And thirty of them are pissed off that all their ideas got dumped to produce a compromise." Klain was actually understating the ugly truth: Forty-eight senators were pissed off that they had to bend to the will of just two: Joe Manchin and Kyrsten Sinema.

Not for nothing is the chief of staff called the president's javelin catcher. The projectiles were coming from every direction. One of those forty-eight senators, Bernie Sanders, didn't understand why Joe Manchin's vote counted more than his vote. And everyone had different priorities. Senator Sheldon Whitehouse (D-RI) cared about climate change provisions. Senator Bob Casey (D-PA) didn't understand why home-based care was cut. Senator Elizabeth Warren (D-MA) didn't understand why there was a means test for childcare. Senator Amy Klobuchar (D-MN) didn't understand why the provision for lowering prescription drug prices came out.

The latest tussle pitted Manchin against Sanders. Manchin was against anything that was, in his mind, tantamount to paying somebody not to work, or anything he considered a freebie. That meant not only family leave but also glasses for seniors. But Sanders's attitude was "why is his position more privileged than mine?"

Klain liked Joe Manchin personally and understood where he came from. Early on, he'd paid a visit to the West Virginia senator on his houseboat, tied up on the Potomac. "I spent a lot of time talking about why we need this. And he's like, 'Well, you don't need every single thing that the left wants.' I said, 'Okay, but we need some things.' He cares genuinely about public service. He's here to serve. And when you say to him, 'Look, here's a bill that's going to give every kid in your state universally free preschool, that's going to lift those kids up,' he gets it. He has a perspective that he feels very strongly about. Services for people. Put them to work. Educate them. He's not willing to vote for checks and handouts for people."

Of course, choosing to see certain legislation—such as BBB—as "handouts," even if it were a sincerely held belief, played well politically in conservative West Virginia. Biden had lost the state by thirty-eight points. And so the president had little leverage to turn Manchin around. If he offered to go to the senator's state and campaign with him, Manchin would probably lose by *forty-two* points.

Kyrsten Sinema was harder to understand. She was from a state Biden carried—but not by much. She fancied herself the next John McCain—a bipartisan maverick for whom moderation was the thing. But McCain was a mostly predictable fiscal conservative who favored strong defense. By contrast, Sinema's core beliefs were a mystery. Other than being against taxing the rich, she was all over the map.

Klain was worn out by the legislative wrangling. He understood the political toll it inflicted on the president—because voters seemed to care more about short-term pain at the gas pump than about long-term gain represented by bridges and childcare. "The most frustrating part is that we are in this morass on Capitol Hill, no margin for error, and it sucks up so much of our time and so much energy and so much political drama," Klain said. "And it's a very important agenda. It's an agenda we have to fight for, an agenda we believe in. And in the long run it matters a lot. But right now, people wish we were more focused on gas prices and hamburger prices than whether or not we're going to build bridges or have free pre-K."

Yet there was little Biden could do about gas prices beyond persuading OPEC to pump more oil or tapping the Strategic Petroleum Reserves. And both moves, even if they could be executed, were temporary holding actions whose effect would soon wear off.

As for BIF and BBB, in football terms, Biden's team was in sudden-death overtime. "You don't want to quit on the ten-yard line when you've put so much time and energy into getting there," said Klain. "But every week we're on the ten-yard line, or the five-yard line, and we're not getting to the end zone. People are like, 'Yeah, but why isn't the guy doing these *other* things?' I think either we're able to get it over the hump in the House this week, or else it just kind of falls apart."

Looking ahead to the state governors' elections, just three days away, Klain worried that a loss in Virginia by the Democrat, former governor Terry McAuliffe, could bring Biden's legislative agenda crashing down. Biden had carried Virginia by ten points in 2020. "Assuming we lose in Virginia on Tuesday, that'll be a momentum blow," he said. His fatalism about passing Biden's agenda was palpable. "At some point you have to say, 'Look, we tried. We couldn't get it done and it's time to move on to other things.'"

I asked Klain about the U.S. withdrawal from Afghanistan, now that a few months had gone by. He was struck by the hypocrisy of Biden's critics. "Every person who's gone on TV and blasted our handling of this, at some point in the past ten years said, 'The Afghan army is great!' A Democratic senator whacked us last week on this. But back in June he was like, 'We've *trained* that Afghan army. They're going to hold Kabul!'"

How did he feel about criticism from his fellow chief, and ex-boss, Leon Panetta? "I love Leon, but I feel like we've taken a lot of responsibility here," he said. "And I'm waiting for the first person who held a position of power in a previous administration—who signed the checks to buy, equip, and train these people—to say, 'You know what? Maybe we didn't do our jobs of making sure the taxpayers got what they paid for.'"

The holidays were approaching. Klain was bone-tired, and he was thinking about quitting. He loved being White House chief of staff, even when things were going badly, and believed he made Biden more effective. But the workload was relentless and debilitating; that's why the average tenure of White House chiefs was eighteen months. And Klain knew that when it came to departing, timing was everything.

History showed what could happen when a White House chief quit too close to the next midterm elections. Bill Clinton's Mack McLarty had departed in June of his second year, and Barack Obama's Rahm Emanuel in October; each time their successors had little time to prepare for the midterms—and their parties were routed at the polls. Klain wanted to avoid that mistake. He would stay, assuming the president wanted him, until the end of the first or second year; quitting at any time in between was too risky. Klain would talk it over with his wife during Thanksgiving.

My visit had lasted nearly an hour and a half; it was time to go. Biden's chief walked me down the hall past the Oval Office, where the Secret Service still stood watch, and through the West Wing reception room. Out on the North Lawn, before heading toward the exit at the Southwest Gate, I snapped a photo of the White House with my iPhone. Dark clouds were gathering.

―――――

Three days later, Republican Glenn Youngkin routed Democrat Terry McAuliffe in the Virginia governor's race. In New Jersey, Phil Murphy, the incumbent Democrat who'd been favored by sixteen points, was in a contest too close to call (he ultimately prevailed). Media pundits predicted turbulence ahead. "The menacing thunder couldn't get much louder for Democrats," *The New York Times* opined. The election results "raised alarms that the wave of anti-Trump energy that carried them into power has curdled into apathy. . . ."

More ominously, according to the *Times*, the elections had been a bellwether, a referendum on the Biden presidency: "The party's motivation has been replaced by a sense of dissatisfaction with the state of a country that has, despite all of Mr. Biden's campaign promises, not yet returned to a pre-Covid sense of normalcy."

Chris Dodd, the former senator and Biden confidant, sounded a warning. "The reality is, this past fall has been a wake-up call," he told me. "The Democrats' failure to pass all of the Biden legislative agenda has taken a toll. The Democrats must start telling a better story about President Biden's achievements in this unprecedented, perilous year. The Democrats have a job to do—to have a positive impact on the midterm elections and the presidential election of 2024."

Donald Trump hadn't said whether he would run for president again in 2024. But in a poll conducted by his nascent campaign, he was ahead in the key swing states. He'd been impeached twice, fumbled a lethal pandemic, and incited a violent assault on the U.S. Capitol. But at this early stage of the next presidential race, Trump was up in Arizona by 8 percentage points, Georgia by 3, Michigan by 12, Pennsylvania by 6, and Wisconsin by 10.

Meanwhile, halfway around the world, Joe Biden's climate czar was trying to persuade the Chinese to act—before it was too late to save the planet.

FOURTEEN

CODE RED

John Kerry was irritated. It was September 3, 2021, and Joe Biden's special presidential envoy for climate (SPEC) had flown halfway around the world for an important meeting on global warming with Chinese officials. The former Massachusetts senator, U.S. secretary of state, and presidential candidate believed in personal, hands-on diplomacy. But with China in a COVID lockdown, Kerry and his small team were whisked into isolation with their Chinese counterparts in the seaside city of Tianjin. Enclosed in a bubble, emptied of inhabitants, the "resort" was otherworldly; the Chinese wore "moon suits," HAZMAT outfits, and wouldn't come anywhere near the Americans. Senior diplomats spoke with Kerry only by videoconference, while a junior official sat at the far end of an enormous table. Haggling with the Chinese over climate change was always a daunting proposition. But this was ridiculous.

"The Taliban got a better reception," wrote one longtime China observer, referring to a recent visit by a delegation of the Afghan insurgent group. Kerry had been better received on his *first* trip to China, a visit to Shanghai in April; the two countries had issued a joint statement pledging cooperation on some measures to reduce carbon emissions. But this time the Chinese foreign minister gave Kerry a stern lecture about "strategic miscalculation."

Kerry had been laser-focused on China since Joe Biden gave him the climate portfolio back in November 2020. He'd vowed not to return to government for just any assignment, but "when the president of the United States called me up and said, 'I want you to do something,'" Kerry couldn't refuse. For Barack Obama's top diplomat, it meant trading his State Department motorcade and entourage for Ubers and just an assistant or two. But he had cabinet rank and reported only to Biden and Secretary of State Tony Blinken. More important, global warming was an issue Kerry had lived, breathed, and warned about for three decades. "This topic has been near and dear to my heart for a long time," he told me on a virtual call from the American embassy in Paris en route to the Munich Security Conference.

For Joe Biden, climate change was a high priority. As a senator, he hadn't been in the same league as environmental heavyweights like Kerry and Al Gore (D-TN). But Biden could claim authorship of the first bill in Congress to address climate change. Biden's Global Climate Protection Act, which called for setting up a task force on global warming, died in the Senate in 1986, but it passed as part of the Foreign Relations Authorization Act on December 12, 1987.

During his presidential transition, Biden asked his old friend Kerry to head a climate task force combining his own experts and those of Bernie Sanders's defunct campaign. "Biden was already interested in the issue, but by the time he got to the White House he was completely revved up and ready to go," said Todd Stern, Obama's ex–State Department climate envoy. Both the progressive and centrist wings of the Democratic Party were committed to the cause.

On January 20, with Kerry at his side, Biden had signed an executive order reentering the U.S. into the landmark Paris Agreement, signed by 196 countries in December 2015. He'd set ambitious climate targets—committing the U.S. to converting to clean energy consumption by 2035 and reducing greenhouse gas emissions to net zero by 2050.

There was no time to lose. Forest fires in the West were devouring entire towns. Severe storms with monster tornadoes had become commonplace. The U.S. had spent $100 billion recovering from natural disasters in 2020 and, an indication of how bad things could get, temperatures in Death Valley had hit 130 degrees Fahrenheit. The Paris Agreement, negotiated by Kerry as Obama's secretary of state, had put the world on a path to limit the global temperature rise to less than 2.0 degrees Celsius (2.0°C) over preindustrial (revolution) levels. But since then global warming had accelerated; pledges to reduce emissions were one thing, but action to follow through on them was another. In August 2021, the U.N.'s Intergovernmental Panel on Climate Change (IPCC) sounded an alarm, declaring a "code red for humanity." Its report concluded that the target set at Paris fell short; even a rise of 1.5°C in the earth's temperature would have catastrophic effects.

The consequences of rising global temperatures were sobering to contemplate. In 2021, the earth's temperature had already spiked 1.2°C over preindustrial levels. If the temperatures reached the 1.5°C threshold, nearly a billion people worldwide would suffer in life-threatening heat waves; hundreds of millions would experience severe drought; sea levels could rise ten to thirty inches, affecting five hundred million more. Seventy percent of coral reefs would die, eliminating fish habitats; huge swaths of earth's land area would shift from one biome to another—turning grasslands, for example, into deserts. If temperatures rose by 2.0°C, many of these effects could be doubled. Most frightening of all, perhaps, there was no way of knowing when rising temperatures would reach a tipping point, making climate damage irreversible, a point of no return. Such a tipping point might be the destruction of the Amazon Rain Forest or the melting of the Arctic Glacier.

Since January 20, Kerry, seventy-seven, had traveled to eighteen countries, exhorting his foreign counterparts to make "nationally determined contributions," or NDCs—pledges to lower emissions of carbon dioxide. The world would have to raise its game in order to reduce warming and avert global disaster. This was Kerry's message, which he took to heads of state and foreign ministers around the planet.

Kerry was famously indestructible. "He'll break his leg, he'll screw up his knees, he'll go back to snowboarding and skiing and I don't know what the hell else," said a veteran diplomat. "The guy's a phenomenon." Gina McCarthy, Biden's White House national climate adviser, Kerry's domestic counterpart, agreed. "I don't know how this man actually does what he does." McCarthy was as close to Biden's climate envoy as a little sister. They were both Irish Bostonians—though McCarthy, sixty-seven, was a foot shorter and spoke with a working-class brogue. Biden's top climate officials were an odd couple: the blue-collar bureaucrat and the to-the-manor-born, Yale-educated plutocrat who'd married into the Heinz ketchup fortune; he and his wife, Teresa Heinz, had met in 1990 at an Earth Day rally in Washington, D.C. Kerry had taken his share of ridicule for his self-regard over the years—a 1971 *Doonesbury* cartoon portrayed him thinking, "You're really clicking tonight, you gorgeous preppy." But, a half century later, he took himself less seriously, and he brought unrivaled credibility, expertise, and influence to the cause.

McCarthy described their mission: "The first goal was to show that on climate the United States, under President Biden's leadership, is back," she said. Having someone of Kerry's stature as global climate czar went a long way toward demonstrating that. "And the second was that we needed to keep this one-point-five Celsius number in play, and we were nowhere close to having the kind of commitments that would get us on track for that."

Kerry was almost evangelical on the subject. While Biden framed global warming as an opportunity to create jobs, Kerry talked about it as an existential threat. "We have to reduce emissions by forty-five percent over these next few years in order to achieve two things," he told me. "One, to hold the earth's temperature increase to one-point-five C, and two, to have the possibility of getting to 2050 net zero. Twenty countries generate eighty percent of all emissions. And if you can't get them on board, if you can't get people moving, we're screwed."

On April 22, from the White House, Kerry and Biden convened a virtual meeting of the Major Economies Forum on Energy and Climate, or MEF, an acronym for "the Major Emitters Forum." It included the world's twenty largest economies and greenhouse gas emitters and forty world leaders, who pledged to make NDCs that would keep the target of 1.5°C within reach. "So we had the EU, we had the U.K., we had Canada, Japan, South Korea, all making a commitment," said Kerry. But one country came up conspicuously short. "China simply refused from day one to move their NDC. They'd come out with a plan and chose a 2060 date—which doesn't cut it for us or for anybody. And we were trying to move them for most of the year, but it became clear that they weren't going to move."

Kerry went on: "When you have a country that represents thirty percent of the world's emissions all by itself, that is using more coal than all thirty-eight of the OECD [Organisation for Economic Co-operation and Development] countries put together, that is opening more coal plants next year than exist in the United States—when you see that, you have to figure out, how do we stop that?"

———

Arguably, Kerry was uniquely qualified to crack the Chinese code. As Obama's secretary of state, he'd been the driving force behind secret negotiations with Chinese leadership that ultimately led to the break-through in Paris. "Kerry is a person of the big gesture," said Stern, the Obama climate envoy. "He wants to go and talk to the president and the secretary of state and foreign ministers and he wants to come up with big things. That's tremendously to his credit and it paid off in the case of China."

When he replaced Hillary Clinton as Obama's secretary of state in 2013, Kerry was forewarned about Chinese intransigence. "The folks on my staff said to me, 'You know, this isn't going to work. You can't get China to agree to anything that quickly. They've got to go through their process.' And I said, 'No. I don't believe that.' I'd been a senator for twenty-eight years. I knew them. They knew me. So we went to China and boom! President Xi, one-on-one, listened, talked, agreed—and said, 'Yeah. That makes sense. We'll do that task force.'" Kerry put together a U.S.-China climate task force and a year later, on November 12, 2014, Barack Obama and Xi Jinping stood in the Great Hall of the People in Beijing and announced a major U.S.-China agreement to reduce greenhouse gases. It became the impetus for the Paris Agreement the following year.

But since then U.S.-China relations had worsened dramatically; Donald Trump's trade war had poisoned the atmosphere. And then there were the contentious issues of Taiwan's sovereignty, Hong Kong's democracy, a military buildup in the South China Sea, and human rights for the country's abused minority, the Uyghurs—the U.S. had labeled their treatment genocide. Moreover, the chaotic U.S. retreat from Afghanistan, and Biden's anemic approval rating, had seemed to harden Xi's arrogance.

Todd Stern explained Kerry's challenge with the Chinese: "He's not going to wear them down. Not even if our relationship with China was at the level it was with Obama, which was not easy, but nothing like it is now. They don't want to do something that looks like they're giving in to the United States. So this is superhard." Kerry agreed: "The more you hammer them publicly and tell them you're going to do this and you're going to do that, the less you're going to get out of them. They don't work that way. That's not Chinese."

Kerry's Chinese counterpart, Xie Zhenhua, had come out of retirement to negotiate with his old friend. The two veteran diplomats had forged the agreement that led to the 2015 breakthrough in Paris. But Kerry sensed that this time Xie wasn't calling the shots. "I don't think we can do this if President Xi doesn't invest in it," he told me. "I'm told, through my channels and my understanding of China, that Xi is making these decisions. Nobody else. President Xi is personally deciding what they will do and when and how."

The year's most consequential event was COP26, scheduled to take place in Glasgow, Scotland, from October 31 to November 12, 2021. The gathering would be a kind of global reality check, a chance to see whether the world's nations could commit to lowering their emissions in time to avert disaster. COP26 would be not just virtual but also in person; despite the continuing COVID pandemic, world leaders would be flying in to attend. But two of the most important would be there only via video screen: Russian president Vladimir Putin and Chinese president Xi Jinping.

Joe Biden was scheduled to appear in person at the conference on its second day, en route from Rome, where he'd visited the pope and attended a meeting of the G20.

Upon his arrival, the president called his team together—Kerry, McCarthy, Jake Sullivan, Tony Blinken, and speechwriter Carlyn Reichel. Biden told them that he wanted to address the elephant in the room: the fact that, under Trump, the U.S. had been AWOL on climate change. Trump had dismissed the whole idea as a Chinese hoax and withdrawn the U.S. from the Paris Agreement. Biden thought the U.S. owed the world an apology.

"How do we make sure that we don't come in saying, we're the best?" the president asked. "That we don't come in acting like we've earned the leadership position again." Kerry and McCarthy agreed that Biden should say something; they'd spent the better part of a year trying to convince their foreign counterparts that the U.S. could be trusted after Trump's abdication of leadership. "It was a terrible, embarrassing, horrible four years," said Kerry. "It was destructive to the world. And the president welcomed the humility that needed to come with our position."

There was something else to be humble about. Biden had wanted to have BBB, and its sweeping climate provisions, passed into law before he arrived in Glasgow. Instead, he'd come empty-handed. In a sense, Kerry's hands were tied without it. It was the only way to show the world that they were serious. "I remember saying to the president that the single biggest thing we could do to deal with China is pass Build Back Better. And he said, 'I agree!' He really got animated. He knows. We've got to show them that we're effective, we're getting things done, we're putting billions of dollars into research and development, and we're moving the world."

Biden was fed up with the gridlock on Capitol Hill, and Kerry knew it: "He's obviously frustrated. Who isn't? I mean, there's a terrible situation in Washington right now. And we don't look good in the world. And that hurts us." In a sidebar at the conference, Indonesian president Joko Widodo asked Biden how he was doing. "There's this old joke," Biden replied. "A guy jumps off a 100-story building. As he passes the 50th floor, they ask him how he's doing. And he says, 'So far so good.'"

Still, at Glasgow, Biden was eager to make his case to the world. "He was hot to trot," said Kerry. "He wanted to go out and do it."

Removing his mask as he stepped up to the podium, Biden began:

We meet with the eyes of history upon us and the profound questions before us. It's simple: Will we act? Will we do what is necessary? Will we seize the enormous opportunity before us? Or will we condemn future generations to suffer? This is the decade that will determine the answer. This decade. The science is clear: We only have a brief window left before us to raise our ambitions and to raise—to meet the task that's rapidly narrowing.

Then Biden acknowledged the elephant in the conference hall:

We'll demonstrate to the world the United States is not only back at the table but hopefully leading by the power of our example. I know it hasn't been the case, and that's why my administration is working overtime to show that our climate commitment is action, not words.

Biden departed the next day—but the U.S. delegation was energized. At one point, rushing through a restaurant, McCarthy spotted Kerry having a salad. "Oh, you're sitting down!" she needled him. "Gina," Kerry replied, "this is the first meal I've had in three days."

The agreements reached at Glasgow were substantial. More than 190 countries—including the U.K., the EU, the U.S., Japan, Canada, and South Korea—had agreed to ramp up emission reduction targets for 2030. What's more, the U.S. and 109 other countries, which collectively possessed eighty-five percent of the world's forests, agreed to measures aimed at ending deforestation by 2030. And a significant agreement was struck on reducing emissions of methane. On his way to Glasgow, Biden had been told that about thirty countries would agree to the Global Methane Pledge. In the end, 105 countries were onboard. Kerry and his team's relentless efforts had paid off.

Toward the conference's end, Kerry even managed to cobble together an agreement with China. The absence of President Xi had made a major breakthrough impossible. But, working through the final nights, Kerry and his Chinese counterpart, Xie, hammered out a bilateral deal. "It took until three in the morning—going back to Beijing and going back to Washington on the last night," said Kerry, "but China came back with a proposal which we then succeeded in changing a bit. And we finally reached an agreement." China pledged to phase down coal consumption and to develop a methane plan before the next conference.

Still, the target of reducing global warming below 1.5°C had been missed. "We've got twelve countries that are legitimately chasing the one-point-five C target in the next eight years," Kerry told me, "but we also have this other group—China, Russia, India, Mexico, Brazil, Indonesia, South Africa, Saudi Arabia—that are not there. And that kills us. If we can't get them to move faster, the planet is in super-trouble."

"Glasgow was disappointing in a lot of important ways," said Todd Stern. "But if you change the behavior of one country, it could have been a smashing success. China could have done the big thing that the Glasgow conference was looking for—right now, this decade, in a way that will keep alive the hope of holding temperatures to one-point-five C. And China didn't."

The world's leaders had only a decade left to prevent the worst-case catastrophe of global warming. Joe Biden and his Special Envoy Kerry had much less time than that.

FIFTEEN

INFRASTRUCTURE WEEK

When Joe Biden stepped off Air Force One at Joint Base Andrews on November 3, on his return from Glasgow, the political landscape had changed. Terry McAuliffe's loss in the Virginia governor's race to underdog Republican Glenn Youngkin had concentrated minds among Democrats who feared disastrous midterms to come. McAuliffe's loss likely had more to do with culture war issues like critical race theory and his own campaign gaffes than with Biden's failure to pass an infrastructure bill. But the mood in the president's party was bleak.

Instead of stalling Biden's legislative momentum, as Ron Klain had feared, McAuliffe's defeat had a galvanizing effect. Speaker Pelosi, Majority Leader Schumer, and Klain went to work on the Democratic caucus, trying to corral votes for BIF. Meanwhile, Biden's team had made progress paring down the cost of BBB. As a senior White House adviser put it, "A little bit of political necessity and a little bit of progress on right-sizing Build Back Better enabled these things to move forward on separate tracks."

Pelosi called the president multiple times a day, pushing him to call for a vote on BIF once and for all. But on Thursday, November 4, Pelosi tapped the brakes, concluding that at least a dozen moderate

Democrats were holding out, once again refusing to say they would later support BBB.

The breakthrough came that evening. Over dinner, the Majority Whip, Representative Jim Clyburn (D-SC), told a White House aide that the Congressional Black Caucus (CBC) would agree to vote for BIF and put off the BBB bill for another day. "A lot of people trusted, and trust, Jim Clyburn," said a senior White House adviser. "And so he and Representative Joyce Beatty (D-OH) came up with the final idea, which was actually the idea that passed."

Clyburn dispatched Representative Beatty to present the idea to the progressives. They were still wary, suspecting a betrayal. If they voted for BIF, what assurance did they have that BBB would ever be passed?

As the clock kept ticking, Biden canceled his weekend plans in Wilmington and vowed to stay until a deal was done. "At six o'clock or so, we went upstairs to the residence," recalled Klain. "Started to make calls. The president ordered us pizza. We ate, we called, we called, and we ate." It was a full court press—as Klain; Ricchetti; Louisa Terrell, director of the Office of Legislative Affairs (OLA); Susan Rice, director of the Domestic Policy Council (DPC); and Brian Deese, director of the NEC, worked the phones over pizza, Coke, wine, and Dove bars. The president had a giant freezer stocked with them. A little after 7:00 p.m., Vice President Kamala Harris arrived and started making calls.

Klain called Representative Pramila Jayapal (D-WA), the leader of the progressives, to plead Biden's case. "We got to the point around eight o'clock where we were stuck," he said. "Rep. Jayapal and her group weren't budging, and House leadership called us and said, 'Hey, you've got to move the progressives.' And so I continued to work it for a while. The vice president made some phone calls."

Tempers were flaring. Joe Biden was on a short fuse. Early in his term he had reserved the f-bomb mostly for discussions of the southern border, but lately he was using it more often. Nancy Pelosi was angry with the White House staff; there was tension between the Speaker and Jayapal; and some Democrats were frustrated with Klain, accusing him of coddling Jayapal.

They were getting nowhere. Biden told Klain he wanted to speak directly to Jayapal and her caucus.

From the Treaty Room, on the second floor of the residence, the president was connected with Jayapal; she put him on speakerphone with her caucus. The president gave them the Biden treatment. "Look," he told them. "I will get this done. It's going to take a while, but I will get Build Back Better done. We're risking even more fissures inside the party. People want to see us deliver. I understand this leveraging strategy, but voters, even though our supporters are Democrats, don't understand why we're not moving forward on lead pipes just because we're trying to get childcare also. Why shouldn't we just move forward on things that are ready?"

"The president had a number of direct conversations, both with the caucus itself and with individual members and with Republicans, to get this across the finish line that night," Steve Ricchetti told me. "And we didn't know for sure whether we had the votes until well into the evening."

The irony was not lost on Biden or his aides that the president had to prove his devotion to BBB. "I mean, Build Back Better is *his* plan," complained a senior White House adviser. "He doesn't have to promise anyone that he's fighting for *his* plan. I mean, with all due respect to the progressive caucus, we wrote Build Back Better when they were all trying to get Elizabeth Warren elected president. So the idea that they could now love this better than we do is ridiculous."

Biden's appeal, on bended knee, was the price of getting the progressives to go along with a vote on BIF. "He basically pushed in a gentle but firm way," said Peter Baker. "That said, it was, 'Time's up. Gotta do it.' And the appeal might not have worked in August. It might not have worked in September or October."

But now it worked. At 10:55 p.m., the president and his team watched on C-SPAN as the House began voting on H.R. 3684, the Infrastructure Investment and Jobs Act. When the "yes" votes passed 218, ensuring the bill's passage into law, Biden and his team broke into cheers, sharing high fives and hugs.

———

Ten days later, on a blustery afternoon on the South Lawn, Joe Biden presided over a signing ceremony for the 2,702-page bill. Eight-hundred people gathered to watch the president sign into law the once-in-a-generation infrastructure package. It provided more than half-a-trillion dollars for roads, bridges, water pipelines, broadband internet, and other critical needs. Perhaps as important, it was the kind of bipartisan achievement that was thought impossible in a polarized era, but which Biden had promised during his campaign.

The signing also came just before a virtual summit between Biden and Chinese president Xi Jinping. BIF would put the U.S. on a path to spend more on infrastructure than China over the next decade, a striking reversal of recent history. It represented points on the board in the contest between democracy and autocracy.

Sitting at a desk that had been hauled out on the South Lawn, flanked by the Democratic leadership, Pelosi and Schumer, and the "Gang of Ten" senators who'd celebrated the initial agreement at the North Portico with the president back in June, Biden signed the documents. The celebration was spirited but not without glitches. Biden squinted into the sun. Then, spotting Kyrsten Sinema, the president said, "Hello, *Kristen!*" Josh Bolten, who was within earshot, cracked: "He really should know the first name of the second most important person in his caucus [after Manchin]."

"There were moments of peril and setbacks and frustration along the way for months," Ricchetti told me, "and we just kept our heads down and tried to overcome any adversity to get this done." Ron Klain was fed up with the second-guessers. "Five presidents tried to pass generational infrastructure investment and one president got it done," he said. "And so maybe we should have asked for the vote on October 1 or maybe we should have asked for the vote on October 28, or maybe I shouldn't have called Jayapal, or maybe this or maybe that. People can second-guess each step, perhaps fairly. But in the end it comes down to this: We're the only folks who actually got this done."

But where did this leave the BBB bill? Months of Democratic feuding had left the public confused about what was in it. On November 22, David Axelrod tweeted a warning to the Democrats:

> *Ds should stop referring to the BBB as huge, historic and "transformative," emphasizing instead how it is RESPONSIVE to some of the everyday challenges people are facing. Practical answers to real life problems like the cost of childcare. No one's asking to be "transformed."*

Axelrod had a point. The elements of BBB, when you broke them down into separate parts, were enormously popular not only with Democrats but with most voters. But after months of haggling over arcane congressional rules and votes that never got taken, the only thing most voters grasped was its eye-popping price tag: $6 trillion at the start, it had now been trimmed to $2.1 trillion.

———————

On December 18, Klain and I spoke again by phone. During our previous talk, at the White House, he'd put the chances of passing BIF and BBB at fifty percent. What were the prospects now for Build Back Better? I asked him. "I'll put BBB at sixty percent; how's that?" he said.

"Is it Manchin again?" I asked.

"It's Manchin. The challenge is, the bill was tilted in a way to make everyone else happy—and we've got to keep our word to him. The president and Manchin struck a deal. That deal was for one-point-seven-five trillion dollars. The House passed a bill that was two-point-one trillion dollars. Manchin is not unreasonable to say, 'Hey, that's not my deal.'"

Klain was confident that Manchin would honor the agreement he'd struck with the president. All they had to do was cut $400 billion from the package.

"So you've got to get back to one-point-seven-five?" I asked.

"We've got to get back to one-point-seven-five."

The next day, Sunday, December 19, Joe Manchin was a guest on *FOX News Sunday*, hosted by Bret Baier. Asked if he'd vote for the Build Back Better Act, the West Virginia senator cited his concerns about inflation, the national debt, geopolitical unrest, and the pandemic. Then Manchin lowered the boom: "I cannot vote to continue with this piece of legislation. I just can't. I've tried everything humanly possible. I can't get there."

"You're done. This is a no," Baier said.

"This is a no on this legislation," Manchin replied. "I have tried everything I know to do."

Joe Biden was furious. He told Press Secretary Jen Psaki to put out a statement:

Senator Manchin promised to continue conversations in the days ahead, and to work with us to reach that common ground. If his comments on FOX and written statement indicate an end to that effort, they represent a sudden and inexplicable reversal in his position, and a breach of his commitments to the President and the Senator's colleagues in the House and Senate.

Why had Manchin blindsided Biden and his team? Apparently, he'd been angered by an earlier White House statement that he felt had singled him out as an obstacle.

Josh Bolten, head of the Business Roundtable, blamed the White House staff, not Manchin. "I think they overreached with Build Back Better," he said. "They overpromised to the left and then fumbled the critical negotiation with Manchin and Sinema. They should have set expectations better about what they could get out of Manchin. It's not like Manchin didn't tell them. And I think they felt like they needed to demonstrate to the left that they weren't going to take it lying down. But the result of that is they look weak, and they bungled what could have been a path to three quarters of a loaf. Even for the left, that would have been cause for celebration."

The Build Back Better bill, with its ambitious climate provisions, was all but dead.

SIXTEEN

THEY WANT ME TO BE PRESIDENT

As the first anniversary of the January 6 attack on the U.S. Capitol approached, Joe Biden was frustrated. Uniting the country, as he'd promised to do, meant turning the page on Trump, dialing down the temperature, restoring civility, and reaching across the aisle to do bipartisan things. Biden had tried that; he'd delivered emergency COVID relief, created more jobs than any other president in his first year, and placed more judges on the bench than Ronald Reagan. He'd passed a historic bipartisan infrastructure bill. But no Republicans appeared willing to work with him on anything else. Biden was fed up with their obstruction, their willingness to parrot Trump's lies about the 2020 election, and their complicity in subverting future elections. With a few obvious exceptions, they stood for nothing—except clinging to power and making it impossible for Biden to govern.

Most frustrating of all, while trying to govern, Biden had been forced to fight a rearguard action against Trumpism. The ex-president might be lying low in Mar-a-Lago, but his followers were inflicting real damage—in the form of vaccine resistance; voter suppression and election subversion; doubt among foreign leaders about the viability of American democracy; and, most dangerous, the threat posed to national security by Trump's violent acolytes.

Biden hadn't wanted to give a speech blasting Trump; he'd be accused of being divisive, of sinking to the ex-president's level. But the door that had been opened at Charlottesville hadn't been shut. The time had come to speak plainly about the man who'd unleashed America's darkest forces.

———

It all went back to August 11, 2017, when hundreds of white supremacists had gathered brazenly and in broad daylight in Charlottesville, Virginia. Afterward Trump had given them cover with his talk of "very fine people on both sides." Biden had called Mike Donilon, his confidant and wordsmith, at his home in Virginia. "He said, 'I have to speak out,'" recalled Donilon. "'I can't let this go.' I think he saw something that wasn't just offensive; he saw something that was dangerous." Up to this point, Biden had been on the fence about running for president; he'd just written a book and had two institutes in Delaware to run. But Trump's remarks, during a press gaggle in the Trump Tower lobby, changed everything.

The unofficial campaign had begun—with an article the following week under Biden's byline in *The Atlantic* magazine, written with Donilon. The piece opened with Biden standing at the railroad station in Wilmington, Delaware, in January 2009, waiting for a train carrying Barack Obama, the first African American elected president. But Biden was flashing back to another time, 1968, when, from the same spot, he'd watched the flames of buildings being torched in response to the assassination of Martin Luther King by a white racist:

In Charlottesville, that long trail emerged once again into plain view not only for America, but for the whole world to see. The crazed, angry faces illuminated by torches. The chants echoing the same anti-Semitic bile heard across Europe in the 1930s. The neo-Nazis, Klansmen, and white supremacists emerging from dark rooms and remote fields and the anonymity of the Web into the bright light of day on the streets of a historically significant city.

If it wasn't clear before, it's clear now. We are living through a battle for the soul of this nation.

There it was: the rallying cry that Biden would deploy in his campaign and in his presidency. And though he didn't know it yet, he was also foreshadowing a struggle to come against a revanchist dictator named Vladimir Putin.

Biden was fighting "the oldest and darkest forces in America."

Are we really surprised they rose up? Are we really surprised they lashed back? Did we really think they would be extinguished with a whimper rather than a fight?

The "battle for the soul of the nation" would be long-lasting, Biden wrote, because "when it comes to race in America, hope doesn't travel alone. It's shadowed by a long trail of violence and hate."

Biden's campaign operatives had panned the new rallying cry. "There weren't a lot of people in the campaign who were crazy about it," recalled Donilon. "Pollsters were like, 'It's nonsense!' And you know what? The truth was, political insiders didn't get it." Too bad; Biden and Donilon were sticking with it. "We said, 'Look, this isn't some jump ball. This is why he's running. There are no bromides here.' And it helped to get us through really hard times in Iowa and New Hampshire." Donilon felt reassured by reports he was getting from the campaign trail. "A couple of folks told me that when they were knocking on doors, people were saying to them, 'We're in a battle for the soul of the nation.' That's when I thought, 'Okay!'"

The power of the phrase, Donilon thought, was its clarity. "The country's got to figure out why you're in it, what you're saying. And for Joe Biden, it was a great anchor. A real kind of moral compass. And by the way, I think it's one of the reasons he won."

———

Now, after a year of floating above the fray as president, Biden was ready to sound the battle cry again. "He watched for a year as Trump and his supporters just really doubled down on the Big Lie," said Donilon. Toeing the line, parroting that falsehood "had become an almost definitional, threshold question for Republicans to survive Trump's wrath." Echo chambers like Fox News had spread the Big Lie far and wide. Biden had called it out in his inaugural address but not much since then. "Look, there's truth and there's lies," said Donilon. "And that's why the essential setup of his January 6, 2022, speech was that the muse of history looks over the Rotunda today." In the same spot where Trump's rioters had battled Capitol Police a year earlier, Biden looked into the camera and began:

I'm speaking to you today from Statuary Hall in the United States Capitol. This is where the House of Representatives met for fifty years in the decades leading up to the Civil War. This is—on this floor is where a young congressman of Illinois, Abraham Lincoln, sat at desk one-ninety-one. Above him—above us, over that door leading to the Rotunda—is a sculpture depicting Clio, the muse of history. In her hands, an open book in which she records the events taking place in this chamber below.

Clio stood watch over this hall one year ago today, as she has for more than two hundred years. She recorded what took place. The real history. The real facts. The real truth. The facts and the truth that . . . you and I and the whole world saw with our own eyes.

Biden went on to describe the bloody events of January 6, and then delivered a blistering attack on Donald Trump:

And here is the truth. The former president of the United States of America has created and spread a web of lies about the 2020 election. He's done so because he values power over principle, because he sees his own interests as more important than his country's interests and America's interests, and because his bruised ego matters more to him than our democracy or our Constitution.

Trump's behavior, and the GOP's acceptance of it, was so numbingly familiar that it was easy to forget how unprecedented it was. The Republican Party could have broken with Trump the day after the assault on the Capitol. Biden couldn't understand why his Republican colleagues hadn't tossed Trump into the dustbin of history. So he called out Trump's enablers now:

I did not seek this fight brought to this Capitol one year ago today, but I will not shrink from it either.

*I will stand in this breach. I will defend this nation. And I
will allow no one to place a dagger at the throat of our democracy.*

Watching from his home in California, Leon Panetta, Bill Clinton's former chief of staff, was impressed. "It was the best speech
of his presidency because he was speaking truth to the American
people," he told me. "And you just got a sense that he was really
being very honest about what had happened. I thought it was very
important. He was willing to say things that needed to be said, and
that's what presidents should do. So I thought, 'That's an important
turning point for him.'"

Sometimes a speech can resuscitate a presidency. In Panetta's
view, that's what had happened to Bill Clinton during his third year
in office. On April 19, 1995, a massive explosion had rocked the
Alfred P. Murrah Federal Building in Oklahoma City, killing 168
people and wounding 851. Like the MAGA insurrection at the
U.S. Capitol a quarter century later, it had been the handiwork of
homegrown, far-right extremists—in that case, one led by a man
named Timothy McVeigh.

At that point, Clinton's presidency had hit rock bottom. The administration's effort to reform health care had failed. The Republicans had won the House in a landslide, creating their first majority
in forty years. Newt Gingrich, the Republican Speaker who was then
championing a series of conservative proposals dubbed "Contract with
America," was ascendant. Almost plaintively, Clinton insisted that "the
president is relevant . . . the Constitution gives me relevance."

But at the memorial service in Oklahoma City, Clinton changed the
narrative. "You have lost too much, but you have not lost everything,"

he told the victims' families in a nationally televised eulogy, biting his lip, displaying his trademark empathy. "And you have certainly not lost America, for we will stand with you for as many tomorrows as it takes." After this stellar turn as consoler in chief, Clinton's fortunes began to change. Within months he'd bested Gingrich in a showdown over the federal budget and was on his way to reelection.

Panetta believed that Biden could take a page from Clinton's book. "Everybody thought Bill Clinton was going to lose the election and everything was going to go to hell," he recalled. "But the reality is that you can turn it around; it isn't written in stone. You have the ability to determine your own destiny, and that, in the end, is what can make a difference."

In 2021, Biden was calling out forces that were more fundamental and intractable than those faced by Clinton. The people who blew up the Murrah building didn't represent a quarter of the country. But that was how many people believed that Trump had won and Biden lost the 2020 election. They'd turned the people who stormed the Capitol on January 6 into martyrs, and Trump into their leader. It was as if, in 1995, George H. W. Bush had been going around the country saying that Timothy McVeigh was a hero.

Times had changed since 1995. Rather than bringing the country together in mourning, as the Oklahoma City bombing had done, the assault on the Capitol in 2021 seemed only to harden America's divisions.

Still, though Biden might not be able to unite the country, he *could* draw a clear line between autocracy and democracy. And he could call out those who stood on the wrong side.

———

The Capitol riot on January 6 hadn't ended the Trumpian assault on democracy. That had continued—in the form of Republican attempts to suppress and subvert the vote. More than two hundred bills had been introduced across the country that would give GOP partisans the ability to rig elections by replacing legitimate slates of electors with their own.

Two bills before Congress, the John Lewis Voting Rights Advancement Act and the Freedom to Vote Act, or a combination of the two measures, would protect against voter suppression and election subversion. But they stood no chance of passing the Senate with the sixty votes required to defeat a filibuster. Manchin and Sinema made it clear that they wouldn't agree to eliminate the filibuster entirely. But what about a onetime "carve-out" for voting rights alone? Such an exception—a "special rule"—had just been used to lift the debt ceiling so that the country's credit wouldn't go belly up. Wasn't protecting the right to vote in a democracy just as important?

The trick, said a senior White House adviser, was "to find a formula that allows everyone to stand by their principles, but still get this done."

On January 11, 2022, Joe Biden traveled to Atlanta, Georgia, to deliver a major speech on voting rights. Demanding action by Congress to amend the filibuster was a gamble—because he had no assurance that Manchin or Sinema would support a carve-out and he needed both of them to prevail. By putting the full force of the presidency behind this vote, Biden would be climbing out on a limb, which might well be sawed off behind him.

It's an axiom of politics on Capitol Hill that you don't push for a vote you know you will lose. Nancy Pelosi had made a career out of following this rule. Leon Panetta had learned it the hard way. "There are always people in the White House who say, 'Well, you know, even if you lose, it's okay,'" he told me. "Losing is not okay!" He let out his booming laugh. "And when you do that, the American people get one message: You can't get it done!"

During an Oval Office meeting before his trip to Atlanta, Biden was adamant. "Look," the president said. "There are millions of voters, particularly Black voters, who, at incredible cost to themselves, at risk in a pandemic, made the extra effort to go and vote on election day 2020. Even if I pay a political price for this, even if I take a hit in the polls, how can I do anything less for these people than they did for me?"

Biden had decided that, win or lose, he was going to do nothing less.

The president's speech picked up where his remarks in the Capitol's Statuary Hall had left off:

> *Today we come to Atlanta—the cradle of civil rights—to make clear what must come after that dreadful day when a dagger was literally held at the throat of democracy. . . .*

Biden described the Senate filibuster as a cudgel historically wielded against civil rights for Black Americans. And then he argued for a "carve-out" for voting rights:

> *State legislatures can pass anti-voting laws with simple majorities. If they can do that, then the United States Senate should be able to protect voting rights by a simple majority. Today I'm making it*

clear: To protect our democracy, I support changing the Senate rules, whichever way they need to be changed—to prevent a minority of senators from blocking action on voting rights.

He posed a question:

So I ask every elected official in America: How do you want to be remembered? At consequential moments in history, they present a choice: Do you want to be on the side of Dr. King or George Wallace? Do you want to be on the side of John Lewis or Bull Connor? Do you want to be on the side of Abraham Lincoln or Jefferson Davis?

His words struck a nerve. The next day, Republicans cried foul. On the Senate floor, Minority Leader Mitch McConnell called Biden's speech "profoundly unpresidential" and added, "I have known, liked, and personally respected Joe Biden for many years. I did not recognize the man at the podium yesterday." Andy Card, George W. Bush's ex-chief, agreed. "I thought his speech in Atlanta was terrible," he told me. "I thought it was not an inclusive speech. It was an exclusive speech. And I had an expectation that he would be an inclusive president."

But Biden had simply told an inconvenient truth. It was as though the great conciliator had become a twenty-first-century version of "Give 'em hell, Harry" Truman. He was putting every U.S. senator on notice that history would judge his or her vote on changing the filibuster. Including Kyrsten Sinema and Joe Manchin.

The vote on the filibuster was scheduled for two days later, on the afternoon of January 13. That morning the John Lewis and Freedom to Vote bills had been combined and passed by the House; the decisive Senate vote would come later. Just after noon, Kyrsten Sinema took the floor of the Senate. What followed was a remarkable act of defiance against a president of her own party, and a dagger through the heart of voting rights.

Sinema said she was troubled by voter suppression committed by Republicans in some states. But Democrats had not tried hard enough to win Republican support for their bills. And she insisted that a partisan change in the filibuster, allowing voting rights to pass with a simple majority, would only fuel political division. Then she dropped the hammer: "I will not support separate actions that worsen the underlying disease of division infecting our country." She was a "no" on amending the filibuster.

Sinema's argument seemed to ignore incontestable facts—Democrats, including Joe Manchin, had spent months trying to corral Republican support for voting rights to no avail, and exceptions to the filibuster had been made for less urgent causes. But the maverick Arizona senator was immovable. It was all the more exasperating because of her timing; not only was the vote on the filibuster scheduled for that afternoon—but Joe Biden was about to visit the House caucus to make a last-ditch personal appeal.

When he arrived, Biden largely ignored Sinema's defiance; instead, he reminisced about his days in the Senate and bemoaned the demise of bipartisanship. A senior White House adviser insisted that Biden didn't take Sinema's act personally. "He was disappointed. But it's not like, 'Oh, she dissed me.' He's not Donald Trump. It's just that you'd expect that first- or second-term senators would line up behind the president in the direction the party's going. And he's old-school. The president comes from an era when, if the president of your party made the kind of push that Joe Biden made on this, the party would line up behind him. And, obviously, we're in a different time."

Biden and his team hadn't been blindsided; they'd known exactly what Sinema and Manchin were going to do. (Manchin was also a "no" on changing the filibuster.) "We were going to do our thing, which was to make the maximum case for their vote," said the senior adviser. "They were going to do their thing, which was not vote with us. Sinema thought the best way to do that was to make her position public before the president had gone to the caucus."

Emerging from his huddle with the Democrats, Biden spoke to the TV cameras and tried to put a good face on his imminent defeat on voting rights. "Like every other major civil rights bill that came along," he said, "if we miss the first time, we can come back and try it a second time. We missed this time."

Why did Biden and his team forge ahead—calling for a vote not only on the filibuster but also on the doomed voting rights bill? Klain wasn't in the habit of pushing for votes on lost causes. Tilting at windmills was not his thing. Bernie Sanders was constantly exhorting him to take bills to the floor even when they didn't have the votes, and then take their message to the country. Klain would have to explain to Sanders that that wasn't the way the White House did things.

But Biden's chief of staff was trapped. "We knew we didn't have the votes. But the president felt he couldn't look those voters in the eye if he didn't do every single thing he could to try to protect their right to vote in the future. Even knowing that we were likely to lose, and that we were paying a political price for losing."

———

On the afternoon of January 19, the president held a press conference, his first in six weeks. "All of us who are his supporters cringe whenever he gets in front of the camera," a Democratic senator told me, "because you don't know where it's going to go." It wasn't that Biden didn't have his wits about him; anyone who'd dealt with the president knew that he was mentally sharp. The trouble was that even the slightest stammer or verbal tic would be blown out of proportion by Fox News, the *New York Post,* and other right-wing media. (Much of the European press, perhaps remembering Reagan's dotage, seemed to assume that Biden was senile.)

But it was also true that when speaking Biden could wander off in unexpected directions. And on this day no one—not Klain, Jen Psaki, or Kate Bedingfield, the communications director—had any idea that the president was about to go toe-to-toe with the combative Washington press corps for nearly *two hours.*

Biden hit his first rough patch when he was asked about the simmering crisis in Ukraine. Russian president Vladimir Putin had stationed more than 100,000 troops on the country's borders, threatening an invasion. "Russia will be held accountable if it invades," Biden said. But then he added a caveat: "And it depends on what it does. It's one thing if it's a minor incursion and then we end up having a fight about what to do and not do, et cetera."

At the NSC, officials were slapping their foreheads. This was the kind of speculation a senator might offer—not a U.S. president who needed to draw a line against *any* Russian incursion. Biden's slip would trigger unease in Kyiv and other European capitals, and Jen Psaki would later issue a clarification: "If any Russian military forces move across the Ukrainian border, that's a renewed invasion, and it will be met with a swift, severe, and united response from the United States and our allies."

As the news conference continued, Biden regained his stride. Asked by a reporter about Republican Minority Leader Mitch McConnell, he said:

*I actually like Mitch McConnell. We like one another. But . . .
I think the fundamental question is: What's Mitch for? What's he
for on immigration? What's he for? What's he proposing to make
anything better? What's he for, dealing with Russia, that's different
than I'm proposing? . . . What's he for on these things? What are
they for?*

*I've had five Republican senators . . . who've told me that they
agree with whatever I'm talking about for them to do. "But, Joe, if
I do it, I'm going to get defeated in a primary."*

We've got to break that. That's got to change. . . .

"Can you tell us who those five Republican senators are?" a reporter asked. "Sure," Biden replied with a laugh. "No. Are you kidding me?"

The senators who privately admitted that they agreed with Biden's
positions but were cowed by Trump varied from week to week—
though they almost certainly included Mitt Romney, Susan Collins,
Lisa Murkowski, and Rob Portman.

Biden had been in the ring for an hour now, but instead of getting
tired, he seemed to be gathering strength.

Talking for two hours hadn't been the plan. The plan was for
Biden to take nine or ten questions, ending with Kristen Welker of
NBC News. "But he just felt it," said a senior White House adviser,
"and so he just kept going. His gut was, 'Look, I'm doing well, and
everyone says I'm too old or too weak or too this or too that, and I'm
going to stand here and hold the longest press conference in American history. And then we'll see what people think.'"

"You put Vice President Harris in charge of voting rights," a reporter said. "Are you satisfied with her work on this issue? And . . .

do you commit that she will be your running mate in 2024, provided that you run again?"

> *Biden: Yes and yes.*
> *Reporter: Okay. You don't care to expand?*
> *Biden: No, there's no need to.*
> *Reporter: On voting?*
> *Biden: I mean, she is going to be my running mate, number one. And number two, I did put her in charge. I think she's doing a good job.*

This was a good answer—though it wasn't strictly true. Biden still thought Harris was a work in progress, finding her bearings as vice president. Whether the president's response was off-the-cuff or rehearsed was hard to tell.

It was almost 6:00 p.m. Biden hadn't stepped on any landmines since his flubbed answer about Ukraine.

"Is the country more unified than when you first took office?" a reporter asked.

> *I'd say yes, but it's not nearly unified as it should be. Look, I still contend . . . that unless you can reach consensus in a democracy, you cannot sustain the democracy. And so this is a real test—whether or not my counterpart in China is right or not when he says autocracies are the only thing that could prevail because democracies take too long to make decisions and countries are too divided. . . .*
>
> *And the question is: Can we keep up with it? Can we maintain the democratic institutions that we have, not just here but around*

the world, to be able to generate democratic consensus of how to proceed?

It's going to be hard, but it requires leadership to do it. And I'm not giving up on the prospect of being able to do that.

Nearing the end of the marathon conference, Biden suddenly offered a telling glimpse into how he thought about his leadership so far, and how it might change going forward. It came in answer to a question about polling.

One of the things that I do think that has been made clear to me—speaking of polling—is the public doesn't want me to be the "president senator." They want me to be the president and let senators be senators.

This was advice that Biden's aides had given him: For months the president had been locked behind closed doors negotiating with senators, dotting every *i* of his legislation. He should let the staff do that and get out in the country and focus on national security, and "not be sitting around a table with Kyrsten Sinema for hours going over her spreadsheet."

Biden's aides had told him this privately, not expecting him to share it with the whole world. But Biden being Biden, he'd blurted it out. A senior aide couldn't help chuckling as he explained: "One of the things I love about the president but which is a little frustrating is that if you tell him something that you intend to be stage directions, the odds are extremely high that he will read them aloud. And what you see is what you get, and what you get is what you see."

Later that evening, after ten hours of heated debate, the Senate would reject Biden's bill to amend the filibuster, 52–48. And Republicans would block consideration of the voting rights bill.

Biden's remark about being president was telling. On one level, he was merely saying that he wanted to get out of the Washington, D.C., bubble and interact with real people. But on another, he was talking about presidential leadership. It wasn't enough to reprise your successes as senator or vice president or hammer out deals behind closed doors with your former Senate colleagues. You had to get out and lead the country. Years before, Panetta, as CIA director and secretary of defense, had seen Bill Clinton and Barack Obama grow into the office at pivotal moments. "When you've been a senator for as long as Joe was—and even as vice president, I think he continued to *think* as a senator—it's hard to get it out of your system," Panetta told me. "And then suddenly you realize that you're not a senator, you're president of the United States."

Sometimes a cataclysmic event could drive that realization home. Such an event was looming for Biden.

SEVENTEEN

EVERYONE'S GOT A PLAN

Mack McLarty had warned Ron Klain about UFOs: unforeseen occurrences. The UFO Joe Biden was about to confront would be one for the ages. It would upend the postwar international order, shake up his presidency, and ultimately determine his place in history.

The first hint of trouble came in early 2021. Satellite images showed Russian troops amassing along Ukraine's borders. The PDB noted that this could signal a full-scale Russian invasion. But then Putin's armed forces retreated toward their barracks. U.S. and allied intelligence analysts breathed a sigh of relief.

By the fall, Russian troops were encircling Ukraine again. The signs of a full-scale invasion, detailed in the first half of the PDB, were cumulative and overwhelming. "Every day there was one more stick on the camel's back, or whatever that childhood game was," said a senior White House adviser. This wasn't going to be a repeat of Russia's occupation of Crimea in 2014. Bill Burns, the CIA director, saw a clear pattern. "It's a puzzle when you're trying to put it together, but early on we had a pretty significant number of the pieces," he told me. "What was emerging was not another kind of limited incursion but something much bigger."

In late October, a group of colonels from the Pentagon's J2 intelligence section, led by a three-star admiral, went to see General Milley at his office. They brought detailed maps and showed him the indicators of an imminent Russian attack. "This is much bigger than normal," the admiral told the Joint Chiefs chairman. All the "warning indications" were there—the size, scope, scale, and ammunition were dead giveaways. Shortly thereafter, Milley and Defense Secretary Austin went to see Joe Biden in the Oval Office. Milley spread out his maps and briefed the president on the geography and history of Ukraine, the country's defenses, and the order of battle of the Russian military. When Milley was finished, Biden asked him if he thought Putin would invade. "Yes, I do," Milley replied. "I think it's more probable than not that there's going to be an invasion and this will be really big."

On October 28, the president flew to Rome for a meeting with the G20, where Putin would be in attendance. While there Biden conferred in a private "pull-aside" with the heads of state of the so-called Quad: Boris Johnson of the United Kingdom, Emmanuel Macron of France, Mario Draghi of Italy, and Angela Merkel, the outgoing chancellor of Germany. Merkel had brought along her successor, Olaf Scholz. The meeting's ostensible subject was Iran, but the more urgent matter was Ukraine. Flanked by Tony Blinken and Jake Sullivan, Biden briefed the allies on the latest intelligence: Russia was poised to invade a democracy in the heart of Europe.

Except for Britain's Johnson, the Quad's leaders were not only skeptical but incredulous. They found the idea of an invasion unbelievable, irrational. "When we would lay out the case, they'd say, 'We think you guys are crazy,'" said a senior State Department official. "'This is not happening. This is a normal buildup. They do these exercises every year. There's no way they would take this type of step.'" Putin's troop movements were a trick, they said, designed to pressure the West into making concessions on security arrangements.

Still, Blinken felt they'd gotten the European leaders' attention. "It was an eye-opener for them because they had some visibility on the movement of Russia's forces," Biden's secretary of state told me. "What some didn't have, which we were able to share, was the detailed Russian planning that we'd picked up. You put those two together and it created a very chilling picture." Blinken and his NATO counterparts went to work developing strategies to 1) deter Putin from invading Ukraine and 2) impose severe consequences if he went ahead. The head start they got in Rome would pay dividends in the crisis to come.

Skeptical or not, the normally reserved Merkel decided to take matters into her own hands. At the next opportunity during the G20 conference, she took Vladimir Putin aside, alone. "Hey," she said to her old nemesis, according to a senior State Department official, "if you do something like this, it's a whole new ball game."

Biden wanted to fire a shot across Putin's bow. So before departing for Rome, he asked CIA director Bill Burns to make a special trip to Moscow. CIA directors normally avoid high-stakes diplomacy, serving instead as "honest brokers" of intelligence. But Biden considered Burns a unique asset: not only his spymaster but an überdiplomat who could deliver tough messages to heads of state. During the evacuation from Afghanistan, Burns had flown to Kabul to meet with Taliban leaders and help arrange for the safe exit of American troops. (Unfortunately, neither Burns nor the Taliban could prevent the infiltration of a suicide bomber from the terrorist group ISIS-K.) A legendary foreign service veteran, Burns had met with the Russian autocrat more than a dozen times. Few people had studied him more thoroughly, or at such close range.

Burns's message to Putin would be blunt: We know what you're doing, so don't even think about invading Ukraine.

On November 2, traveling in the unmarked jet that he used to travel inconspicuously, Burns touched down in Moscow. At the Kremlin, Biden's CIA director met with Russia's secretary of the Security Council, Nikolai Patrushev. Burns gave Putin's apparatchik a detailed, dead-to-rights account of Moscow's invasion plans. He was blunt about the consequences that would follow a Putin invasion. This would not be like 2014, Burns warned; the costs to Russia would be profound.

To the CIA director's surprise, Patrushev was surprised, even shocked. Was he playacting? Burns thought not; evidently Putin had kept Patrushev in the dark about his war plans. Recovering his composure, Patrushev treated Burns to a litany of complaints about U.S. behavior and bravado about the might of the Russian military. While Russia might not compete with the United States as an economic power, Patrushev warned him, its modernized armed forces were now a match for America's.

Afterward Burns met with three other members of Putin's inner circle: Alexander Bortnikov, head of the Federal Security Service (FSB), Sergey Naryshkin, director of the Foreign Intelligence Service, and Yuri Ushakov, a foreign policy adviser. All three reacted to the CIA director's warning with stolid indifference. Yet Burns was struck by the fact that none bothered to deny that planning for an invasion was under way.

Finally, the CIA director spoke with Putin himself. Since the onset of the COVID pandemic, the reclusive autocrat had rarely met visitors in person. True to form, Putin agreed to speak with Burns only by telephone. The Russian leader listened impassively to Burns's presentation. When he'd finished, Putin replied with a cold-eyed lecture about American betrayals and Ukrainian malfeasance. Burns's Russian was fluent but rusty, so he spoke English and waited for the translator. ("I didn't want to risk World War Three by screwing it up," he joked.) "I've talked to Putin a lot over the years," Burns told me, "and he was very tempered; there were no histrionics." This was the Putin Burns had known for decades, but even more steely and menacing. To Burns's description of his war plan, Putin matter-of-factly replied that Russia was conducting military exercises in its sovereign territory and trying to protect itself from Ukraine. It was a stubborn, ex–KGB spymaster's logic, oblivious to facts on the ground.

As he rode in his car to the airport, Burns had a sinking feeling. "I just came away convinced," he told me, "that there was a growing danger that Putin was going to launch a major invasion."

Upon his return to Washington, D.C., Burns went to the White House to brief the president and his national security team. Putin was leaning toward an irrevocable decision to invade Ukraine, he told them. The Russian autocrat kept his game face on, because he was professionally trained to do that, Burns told the president. But Putin was utterly contemptuous toward Ukraine—and dismissive of Burns's warnings. He wasn't spooked by the potential economic consequences of aggression; he'd built up a war chest of hard currency reserves that would insulate him. Nor did he believe the Europeans, especially the Germans, would impose serious sanctions. In the end, Putin was driven by grievance and a sense of mission.

Tony Blinken listened intently. Biden's secretary of state was prepared to do whatever he could to find a diplomatic way out. But he wondered: "Was that really what this was about or was it theological—by which I mean, Putin's view that Ukraine is not a sovereign, independent country." Burns's briefing helped convince him it was the latter.

Burns had only confirmed what Biden had known in his gut: Putin was going to invade.

One thing was clear: When it came to understanding the Russian tyrant, Western leaders had spent decades with their heads in the sand. Biden had understood the former KGB lieutenant colonel better than most.

———

Putin's malevolence should have been obvious. From the moment he'd taken office in 1999, Boris Yeltsin's protégé had demonstrated his ruthlessness in pursuit of power. Evidence strongly suggested that Putin staged the bombings of several Moscow apartment buildings, killing more than two hundred Russian civilians; he blamed the carnage on Chechen terrorists. This terrified Muscovites and gave Putin a pretext to send Russian troops into Grozny, the Chechen capital; they pulverized the city with a scorched-earth military campaign, killing tens of thousands of innocent civilians.

All the while, the Western world slept. President Bill Clinton had been too busy celebrating the Soviet Union's demise to worry much about the ex-spy whom Boris Yeltsin had picked to succeed him. Clinton's successors tried to do business with Putin. At his first meeting with George W. Bush in Slovenia in June 2001, Putin was reaching for his note cards when Bush leaned over, put his hand on the cards, and said, "Can I ask you a question?" Was it true, Bush asked him, that after his mother's dacha caught fire and burned to the ground, Putin had scoured the rubble—and found something glittering in the ashes? Putin sat back suddenly, surprised that Bush knew this family lore. Then he leaned forward and said, "It was the cross my mother gave me." Looking him in the eye, Bush replied, "That's the power of faith."

Afterward Bush said that he'd found Putin "trustworthy." He'd looked the Russian leader in the eye and got "a sense of his soul." Bush thought he'd bonded with Putin over their shared religiosity.

But the bond quickly frayed. In 2008, with no notice, Putin invaded the Republic of Georgia and seized a northwestern province.

Garry Kasparov—the Russian chess grandmaster who, upon immigrating to the U.S., became a human rights campaigner and fierce Putin opponent—had been warning about him for decades: "Every dictator knows the game: He takes a step, looks around, and if no one stops him, he takes another step."

Having carved off a slice of Georgia with impunity, Putin took another step. In 2014, he invaded and annexed Ukraine's Crimea and occupied the Russian-speaking provinces of Donbas and Luhans'k. In July of that year, Russian-backed separatists shot down a Malaysian civilian airliner, killing 298 passengers. Barack Obama, whose secretary of state, Hillary Clinton, had tried to launch a "reset" of U.S.-Russian relations, felt betrayed. But Obama and his foreign policy team concluded that they couldn't afford to wage war, militarily or economically, over Ukraine, a non-NATO country thousands of miles away. Obama ended up imposing mild financial sanctions on Russia. Putin shrugged them off.

Meanwhile, Putin intervened on the side of Syria's Bashar al-Assad in his barbaric civil war. Russia's military turned the city of Aleppo into rubble. At home, Putin imprisoned and murdered his opponents; Boris Nemtsov, an outspoken Putin critic, was shot and killed just outside the Kremlin walls. Abroad, assassins from Moscow's GRU intelligence service had murdered a Russian dissident, Alexander Litvinenko, with radioactive polonium-210 in 2006, in London; twelve years later, they tried but failed to kill a former Soviet spy, Sergei Skripal, with A-234, a military-grade nerve agent, in Salisbury, England.

From almost the beginning, Putin had made no secret of his ambition to reverse the dissolution of the Soviet Union, an event he described in 2005 as history's greatest geopolitical catastrophe.

Some members of the American foreign policy establishment argued that the U.S. had planted the seed of Putin's aggression by encouraging NATO's eastward expansion in the early 1990s. According to this theory, NATO's steady encroachment had turned Putin into a paranoid autocrat. But this was tortured logic. Anthony Lake, Bill Clinton's former national security adviser at the end of the Cold War, pointed out that Russia could have *joined* NATO, if it had met its conditions for membership. "The issue is whether Putin was a delicate flower and a nice guy who was so enraged by NATO enlargement that he became Putin," he told me. "Or whether Putin was Putin all along. I subscribe to the latter."

The Russian leader only respected force. This was obvious to many observers, but not to U.S. presidents. In his book *Winter Is Coming*, Kasparov described their dangerously naive behavior toward Putin and his followers:

> *. . . instead of standing on principles of good and evil, of right and wrong, and on the universal values of human rights and human life, we have engagement, resets, and moral equivalence . . . we continue to engage them, to negotiate, and even to provide these enemies with the weapons and wealth they use to attack us. To paraphrase Winston Churchill's definition of appeasement, we are feeding the crocodiles, hoping they will eat us last.*

Kasparov continued:

Putin fomented a war in . . . Ukraine and became the first person to annex sovereign foreign territory by force since Saddam Hussein in Kuwait. The same world leaders who were taking smiling photos with Putin a year ago are now bringing sanctions against Russia and members of its ruling elite . . . a metaphorical mafia state with Putin as the capo di tutti capi *[boss of all bosses] has moved from being an ideologically agnostic kleptocracy to using blatantly fascist propaganda and tactics. The long-banished specter of nuclear annihilation has returned.*

Kasparov wrote this *in 2015*, after Putin's annexation of Crimea the previous year.

His point was that only action would stop Putin, and every day action was delayed only made the Russian tyrant bolder and more aggressive.

Joe Biden had known Putin for more than a decade. During their first official encounter, in 2011, when Biden was vice president, he told the Russian leader, "I'm looking into your eyes, and I don't think you have a soul." Putin looked back at him and said, "We understand one another." In March 2021, Biden, the newly elected president, was asked by ABC News if he thought Putin was a killer. "I do," Biden replied. In response, Russia temporarily recalled its ambassador and Putin shot back that Biden's name-calling was a projection, like that of a bully on a playground.

Still, Biden and his team—and the rest of the world—had underestimated Putin's gathering threat. Three months later, in Geneva, Switzerland, Biden held his first summit with the Russian president.

It came on the heels of a G7 gathering in Cornwall, England, and a NATO ministerial meeting in Brussels, Belgium. The encounter was almost perfunctory. "In some ways it's the least important thing on his agenda," said a senior White House adviser, reflecting the low priority of U.S.-Russia relations in the administration's plans. "There's no expectation for any kind of agreements or progress. We're the world's two great nuclear powers—so it's important for the leaders of those two countries to sit down periodically and look each other in the eye."

Putin treated Biden to an aggrieved history of NATO's encroachment on Russia's traditional sphere of influence. Biden warned the Russian president that he'd be held accountable for future Russian government-sponsored cyberattacks on U.S. infrastructure or companies like the U.S. Colonial Pipeline. And the U.S. would also consider Putin responsible for any cyberattacks by hackers on Russian soil, he told him.

Biden wasn't looking for a "reset" or any strategic breakthrough; his goal was to make U.S.-Russia relations "stable and predictable," to keep Putin in a box. That would give Biden and his team time and space to focus on their bigger geostrategic adversary, China.

So much for Biden's agenda. It was almost as though Putin had decided to show him that attention must be paid. The coming events would validate one of Jake Sullivan's favorite sayings, borrowed from the boxer Mike Tyson: Everyone has a plan until they get punched in the mouth.

EIGHTEEN

CHRONICLE OF A DEATH FORETOLD

In November 2021, Joe Biden and his national security team watched with concern as Putin's troops prepared to invade Ukraine. To deter an invasion, but also to prepare for the worst, they decided on a three-pronged strategy.

First, Biden agreed to share intelligence with U.S. allies. Avril Haines, the Director of National Intelligence (DNI), would soon depart for Brussels to brief her NATO counterparts.

Second, and more daringly, Biden and his team launched a brilliant and audacious campaign to declassify—and publicize—sensitive secrets about Putin's war plans. American intelligence officials had caught Moscow red-handed plotting "false flag" provocations—bogus stunts that it would blame on Ukraine's forces to justify Russian aggression. Some of these provocations bordered on the ludicrous; they involved staging and videotaping fake attacks, using actors and dead bodies. Joe Biden could scarcely believe what he was hearing when he was briefed on the plots by General Milley. "Is that all true?" the president asked him. "Absolutely, Mr. President," Milley replied. "Can you put that out in public?" Biden asked. "Well, I don't have authority to declassify the information," Milley replied, "but *you* do and *Avril Haines* does." DNI

Haines and the rest of Biden's team agreed to the idea. The plan was to thwart these false flag operations ahead of time.

Biden's team had learned from the Ukraine-Russia crisis in 2014. "One of the things that frustrated me deeply," recalled Tony Blinken, then the vice president's national security adviser, "is that we had some extraordinary intelligence during the Russian seizure of Crimea and the aggression in Eastern Ukraine and the Donbas that we couldn't share with allies and partners." That was because intelligence officials zealously guarded their sources and methods; Obama was reluctant to overrule them. The closely held secrets included information about the downing of Malaysia Airlines Flight 17 by Russian-backed separatists. Blinken didn't want to make the same mistake twice. "A lot of us came into this chapter believing we had to make an extra effort to see if we couldn't put more of this before our allies and partners and ultimately the public," he told me. "And we needed to find ways of making sure that our credibility was enhanced."

The allied information campaign threw a wrench into Putin's invasion plans, as U.S. intelligence officials confirmed. "You could see the Russians kind of floundering," said Burns, "trying to follow through on these false flag operations even after they'd been publicized." Biden and his team had knocked Putin off stride, exposing what Burns called his "body of lies and false narratives."

Third, Biden and his team launched a campaign to send lethal weapons to Ukraine. Persuading NATO allies to do so wouldn't be easy. Ukraine's European neighbors didn't want to provoke Putin. Germany, haunted by Hitler's invasion of Russia during World War II, initially not only refused to provide weapons to Ukraine but also blocked Estonia, which required its permission, from supplying old German howitzers. Still, after relentless lobbying by the U.S. and

Britain, NATO countries began to come around. Latvia, Estonia, and Lithuania rushed anti-armor missiles and other U.S.-made weapons to Kyiv. Great Britain agreed to supply light antitank weapons.

———

During the Afghanistan withdrawal crisis, Blinken had appeared dazed, almost shell-shocked, in press conferences and on television. "It looked like he hadn't slept in a week," said Richard Clarke, the veteran former NSC official. "He had all the personal gravitas on camera of a limp noodle. He let the reporters talk over him. He just didn't come across as the sort of commanding presence that you want to convey when you're trying to intimidate a nuclear power into not going to war."

But in the walk-up to the Ukraine invasion, Blinken rose to the occasion.

He'd been preparing for it since Inauguration Day. "The first and most important instruction I got from Joe Biden on Day One was to do everything possible to reengage and reenergize our core alliances and partnerships," Blinken told me. Joe Biden was a dyed-in-the-wool believer in partnerships and alliances as unique multipliers of U.S. strength. And the most important alliance of all was NATO. During a visit to China when he was vice president, Biden had been lectured by President Xi Jinping; he'd denounced U.S. alliances as useless relics of the Cold War. This only strengthened Biden's commitment to them. Blinken, then his national security adviser, was also a true believer and a staunch Europeanist.

The son of an ambassador, Blinken had spent part of his childhood in Paris and was fluent in French and at home in European capitals. His mother was close to French president Emmanuel Macron, whom the family had known for years. "There was really no human better able to ramp up the effort around Ukraine than Secretary Blinken," said a senior State Department official, "because of his knowledge, his relationships, and because he's a trusted interlocutor across Europe."

Blinken had devoted countless hours to courting NATO leaders. Two of his first three trips as secretary of state had been to Brussels, Belgium, to consult with NATO allies. "I've spent more time in Brussels than in any city in the world other than Washington, D.C.," Blinken said. "And a big part of this is showing up."

After the ill-starred U.S. withdrawal from Afghanistan, Blinken would need all of those advantages. Macron was furious. Blindsided by the Americans' sudden exit and seething over the cancellation of France's submarine deal with Australia, the French president wasn't speaking to Blinken, family friend or not. Macron had withdrawn his American ambassador in a fit of pique. The U.S. secretary of state had to communicate with the ambassador quietly until Macron came down off the ledge.

Blinken got a major assist from Kamala Harris. In early November, the vice president had flown to Paris for a previously scheduled meeting with Macron and a speech on inequality and multilateralism at the Paris Peace Forum. Harris's public appearances were dutifully and superficially chronicled by the press. But her real work had gone on behind closed doors.

Harris liked Macron; one of her first phone calls as vice president had been to the French president. And the chemistry was mutual. Macron met with Harris for two hours at the Élysée Palace and made a point of escorting her to a dinner that evening, where she had the seat of honor among twenty-five heads of state (and dibs on making the first song request to the band). The next day, when Harris spoke at the Paris Peace Forum, Macron sat in the front row.

In private, the vice president pressed the administration's case against Putin. The day before her arrival, her national security team shared the latest intelligence on the impending invasion with Macron's advisers. "Our teams have met," Harris told the French president. "We've shared our intelligence with you. We really think people need to take this seriously because all the signs we're seeing are that Russia is going to go in." Macron agreed to give the intelligence a serious review.

Still, Harris couldn't catch a break from her traveling press corps. They reported that she'd gone on a Parisian "shopping spree." (The VP bought a $367 copper serving dish at a shop once frequented by the American chef Julia Child.) In truth, Harris's visit had gone a long way toward smoothing the ruffled feathers of the U.S.-France relationship.

Just after Thanksgiving, Blinken flew to Stockholm, Sweden, for the annual meeting of the Organization for Security and Co-operation in Europe (OSCE). At the introductory dinner for fifty-seven member nations, Sergey Lavrov, Russia's veteran debonair foreign minister, launched into a vodka-fueled rant. "Lavrov was drunk and very bellicose and started spouting unfounded claims about Ukraine in 2014 having been taken over by a Nazi cabal," said a senior State Department official who was present.

This was the kind of kerfuffle diplomats usually let pass, not wanting to make a scene. But Blinken had had enough of Lavrov's bald-faced lies. Biden's top diplomat delivered a withering point-by-point rebuttal that left the Russian foreign minister staring at his plate. "Tony just shut him down in front of all of their peers," said the official. "It was unscripted and it was raw. He just completely ripped to shreds all the arguments that Lavrov was using."

Between November and January, Joe Biden worked the phone constantly to NATO leaders. For his part, Blinken conducted two hundred "engagements" on Ukraine—videoconferences and in-person meetings. "Tiger Teams"—interagency groups of NSC, State Department, and other officials—were formed to game out every possible Russian move and plan the U.S. response.

The secretary of state tried to meet reluctant allies where they were. As a senior State Department official explained: "We would tell them, 'Look, we understand, this may not be rational, but you have to understand that Putin's rationality is not necessarily our rationality. He's in a parallel universe, almost a medieval mind-set of conquest and land grabs and amassing territories. It's not the way most modern leaders think.'"

It was a race to rally NATO countries to impose real sanctions in the event of war. At a meeting in Liverpool, during the first week of December, Blinken got the G7 countries to pledge that a Russian invasion would trigger "massive consequences and severe cost in response." The sanctions could include severing Moscow's major banks from the SWIFT financial-messaging system, which enabled them to trade in dollars, and seizing the assets of the oligarchs close to Putin. And then there was the fraught issue of cutting off Russian coal, oil, and gas. "Some of the ministers in the room were like, 'I don't know that we'll ever be able to get the EU to go along with some of these things,'" said a senior State Department official.

Putin was banking on Europe's dependence on Russian energy. While the U.S. imported eight percent of its oil from Russia, Europe depended on Moscow for roughly twenty-nine percent of its crude. Germany's chancellor, Olaf Scholz, who'd recently replaced Merkel, was wary of sanctions. Germany was a heavy importer of Russian oil and reluctant to jeopardize its Nord Stream 2 pipeline to Russia, which was almost completed. Moreover, Europe had already had its share of crises: Brexit, Syrian refugees, and the rise of far-right nationalism. It didn't help that NATO had been lulled into complacency by seventy years of peace on the Continent, and that its forged-over-the-decades trust in the U.S. had partially drained away due to four years of abuse at the hands of Donald Trump, who'd tried to sabotage the alliance.

In late December, General Milley called his Russian counterpart, Valery Gerasimov. A legendary general, Gerasimov was considered one of the outstanding military minds of his generation, the architect of Russia's supposedly cutting-edge "hybrid warfare," a blend of cyberattacks and military might. But Milley, a Princeton graduate and keen student of history, wasn't intimidated. He was prepared to call Russia's bluff that its troops were merely practicing maneuvers. "Hey," General Milley said, when he and Gerasimov were finally connected by phone. "This is much bigger than what we've observed before. This is very much looking like an invasion. *What are you doing?* The risk is off the charts. This is crazy. You're going to suffer immensely. These people are going to fight you tooth and nail. You're going to have body bags going back to Moscow." Gerasimov shot back: "No, this is just an exercise—an exercise, an exercise." Milley was having none of it. "Look-it," the chairman of the Joint Chiefs replied. "It's not. You and I know it's not." With that, the call ended.

Secretary of State Blinken would have one last chance to warn *his* Russian counterpart. During a meeting in Geneva with Sergey Lavrov on January 21, Blinken took the Russian foreign minister aside. Lavrov's English was impeccable, so no translator was required. "What are you trying to achieve?" Blinken demanded. "What's driving this? What's motivating this? Is this really about the concerns you've expressed about Russian security? Or is it about the views that Putin's expressed about Ukraine?'" Lavrov wouldn't give him a straight answer. Blinken wondered if Lavrov even knew what the war plan was; had Putin left his foreign minister in the dark?

Blinken and his team kept looking for a diplomatic solution—whether Putin wanted one or not. Karen Donfried, assistant secretary of state for European and Eurasian affairs, traveled to Moscow in mid-December. The Russians presented her with two written proposals. They were maximalist demands that were unacceptable. "But there were places where the Venn diagram overlapped, and so we were ready to engage with the Russians," she said. Donfried and her colleagues kept trying. "What we do is diplomacy," she said. "And you're always trying to find a way out. And we all thought it was worth trying to influence Putin's calculation. We thought, okay, what could change his mind? What are the things he really cares about?"

On December 13, Deputy Secretary of State Wendy Sherman called together the senior staff on the seventh floor at Foggy Bottom. It was still hard for many of them to believe that an invasion was imminent. "It's almost unthinkable that the Russians would go through with this," said Sherman, known as a blunt-talking realist. "But if they do, it will reshape the world. The sanctions response we are contemplating would be unlike anything we've seen before." The diplomats left the meeting sobered by the prospect of war.

Supplying weapons to Ukraine was one thing. But what about sending NATO troops to defend other countries in harm's way? Once again, Germany was gun-shy. A senior State Department official explained: "The attitude of the Germans was, 'What planning is needed? We have some plans. They're already in place and we'll deal with it if the invasion happens.' So there was a big battle inside NATO behind the scenes—with the U.S. saying, 'Deterrence and planning doesn't have to be escalatory, and moving some troops into Eastern Europe before Russia goes into Ukraine doesn't have to be escalatory either.'"

In mid-January came more unmistakable evidence of Putin's intentions. Satellite photos showed Russian forces redeploying from the Far East, leaving those borders undefended.

Even more dramatic, U.S. intelligence now knew just how the invasion would begin.

In mid-January, Burns made a secret trip to Kyiv, a mission that would make all the difference in preparing Ukraine for the battle ahead. Upon his arrival in the capital, Zelensky's security guards whisked the CIA director into the president's office.

In public, Ukraine's president had been dismissing the prospect of a Russian invasion, even suggesting that America's warnings were "creating a panic." Burns had come to give him a reality check. The first thing he told Zelensky was that Russian Special Forces were coming to assassinate him. (Biden had told Burns to share precise details of the Russian plots.) This immediately got Zelensky's attention; he was taken aback, sobered by this news.

The intelligence was so detailed that it would help Zelensky's security forces thwart two separate Russian attempts on his life. But that wasn't the only thing Burns had come to share with Ukraine's leader. The CIA director brought the blueprint of Putin's invasion plan. It called for a lightning strike from Belarus to take Kyiv within forty-eight to seventy-two hours and decapitate the regime. This was all based on the Russians' presumption that Zelensky would flee and the military collapse.

But Zelensky wasn't going anywhere. And Burns gave him a detailed preview of Russia's military plans for the invasion's first day.

Ground zero was Antonov Airport, twenty miles north of Kyiv. This was Putin's key strategic objective in the early hours of the war; if his troops could seize and control it, they could use the airport as a staging area for the decisive assault on Kyiv.

––––––––

On January 24, Biden announced that the U.S. would put 8,500 of its troops in the United States on alert, ready to be deployed on a moment's notice to Europe. NATO reinforced its military presence in Eastern Europe with more ships and fighter jets.

At the opening of the Winter Olympic Games, on February 4, Putin and Chinese president Xi Jinping met in Beijing. It was the first time Xi had been face-to-face with a visitor in nearly two years. The leaders of the world's most powerful autocracies had known each other for a decade and had forged a personal bond. In a joint statement, the Russian Federation and People's Republic of China denounced the NATO alliance, called Taiwan part of China, and proclaimed their friendship had "no limits." They also discussed business. Putin said Russia would increase gas exports to China and accelerate trade. The Chinese reportedly asked the Russians to hold off on invading Ukraine until after the Olympic Games.

On February 15, Biden addressed the crisis again. Stepping before cameras in the East Room, he announced that the U.S. and Ukraine were no threat to Russia, America had no missiles on Ukraine soil, and no plans to put any there. He continued:

To the citizens of Russia: You are not our enemy, and I do not believe you want a bloody, destructive war against Ukraine, a country and a people with whom you share such deep ties of

*family and history and culture. Seventy-seven years ago, our peo-
ple fought side by side to end the worst war in history. World War
Two was a war of necessity. But if Russia attacks Ukraine, it will
be a war of choice. A war without cause or a reason. I say these
things not to provoke but to speak the truth. Because the truth
matters. . . . And make no mistake, the United States will defend
every inch of NATO territory with the full force of American
power.*

Biden pivoted to his domestic audience. Severe sanctions against
Russia, he warned, would have costs at home: "There could be impact
on our energy prices, so we are taking active steps to alleviate the pressure on our own energy markets and offset rising prices."

Three days later, on February 18, Defense Secretary Austin, while
traveling in Poland, phoned his Russian counterpart, Defense Minister Sergei Shoigu. Austin was prepared to read him the riot act. "Hey,
I know what you're doing," General Austin told him. "These are not
exercises. You can talk all you want about exercises, but I know what
you're doing and you just need to come clean."

Shoigu's reply was terse and taunting: "Well, those troops won't be
there for much longer, I can assure you." The message was unmistakable. Austin turned to his assistant, who was riding with him in his car.
"Well, that's that," Austin said. "Now we know."

———————

That same day, Kamala Harris led an America delegation at the Munich Security Conference. It was a sign of Biden's growing confidence
in his vice president that he would send her, along with Tony Blinken,
to the event. This was one of Biden's favorite annual gatherings, held

at the posh Bayerischer Hof hotel, a foreign policy wonkfest known in normal times as "Davos for Defense." But coming just before Putin's invasion, the Munich conference would be a historic and momentous occasion.

It was the city where, more than eighty years earlier, the West had failed to stop a tyrant bent on conquering Europe—when British prime minister Neville Chamberlain agreed to an infamous 1938 pact with Adolf Hitler that became synonymous with "appeasement." Now, post-Trump, America's allies were nervous: Could the U.S. be counted on? Would NATO survive? "Joe Biden, of all people, understands the importance of the Munich Security Conference, and the circumstances were quite extraordinary," said a senior White House adviser. The world would be watching Harris to see if NATO could come together and draw a line against Putin and his invasion.

For Harris, it was a chance to show that she belonged on the international stage. "Her political instincts have been inconsistent; her presidential campaign imploded before a vote was cast, and a staff exodus has raised questions about her prospects," wrote *The Washington Post*. This was "a rare opportunity," it reported, "to project a presidential stature. . . ."

The presence of Volodymyr Zelensky made the conference even more dramatic. Ukraine's president had been warned that flying to Munich was risky; his plane would be in the crosshairs of missile batteries in Russia and neighboring Belarus. But Zelensky was undaunted and arrived with an entourage of aides. On the conference's first night, he delivered a blistering speech, warning the delegates not to let the dark history of the 1930s repeat itself: "Has our world completely forgotten the mistakes of the twentieth century? Where does appeasement policy usually lead to?"

Harris held bilateral meetings with NATO secretary general Jens Stoltenberg; Germany's new chancellor, Olaf Scholz; the leaders of the Baltic states; Israel's defense minister; and the prime minister of Greece. On the conference's second night, she delivered the keynote address:

> *As a defensive alliance, we have deterred acts of aggression against NATO territory for the past seventy-five years. And today, let me be clear: America's commitment to Article Five is ironclad. This commitment is sacrosanct to me, to President Biden, and to our entire nation. . . .*
>
> *. . . We have deployed an additional six thousand American service members to Romania, Poland, and Germany. We have put another eighty-five hundred service members in the United States on a heightened sense of readiness. As President Biden has said, our forces will not be deployed to fight inside Ukraine, but they will defend every inch of NATO territory.*

But Harris's most important session was a one-on-one meeting with Zelensky. Despite his fiery speech, Ukraine's leader still doubted that Putin would actually invade. He'd been briefed about Moscow's assassination plots by CIA director Bill Burns in Kyiv six weeks earlier. But Harris wanted to make sure he understood that those plots were all too real.

They met at a private location across the street from the conference site. "Look," Harris told him, "you really need to take this seriously. Our information is that Russia is really going to do this. They're going to do it and you need to prepare for it." They discussed Zelensky's security, and a plan for continuity of government in case he was captured or killed. Harris also described Putin's plan for a massive land invasion. Zelensky listened intently, but it was hard to read him. No one, including Harris, suspected that he'd soon become an internationally acclaimed symbol of resistance to tyranny. As Zelensky departed, Harris had a chilling thought: There was a good chance she'd never see him alive again.

On February 21, Putin appeared on Russian television. He delivered a rambling, incoherent homage to Russia's ancient national glory. Bizarrely, the former KGB lieutenant colonel who'd risen through the Soviet communist system blamed Marxist leader Vladimir Lenin for concocting the idea of Ukrainian statehood. "Modern Ukraine was entirely and fully created by Russia," Putin declared, "specifically the Bolshevik, communist Russia." In Putin's cockeyed version of history, another villain was the Soviet reformer Mikhail Gorbachev, who allowed Ukraine to slip free of Moscow's grasp. In fact, of course, it was the Ukrainian people who voted overwhelmingly, in a 1991 referendum, to leave the Soviet Union.

Three days later, Putin spoke to the Russian people again on state television. He sat across a room from his inner circle, who fidgeted like Blofeld's lackeys in a James Bond film. Putin declared that Russia was annexing Ukraine's eastern territories, Donetsk and Luhans'k. And he issued a threat:

I would now like to say something very important for those who may be tempted to interfere in these developments from the outside. No matter who tries to stand in our way or all the more so create threats for our country and our people, they must know that Russia will respond immediately, and the consequences will be such as you have never seen in your entire history.

He concluded with an exhortation:

Citizens of Russia . . . It is our strength and our readiness to fight that are the bedrock of independence and sovereignty and provide the necessary foundation for building a reliable future for your home, your family, and your Motherland.

Putin's invasion of Ukraine was a "go."

Biden's team worried that Ukraine wasn't ready for the onslaught to come. On February 22, at the Pentagon, General Milley met with a delegation led by Ukraine's foreign minister, Dmytro Kuleba. Milley looked Kuleba straight in the eye. "This is going to be like nothing you've ever seen before," the general warned. "They're going to storm across your borders. You've got to get yourself ready for this. You guys have got to take this seriously." An observer described the scene: "Milley was just laying forth how bad this was going to be for Ukraine. And he was convinced that they just weren't ready. And the Ukrainians were sitting there gobsmacked on the other side of the table. They were like, 'Holy crap.'"

At the White House, Ron Klain thought, *This is less like 'Holy Cow, I can't believe it' and more like* Chronicle of a Death Foretold.

And yet, while Ukraine and NATO braced for a Russian onslaught, the rest of the world's problems wouldn't wait. Global warming was accelerating at an alarming rate. And Biden's climate czar, John Kerry, was impatient for Joe Biden to act.

NINETEEN

NO ONE ELSE CAN DO THIS

J ohn Kerry was anxious. It was early February 2022, and Joe Biden's special presidential envoy for climate was pacing outside the Oval Office. Since COP26, the international climate conference at Glasgow in November, Kerry's job had only become more difficult. A dozen countries were on track to lower their emissions enough to keep temperatures from rising more than 1.5 degrees Celsius. But President Xi had been a no-show, and China, the biggest greenhouse gas emitter, still hadn't made any new commitments. Without its participation, the world would miss its chance of bringing rising temperatures under control.

China wasn't Kerry's only frustration. He sometimes felt that his own government underestimated the urgency of the climate crisis. Global warming wasn't a fringe issue; it was a vital national security matter. And yet Biden's team had been focused on other issues—from Afghanistan to repairing the NATO alliance to navigation rights in the South China Sea. Now, with Putin on the verge of launching a war against Ukraine, the global energy market would be upended and the postwar world order turned on its head. Kerry worried that getting the administration to focus on climate would be almost impossible.

Joining Kerry in the Oval Office were the president, Ron Klain, Jake Sullivan, and Bruce Reed, Biden's deputy chief of staff. Biden's climate envoy got straight to the point about why he'd asked to see the president.

Time was running out to avert a catastrophe, Kerry said. The world needed to raise its game to have any chance of reaching the 1.5 degrees Celsius target; right now it was on track for 2 degrees Celsius or more. That would be catastrophic.

There could be no real progress without China, Kerry explained. But he'd done everything he could with his counterpart, Xie Zhenhua. Kerry's instincts, and his sources, told him that President Xi was calling the shots. Biden needed to show the Chinese president that climate policy was a top U.S. national security priority. "It's been an eye-opener to me the degree to which very rational, incredibly smart, capable people just have a way of being sidetracked," he told Biden. "They'll say, 'Oh, well, we've got to deal with a nuclear weapon here,' or, 'We've got to deal with' this or that. Yeah, we do. But not to the exclusion of what's going to whack you harder than anything that's ever whacked you if you don't get it right.

"I believe we have to change," Kerry told the president. "We're locked into a business-as-usual paradigm right now. We've got to get out of it." Then Kerry pitched an ambitious proposal: a climate summit between Biden and Xi. "I believe the president of the United States and the president of China are the two people who can help bring that about."

"The president is very much for that," Kerry told me later. "He wants to try to change the overall dynamic with Xi and with China. He's really embraced that. But he's got to figure out how to balance a bunch of other things, because he's got more than that on his plate."

Given Xi's fear of catching the COVID virus, Ron Klain thought the prospect of a U.S.-Chinese climate summit was dubious. "The thing that I never understood about this whole pitch was this: President Xi hasn't left China since the pandemic began, and it seems pretty clear he's not going to leave China for some time. And I don't think we're going to China." Moreover, a Russian invasion of Ukraine seemed imminent. For both Biden and Xi, the immediate crisis of war in Europe would trump the existential crisis of global warming. At least for now.

In the meantime, when it came to climate, the U.S. needed to get its own house in order. That meant passing some version of the stalled BBB bill, with its comprehensive measures to mitigate global warming.

Gina McCarthy, Kerry's domestic counterpart, was still bullish on passing BBB. "I'm incredibly hopeful and optimistic that we can make this happen," she said. "I do know that if the U.S. doesn't lead, then we aren't going to get there. We have to start showing everybody that we're going to kick butt. I knew from participating in all the discussions on the Hill that we were going to get this thing done. And I still don't have any doubt about that." Kerry thought only the president could do it. "This is only going to be negotiated by Joe. Nobody else, quite frankly, can pull this off. This requires Joe Biden at his best, and he's good at that stuff. And I think, when the moment is right, it will happen."

Joe Manchin had dealt a crippling blow to BBB—but could he be persuaded to negotiate a scaled-down version? "Is Manchin back at the table?" I asked Klain. "I think we're making some headway," he replied. "We'll see where it winds up."

Kerry was blunt about the urgency for action on climate change: "We only have a decade to get it right to avoid the worst consequences of the crisis. There will still be a planet here, and there'll still be billions of people, but they're going to be living in very different circumstances with very different challenges depending on what happens in these eight to ten years."

Action on global warming would be difficult to achieve, though, if Vladimir Putin invaded Ukraine.

TWENTY

THIS MAN CANNOT REMAIN IN POWER

It was the evening of February 23, 2022, when the first Russian missiles struck Ukraine. Europe's first major land war since 1939 had begun. Joe Biden and his team had been on pins and needles since the night before, when the invasion had been predicted. Now, alerted by the Pentagon, Jake Sullivan rushed into Ron Klain's office. "We've had the first missile strike," he said. "Tonight is definitely the night."

Biden's chief of staff went straight to the Oval Office and broke the news to the president. Though Joe Biden had been expecting the invasion for months, he was nonetheless sobered by it. "The president was painfully aware," said Klain, "that we were entering into a new phase of his presidency, if not also of European and world history. That once started it would be very, very hard to end. It was obvious that a giant tragedy was about to unfold."

CIA director Bill Burns was in his office on the seventh floor of CIA headquarters. "You could see what was going to unfold, an awful lot of destruction and death," he told me. Despite Russia's overwhelming advantage in troops and resources, Burns feared that Putin's war wouldn't end anytime soon. "He was going to run into fierce Ukrainian resistance. And there was no sustainable political endgame for Putin, so I felt sadness as much as anything."

Tom Sullivan, Tony Blinken's deputy chief of staff (and Jake Sullivan's younger brother), was attending an interagency deputies meeting. He immediately called the secretary of state, who then called Defense Secretary Lloyd Austin. Blinken and Austin got on the phone with NATO secretary general Jens Stoltenberg. The three men agreed that it was time to activate the North Atlantic Council's emergency measures—moving troops to bolster the eastern flank of NATO.

General Mark Milley was in his Pentagon office. It had been two weeks since Milley had called his Russian counterpart, General Valery Gerasimov, and excoriated him about the Russian troop buildup. Now the chairman of the Joint Chiefs tried to reach him again. There was no answer.

On paper, Ukraine's armed forces were no match for Russia's vaunted military machine. But as General Milley noted, "There's a big difference between war on paper with computers and real war where people are dying and there's real fear and there's real blood." Volodymyr Zelensky and his ragtag army were about to demonstrate just what a difference leadership and the will to fight could make.

Just as Bill Burns had predicted during his mid-January visit with Zelensky, Russian Special Forces were poised to launch a decisive attack on Kyiv. There were two airports north of the capital; the Russian plan was to seize and hold the one known as Antonov 2—so that they could fly in Il-76 military transport aircraft for the assault on Kyiv. But thanks to the CIA director's briefings, Zelensky's forces were waiting for them.

The Russians' attack helicopters swooped in at low altitude. There were as many as thirty of them, flying in twos and threes, unleashing cannon and machine-gun fire. But Ukraine's Rapid Reaction Brigade, veterans of battles against Russian proxies in the east, fired back. Three Russian choppers went down in flames, struck by Ukrainian missiles. Two others were brought down by a barrage of small-arms fire. The Ukrainians pummeled the airport, cratering the runways. The battle seesawed—with Zelensky's forces and then the Russians gaining the upper hand.

Then came a decisive moment in the Russian advance on Kyiv, which has not been previously reported. Two transport planes, each carrying 150 elite Russian paratroopers, were blown out of the sky. It was a staggering loss, and the Russians retreated in disarray. The lightning strike on Kyiv had been repelled. Putin's plan to quickly decapitate the Zelensky regime was dead.

Putin's invasion was turning into a fiasco. Ukrainians, defending their homeland, were punching way above their weight. To the northeast of Kyiv, a single Ukrainian brigade faced off against fifteen Russian brigades and stopped them cold. Ukrainian citizens not only phoned in intelligence but also joined the battle, armed with Molotov cocktails, guns, mines, and grenades that had been handed out just before the invasion. The muddy terrain helped to hobble the invaders.

Against this spirited resistance, the Russians displayed almost unbelievable incompetence. They failed to achieve air superiority, and they were unable to destroy the Ukrainians' communications. A coordinated bombing and cyber-offensive campaign might have rendered Kyiv's leadership deaf and blind. But Zelensky and his generals had no trouble communicating with one another and the world. Why the Russians failed to black out Ukrainian communications was a mystery to Pentagon officials. "We thought their performance would be much better in electronic warfare," General Milley told me. "They didn't apply all the electronic warfare tools that they had at their disposal to the level of effectiveness we thought they would."

For the Russian military, things quickly went from bad to worse. On the highway from Belarus to Kyiv, a forty-mile-long convoy of Russian tanks and armored vehicles had ground to a halt—its supply lines broken, its vehicles out of gas. Putin's troops were easy targets for nimble Ukrainian forces that struck and disappeared. Russian conscripts were hungry and demoralized.

The Russian military's failures were manifold: its lack of a non-commissioned officer corps (NCOs), poor training, lax discipline, and terrible morale. Another factor was arrogance. As CIA director Burns explained: "They didn't do what the U.S. or any NATO military would have done, which is spend the first two or three days systematically destroying the Ukrainian air defense system. They didn't systematically destroy command and control. They did very little electronic jamming early on. All of that was a signal of hubris. They didn't think they needed to."

On the third day of the invasion, as Russian troops bogged down, Putin announced on state television that he'd ordered his nuclear forces to be put on high alert. Seated at the end of a long table from Shoigu, the defense minister, and Gerasimov, chief of the Russian General Staff, Putin said that "aggressive statements" by NATO had to be answered. "I order the minister of defense and the chief of the General Staff to transfer the deterrence of forces of the Russian army into a special combat duty mode." Shortly thereafter, Pentagon officials *did* detect changes in the Russian nuclear posture—though nothing that was alarming enough to justify raising U.S. nuclear alert levels. U.S. officials also noticed that just before the invasion Russia's nuclear-armed submarines and much of its fleet had been put out to sea. This was a maneuver the Kremlin often made during periods of high tension. But given Putin's nuclear saber rattling, it was cause for concern.

As Putin's tanks and troop carriers sank in the mud, Volodymyr Zelensky rose to meet the moment. Beamed into Western living rooms from his Kyiv bunker, wearing a plain green T-shirt or military fatigues, he was defiant. Offered safe transit by the U.S. to Eastern Europe, Zelensky declared: "I need ammunition, not a ride." The former comedian-actor who'd once merely played the part of Ukraine's president had become a twenty-first-century version of Henry V at Agincourt, vastly outnumbered yet throwing himself into the breach.

Zelensky was more than a showman. Bill Burns was impressed. "He has emerged as a Churchillian-like figure in the midst of this," he told me. "And it's done enormous good for Ukrainians. I think that demonstration of leadership, especially in the first forty-eight hours of the war, once the Ukrainians took the first punch from the Russians and were still standing, infused the whole country with a sense that they could successfully resist."

Until the invasion began, NATO allies had been in denial. Poland's ambassador said, "I have to tell you now, I didn't believe you. I didn't believe this was actually going to happen," recalled a senior State Department official. The morning before the invasion, in the Situation Room, General Milley announced that hostilities would begin in twenty-four to forty-eight hours. "Oh, come on. You're still saying that?" said one of Blinken's European counterparts mockingly. At 1:30 a.m., this person called back. "Well, I guess you were right," he said sheepishly. Blinken replied, "This is one instance I really wish we hadn't been."

"This was Europe's 9/11," said a senior State Department official. "It was not only, 'Oh my God, Putin did this.' It was, 'How could this happen in the twenty-first century?'" Yet months of American warnings hadn't been for naught. At an emergency NATO meeting just after the invasion, delegates from thirty countries sat around a table with U.S. representatives. They were stunned but united. Suddenly a fractious and often slow-moving coalition turned on a dime. A State Department official recalled: "On the morning of the twenty-fourth, you would expect this sort of crisis meeting to be: 'Oh my God, what are we going to do?'" But thanks to U.S. persistence over months, "it was actually sort of anticlimactic how calm it was. Because all the decisions were set."

Sweden, which hadn't taken sides during World War II, was now willing to provide weapons to Ukraine. Even Switzerland, famously neutral in the face of Hitler's aggression, agreed to send arms to Zelensky. "Sweden and Switzerland authorizing arms transfers to Ukraine?" remarked one U.S. official, in amazement. "We're in a whole different world."

Even Germany had done a dramatic about-face. Reversing its long-standing policy of not sending weapons into war zones, Chancellor Olaf Scholz's government announced that it would provide one thousand antitank weapons and five hundred Stinger antiaircraft defense systems. Germany also stopped blocking other countries from shipping weapons it controlled, authorizing the Netherlands and Estonia to send Ukraine rocket-propelled grenade launchers and howitzers, respectively. Even more dramatically, Scholz would soon announce an increase in defense spending to more than two percent of GDP, a commitment the U.S. had been pressing Germany to make for years.

Russia now faced the most severe sanctions ever levied on a modern nation. The U.S. and its allies removed some Russian banks from the SWIFT financial-messaging system; blocked the Russian Central Bank from deploying reserves to undermine sanctions; and launched a transatlantic task force to pursue Putin's oligarchs' ill-gotten gains. Soon the U.S. would halt its imports of Russian coal, oil, and natural gas. "We've never sanctioned the central bank of a G20 country before," said Karen Donfried, the assistant secretary of state for European and Eurasian affairs. "The Russian stock market has been closed for the entirety of the conflict. This is really powerful stuff. And I think it shows how stunned the Europeans were by this and how unacceptable they found Russia's behavior." Chancellor Scholz canceled Nord Stream 2, the $11 billion gas pipeline from Russia to Germany through the North Sea. Western companies began departing Russia in droves; the British energy firm BP ended its shareholding in Rosneft, the Russian oil giant.

For Joe Biden, Volodymyr Zelensky was both inspiring and exasperating. In the first week of the war, the two leaders talked more than a dozen times—with Biden on the receiving end of more than a few Zelensky harangues. Ukraine's president wanted more weapons than Biden was ready to send. "Our interest and his interests are largely aligned but not completely aligned," said Ron Klain. "In the end, Zelensky is the president of Ukraine and Joe Biden is the president of the United States. And we are doing what we can to help Ukraine, but there are things we're not prepared to do because they're not in the interest of the United States. And that obviously creates a certain tension. A tension that's hard to manage when it's a life-or-death struggle in Ukraine."

Nowhere was that tension greater than in the debate over a "no-fly zone." Zelensky was adamant: He needed the U.S. and NATO to control the skies. He and his people would do the fighting, but NATO pilots should defend Ukraine's air space. General Milley said the Pentagon looked at all the options. "We talked about no-fly zones and no-go zones in the ocean and all kinds of options and possibilities," he told me. None of the options were good. "If you do a no-fly zone, how do you do that without entering a war with Russia? It's an active combat zone, lots of missiles flying through the air and lots of planes. So a no-fly zone without confronting and shooting down Russian aircraft is a nonstarter. It's just not going to happen." Joe Biden agreed that such a step would lead to "World War III."

Biden was cold-eyed about Putin. He thought the Russian tyrant personified the evil he'd seen memorialized at Dachau, the German concentration camp he'd visited with his granddaughter Finnegan Biden in 2015. Biden was convinced that now, as then, only the combined might of the world's democracies could stop a vicious dictator.

But Biden worried about a nuclear confrontation with Russia. He couldn't discount the horrible possibility of conflict between the two superpowers. Now that the war for Ukraine had begun, Biden was cautious. He spoke less about what the U.S. would do than what it would *not* do. Pentagon lawyers debated which weapons were "defensive" and therefore acceptable to send to the Ukrainians and which were "offensive" and therefore likely to provoke Putin.

Yet as the stalled invasion turned into a bloody war of attrition, marked by horrific Russian atrocities and war crimes, there was bound to be increased pressure on the U.S. and NATO to act. What if Putin used chemical weapons? Was it wise to take a U.S. military response *completely* off the table? Wouldn't "strategic ambiguity"—not saying exactly what the U.S. military might do—help deter Putin from using unconventional weapons in the first place? Leaving Ukraine to its own devices, and allowing the Russian dictator to bludgeon it with impunity, might just postpone a time of reckoning with the U.S. and NATO—perhaps at the Polish border.

On March 24, Biden arrived in Brussels for a meeting with heads of state of the G7. Afterward he gave a press conference. He was by turns honest, eloquent, and tongue-tied.

The president was asked what he was doing to ensure that Donald Trump wouldn't replace him in two years and undo everything he and NATO were trying to achieve. Biden replied with a reference to Charlottesville, where a young woman protesting racism had been rammed by a car and killed and Americans had chanted the Nazi cry, "Blood and Soil."

No, that's not how I think of this. I had no intention of running for president again until I saw those folks coming out of the fields in Virginia carrying torches and carrying Nazi banners and literally singing the same vile rhyme that they used in Germany in the early twenties—or thirties, I should say. And then, when the gentleman you mentioned was asked what he thought—and a young woman was killed, a protester—and he was asked what he thought. "There are very good people on both sides." And that's when I decided I wasn't going to be quiet any longer.

In Biden's mind, Putin's murderous troops and Trump's "very fine people" were connected. He continued:

I made a determination: Nothing is worth, no election is worth my not doing exactly what I think is the right thing. Not a joke. I'm too long in the tooth to fool with this any longer. . . . the first G7 meeting I attended, like the one I did today, was in Great Britain. And I sat down, and I said, "America is back." And one of my counterparts, colleagues, a head of state, said, "For how long? For how long?"

And so, I don't criticize anybody for asking that question. But in the next election, I'd be very fortunate if I had that same man running against me.

The president took another question—from Christina Ruffini of CBS News.

"Deterrence didn't work," she said. "What makes you think Vladimir Putin will alter course based on the action you've taken today?"

Biden gave her that look he reserves for journalists who are beyond the pale.

"I did not say that in fact sanctions would deter him," he snapped. "Sanctions never deter. You keep talking about that. Sanctions never deter."

Biden was wrong. *Of course*, the point of threatening sanctions had been to deter Russia from invading. The fact that they'd failed wasn't Biden's fault, but that's the way he'd interpreted the question. The president got his back up.

Ruffini persisted. "You believe the actions taken today will have an impact on making Russia change course in Ukraine?"

Trump Senior Adviser Jared Kushner (left) and Christopher Liddell, deputy White House chief of staff. Despite Donald Trump's efforts to prevent Joe Biden from taking office, Liddell, a New Zealand–born business executive, quietly kept the wheels of the presidential transition turning. *(Photo courtesy of Reuters/Alamy Stock Photo)*

Trump supporters storming the Capitol on January 6, 2021. The next morning, Liddell had to be talked out of resigning in order to ensure a peaceful transfer of power from Trump to Biden. *(Photo courtesy of Valerio Pucci/Alamy Stock Photo)*

On Inauguration Day 2021, the president and First Lady walk to the White House amid heavy security. *(Photo courtesy of Adam Schultz/White House)*

Joe Biden and Ron Klain in the Oval Office. The president and his White House chief of staff were like an old married couple: They had their differences, but they clicked. *(Photo courtesy of Adam Schultz/White House)*

National Security Adviser Jake Sullivan and Senior Adviser Steve Ricchetti. Praised by Biden as a "once-in-a-generation intellect," Sullivan was a relative newcomer to the president's team. Ricchetti, who had known the president for decades, wrangled his legislation on Capitol Hill. *(Photo courtesy of Chip Somodevilla/ Getty Images)*

Foreground: Coronavirus Response Coordinator Jeffrey Zients, wordsmith Mike Donilon, Ron Klain, and Senior Adviser Anita Dunn in the Rose Garden. Biden's inner circle was among the best and the brightest but faced the most daunting challenges, domestic and foreign, since FDR. *(Courtesy of Alex Wong/Getty Images)*

The president speaks at the South Portico on the July Fourth weekend in 2021. Joe Biden celebrated a hoped-for return to pre-COVID normalcy, but an outbreak of the Delta variant loomed, and his approval rating, once above 50 percent, began a steady decline. *(Photo courtesy of David Hume Kennerly)*

In the White House Situation Room, the president and his national security team monitor the deteriorating situation at Kabul's Hamid Karzai International Airport in August 2021. Left to right: Joe Biden, Jake Sullivan, Defense Secretary Lloyd Austin, Chairman of the Joint Chiefs of Staff Mark Milley, Ron Klain, and Secretary of State Antony Blinken. *(Photo courtesy of DPA Picture Alliance/Alamy Stock Photo)*

During the panicked evacuation, desperate Afghans crowd into a U.S. Air Force C-17 Globemaster III transport plane for a flight to safety. *(Photo courtesy of US Air Force/Alamy Stock Image)*

The president watches the dignified transfer of U.S. service members killed in a suicide bombing in Kabul by the terrorist group ISIS-Khorasan. Biden was excoriated by several angry family members of the fallen. Later, he told a White House aide, "This is what being president is." *(Photo courtesy of the White House/Alamy Stock Photo)*

Joe Biden and Kamala Harris outside the Oval Office. The vice president got off to a rocky start; allies, including the Second Gentleman, complained that her portfolio was thankless. But Harris later found her footing on national security issues and reproductive rights. *(Photo courtesy of Adam Schultz/White House)*

John Kerry with the president at the Glasgow climate conference (COP26) in 2021. Biden's special presidential envoy for climate believed China was the key to averting a global warming disaster, but Kerry's attempt to broker a summit between Biden and Chinese President Xi Jinping was frustrated. *(Photo courtesy of Reuters/ Alamy Stock Photo)*

Joe Biden and senators at the North Portico as the president announces a deal for a bipartisan infrastructure bill. Months of haggling with senators Kyrsten Sinema (in red) and Joe Manchin (behind her) failed to advance Biden's other, more ambitious priority, the Build Back Better bill (BBB). But in August 2022, after secret negotiations between Manchin and Majority Leader Chuck Schumer, Congress passed a slimmed-down version of BBB, the Inflation Reduction Act, handing Biden a major legislative victory. *(Photo courtesy of Reuters/Alamy Stock Photo)*

Volodymyr Zelensky addressing the world from his office in Kyiv. "I'm not hiding and I'm not afraid of anyone," Ukraine's president vowed. CIA Director Bill Burns warned Zelensky that he and his family were targets of a Russian hit team. *(Photo courtesy of Gavin Rodgers/Alamy Stock Photo)*

Mariupol residents walk past a destroyed building. With a scorched-earth offensive, Putin's troops reduced Ukraine's southern port city to rubble and killed thousands of civilians. *(Photo courtesy of Reuters/Alamy Stock Photo)*

CIA Director Bill Burns. Declassifying and publicizing intelligence about Russian "false flag" operations kept Vladimir Putin on the back foot. *(Photo courtesy of Media Punch, Inc./ Alamy Stock Photo)*

Kamala Harris addresses the Munich Security Conference in early 2022. The vice president's steady performance before NATO allies made up for a widely panned earlier visit to Guatemala. *(Photo courtesy of Reuters/Alamy Stock Photo)*

Jill Biden meets with Olena Zelenska in Ukraine. Despite Secret Service jitters, Dr. Biden insisted on visiting Ukraine's first lady in a war zone on Mother's Day. Said a White House adviser: "No one could talk Jill Biden out of this." *(Photo courtesy of UPI/ Alamy Stock Photo)*

Bodies of civilians killed by Russian troops in Bucha, Ukraine. As evidence of Moscow's atrocities mounted, Biden denounced Putin as a "war criminal" and declared, "this man cannot remain in power." *(Photo courtesy of Sipa USA/ Alamy Stock Photo)*

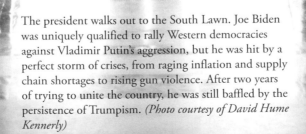

The president walks out to the South Lawn. Joe Biden was uniquely qualified to rally Western democracies against Vladimir Putin's aggression, but he was hit by a perfect storm of crises, from raging inflation and supply chain shortages to rising gun violence. After two years of trying to unite the country, he was still baffled by the persistence of Trumpism. *(Photo courtesy of David Hume Kennerly)*

"That's not what I said; you're playing a game with me. The answer is no. I think what happens is we have to demonstrate—the single most important thing . . . is for us to stay unified and the world to continue to focus on what a brute this guy is."

The press conference was wrapping up. Asked where he was going in Poland the next day, Biden, for security reasons, chose to be coy: "I'll be meeting with a lot of people," he said.

The next day, March 25, Jake Sullivan announced that the president would give a major speech during his visit with Polish president Andrzej Duda in Warsaw.

It was a momentous opportunity, the most important speech of Biden's presidency. The president's top aides and wordsmiths—Blinken, Sullivan, Donilon, and Meacham—all pitched in. Biden's speech would inevitably be compared to another pivotal address by an American president in Europe. In June 1987, at another inflection point in European history, Ronald Reagan had traveled to West Berlin. Standing on a stage at the Brandenburg Gate, next to the infamous Berlin Wall that divided the democratic West from the totalitarian East, Reagan had thrown down a gauntlet to Soviet premier Mikhail Gorbachev. Biden's speech was a chance for him to do the same to Vladimir Putin.

Advance teams had chosen a dramatic venue: the Royal Castle, home to Polish monarchs, a fifteenth-century edifice destroyed by the Nazis and rebuilt after the war. But Biden had another idea. He wanted to go to Ukraine, where Zelensky was leading his country's defense from a bunker. What better place to rally the West and defy Putin than in the heart of the resistance?

The idea was anathema to the Secret Service. In fact, they opposed having the president go anywhere near the Ukraine border. "Even being in Poland, where he was, was dicey," said a senior White House adviser. But Biden wouldn't give up the idea of going to Ukraine; he brought it up again and again before finally relenting.

In Warsaw, on the morning of March 26, Biden met with Ukrainian refugees, mostly women and children; he scooped up one child and held her tenderly while comforting her mother. That morning Russian missiles had crashed into an oil refinery in L'viv, across the Ukraine border, injuring five people and blackening the sky. The strikes could well have been a message from Putin. At 6:16 p.m. Warsaw time, 12:16 p.m. Washington, D.C., time, Biden stepped up to the lectern at the Royal Castle.

"Be not afraid," the president began. The words had been spoken in 1979 by Pope John Paul II upon his return to Warsaw, his hometown, during the Cold War. They were words, Biden said, that had helped the West win the long battle against Soviet authoritarianism.

"Nothing about that battle for freedom was simple or easy," he said:

It was a long, painful slog. Fought over not days and months but years and decades. But we emerged anew in the great battle for freedom. A battle between democracy and autocracy. Between liberty and repression. Between a rules-based order and one governed by brute force . . .

Every generation has had to defeat democracy's mortal foes. That's the way of the world, for the world is imperfect, as we know. Where the appetites and ambitions of a few forever seek to dominate the lives and liberty of many.

My message to the people of Ukraine is a message I delivered today to Ukraine's foreign minister and defense minister, who I believe are here tonight. We stand with you. Period!

Biden reminded his listeners that Russia's aggression toward Europe was part of an old pattern: Hungary and Poland in 1956; Czechoslovakia in 1968; and Poland again in 1981.

Soviet tanks crushed democratic uprisings, but the resistance continued until finally in 1989, the Berlin Wall and all the walls of Soviet domination, they fell. They fell! . . .

Today, Russia has strangled democracy and sought to do so elsewhere, not only in its homeland. Under false claims of ethnic solidarity, [it] has invaded neighboring nations. Putin has the gall to say he's "de-nazifying" Ukraine. It's a lie. It's just cynical, he knows that, and it's also obscene.

So in this hour, let the words of Pope John Paul burn as brightly today. Never ever give up hope. Never doubt. Never tire. Never become discouraged. Be not afraid!

Biden built to a crescendo:

A dictator bent on rebuilding an empire will never erase a people's love for liberty. Brutality will never grind down their will to be free. Ukraine will never be a victory for Russia, for free people refuse to live in a world of hopelessness and darkness. We will have a different future, a brighter future, rooted in democracy and principle, hope and light. Of decency and dignity and freedom and possibilities.

He was almost finished—but not quite. Biden was famous for tinkering with his speeches until the last moment. In that respect he was like Reagan (though Reagan, the former actor, recited his speeches aloud while he fiddled). Thirty-five years earlier, riding in a limousine to the Berlin Wall, the fortieth president came to a line in his text that had been flagged by the State Department as too provocative. Reagan turned to his chief of staff, Kenneth Duberstein, and said: "Ken, it's going to drive the boys at State crazy, but I'm going to leave it in." Minutes later Reagan cocked his head and declared: "Mr. Gorbachev, tear down this wall!"

It was among the most famous presidential declarations of the twentieth century.

Now Joe Biden was about to deliver his own unscripted declaration:

For God's sake, this man cannot remain in power.

In the courtyard of the castle, the crowd applauded. But at the White House, heads were exploding. Staffers' phones lit up. Reporters were calling, demanding to know: Was the president calling for Putin's removal from power? Was the U.S. signaling a change in policy? Was Biden demanding regime change? Minutes later, an anonymous White House official sent out an emailed clarification. It read: "The president's point was that Putin cannot be allowed to exercise power over his neighbors or the region. He was not discussing Putin's power in Russia, or regime change." In other words, Joe Biden hadn't meant what he said.

For the next forty-eight hours, cable television news dissected

Biden's controversial line. The Associated Press called it "a troubling distraction, undermining his effectiveness as he returned home to face restive Americans who strongly disapprove of his performance on issues that matter most to them. . . ." French president Macron chided Biden for jeopardizing potential peace negotiations: "I wouldn't use those terms, because I continue to speak to President Putin, because what do we want to do collectively? We want to stop the war that Russia launched in Ukraine, without waging war and without escalation."

The journalist George Packer, writing in *The Atlantic*, piled on:

Unfortunately, no one will remember anything from that speech except the nine improvised words at its end that expressed a simple wish for Putin to be out of power. That Biden can't give a speech without ruining it by saying something unscripted is not a minor fault. . . . Biden's inability to mobilize the English language on behalf of liberal democracy is one reason he gets so little credit from the public for carrying out a Ukraine policy that has bipartisan support.

Two days later, in Jerusalem, Secretary of State Blinken tried to clarify Biden's remarks *again*, declaring that there was no change in U.S. policy toward Russia.

But Biden wouldn't be muzzled. The following day, at a press conference, asked if he'd misspoken, the president said, "I'm not walking anything back. I was expressing the moral outrage I felt toward the way Putin is dealing—the actions of this man. . . ."

But, his questioner persisted, wasn't the president endorsing regime change? "It's ridiculous," Biden snapped. "*Nobody* believes I was talking about taking down Putin. *Nobody* believes that. . . . I was expressing my outrage at the behavior of this man. It's outrageous. . . . People like this shouldn't be ruling countries but they do."

Biden had gone rogue, off-script. But despite his handlers' protestations, his remark, like Reagan's defiant line, had been just what the occasion called for. It was vintage Biden, a welcome display of unscripted authenticity. I asked several ex–White House chiefs if they would have walked back Biden's ad-libbed line. "Hell, no!" said Leon Panetta, letting out a booming laugh. "Oftentimes staff overreacts and says, 'Oh, my God! He said something that wasn't in the script!' I think his statement that Putin couldn't remain in power is the centerpiece of what this war is all about." The contretemps reminded John Podesta of times when Bill Clinton, veering from the teleprompter, would blurt out a spontaneous thought. "We'd go: '*Uh-oh*, the president has committed *the truth*!'" he said. More often than not, Clinton's advisers let it go.

Joe Biden's prepared speech at Warsaw had been eloquent and polished. Yet his unscripted coda would be remembered long after his written words.

But stirring speeches in foreign capitals couldn't solve Biden's seemingly intractable problems at home.

TWENTY-ONE

BIDEN OF BROOKLYN

On the morning of March 23, 2022, *The New York Times* reported on a violent weekend, marked by nine mass shootings across the country:

> *In Norfolk, Va., an argument outside a pizzeria led to a shooting that killed two people, including a 25-year-old newspaper reporter who was a bystander. In the farming community of Dumas, Ark., a gunfight broke out at an annual car show, killing one person and injuring 27. In downtown Austin, Texas, four people suffered gunshot wounds during the final weekend of the SXSW festival. . . . "We can't endure this anymore, we just simply can't," Dan Gelber, the mayor of Miami Beach, said after two shootings last weekend led the city to impose a midnight curfew.*

The carnage would only get worse in the months to come. Mass shootings in Buffalo, New York, Uvalde, Texas, and other locales represented what the *Times* called "a dark new form of American exceptionalism." For Joe Biden, they were a reminder that despite a crisis in Ukraine, he faced a raft of problems at home. With midterm elections approaching, crime was among the most vexing and politically threatening.

For two years, since the onset of the COVID-19 pandemic, gun violence had been soaring. It had spiked more than thirty percent from 2019 to 2020 and showed no sign of abating (though it was far below the levels of the 1990s). In the wake of George Floyd's horrifying asphyxiation by a white cop kneeling on his neck, Biden had been elected, in part, to put an end to police brutality against people of color. But the wave of gun violence posed an obvious question: Was there a conflict between reforming police behavior and being tough on crime?

During his State of the Union speech on March 1, Biden had declared:

> *I know what works: Investing in crime prevention and community policing, cops who walk the beat, who know the neighborhood, and who can restore trust and safety. Let's not abandon our streets. Or choose between safety and equal justice. Let's come together and protect our communities, restore trust, and hold law enforcement accountable. . . .*
>
> *We should all agree: The answer is not to* defund *the police. It's . . . to FUND* the police with the resources and training they need to protect our communities.

Slamming the notion of "defunding the police," Biden was drawing a line in the sand. He was not going to be tagged with a slogan that had become politically radioactive. For progressives like Representative Cori Bush (D-MO), the phrase was a rallying cry—a call to replace cops with social workers trained to deal with the mentally ill on America's streets. But the slogan had become a cudgel; Republicans were using it to pummel Biden and his party as soft on crime. And the cudgel had drawn blood. Biden's friend James Clyburn, the Majority Whip, thought the phrase was as lethal to Democrats today as the cry "burn, baby, burn" had been back in the 1960s, when Black radicals called for the torching of American cities. "We lost the whole civil rights movement over being tattooed with 'burn, baby, burn,'" he told me. More recently, Clyburn blamed "defund the police" for costing Democrats the South Carolina Senate race in 2020. "Jaime Harrison's campaign plateaued when they tattooed him with that," he said, referring to the attorney-politician who'd lost a race against Lindsey Graham to represent South Carolina in the U.S. Senate. "We lost several seats that I don't think we would have lost."

When I asked Cedric Richmond, a senior adviser to Biden, if he'd consulted with Representative Bush or other progressives before the president gave his State of the Union speech, he replied sharply:

No, we did not and there's nothing to talk about. During the campaign, when he talked about defunding the police, the president said he would put three hundred million more dollars on the ground for more police officers, community-oriented policing. And he's been very consistent about that. He won the election, and this is what he won the election based on.

Richmond continued:

And I'll tell you what, I'll just speak as a Black man who still lives in the same neighborhood I grew up in, that is plagued by violent crime right now. People in my community from all economic levels

want more policing, and just policing. They want safe neighbor-
hoods. And the president has always said that keeping communi-
ties safe is a priority, and especially communities of color. So no, we
didn't preview that. We didn't try to ease it. It's what he believes,
and he's unapologetic about it.

———————

Biden needed an ally in his fight against crime—and he found one in
New York City. A former NYPD cop who'd once worked to end police
brutality, this New Yorker had just been elected mayor.

Eric Adams and Joe Biden had much in common. "Joe brings the
ordinary guy approach to governing," Adams told me. "He understands
it's not about being perfect, it's about being dedicated." Adams liked
Biden's way of "keeping it real." Just as Biden used to ride Amtrak,
Adams, sixty-one, born in the Brownsville section of Brooklyn, rode
the Manhattan subways. They both sometimes struggled for words.
"When you keep it real, sometimes you drop the ball," Adams said.
"Sometimes I wish I would have said something differently. But I'd
rather be authentic and make a mistake than be robotic and be fake."

Adams was the first Black mayor of New York since David Dinkins
in the early 1990s. But he seemed at first glance to have something
in common with Dinkins's Republican successor, Rudolph Giuliani.
Giuliani's police commissioner, William Bratton, had famously pursued a "broken windows" approach to policing, cracking down on
minor offenses that were thought to breed urban lawlessness. Adams
had run on a tough anti-crime program that emphasized quality-of-life
issues. The new mayor wanted to create small NYPD units to get guns
off the streets; similar units had carried out "stop and frisk" practices

that were blamed for unfairly targeting Blacks. But Adams insisted that *his* units would not revive that practice.

Biden and Adams met at a White House event with police chiefs and mayors in July 2021. The president sent word that he'd like to see the Democratic mayoral nominee afterward. Adams felt chills just walking into the Oval Office. And he got the full Biden treatment. The president showed him family photos. "It seemed like we were old friends, just catching up," Adams recalled. "And I'll never forget that he said, 'Eric, I want to help you.'" As Adams was leaving, Biden grabbed him by the shoulders and turned him around. "No, really," said the president. "I want to help you."

Adams told Biden that there was something he could do: Come to New York and visit his crisis management team, which specialized in community violence intervention. "I said that if he could find it in his heart to come, it would mean a lot to them. And he said, 'Eric, let me look into it.'"

Afterward, in the West Wing parking lot, Adams told reporters, "You know, they call me the Biden of Brooklyn."

Biden and his team liked the comparison; after all, Adams had assembled a winning coalition that the president's political staff hoped to duplicate in the 2022 midterms: communities of color and suburban white voters worried about crime. "Adams views himself as a Biden Democrat and wants to work closely with us," said Ron Klain. "It's a good partnership. New York's America's largest city and it's a bellwether for a lot of things."

Unfortunately, some of those things were bad.

Biden kept his promise to Adams. On February 3, he paid a visit to the new mayor at One Police Plaza, NYPD headquarters. Just days before, two New York police officers had been shot and killed on duty.

Standing at a lectern, flanked by Adams and Attorney General Merrick Garland, the president recounted how he'd attended a Catholic school near a small police station and a fire hall. "Everybody that I grew up with either became a cop, a firefighter, or a priest," Biden said. "I wasn't qualified for any of 'em, so here I am." He recounted the grim statistics. Every day in the United States, 316 people were shot and 106 killed. Six NYPD officers had been victims of gun violence already in 2022. Sixty-four children had been shot and twenty-six killed. "It's enough," Biden said. "Enough is enough." He continued:

> *Mayor Adams, you and I agree. The answer is not to abandon our streets . . . the answer is to come together, the police and communities, building trust and making us all safer. The answer is not to "defund the police." It's to give you the tools, the training, the funding to be partners, to be protectors . . . and know the community.*

Biden pledged to send New York $300 million for community policing and an additional $200 million for community violence intervention programs. There would be more funding for anti–gun violence initiatives by the Bureau of Alcohol, Tobacco, Firearms and Explosives (ATF). All U.S. attorneys would be instructed to go after the so-called iron pipeline, the trafficking of weapons across state lines. Finally, Biden promised executive action to restrict "ghost guns"—assembled from parts without serial numbers.

Afterward Biden and Adams rode in the Beast, the armored presidential limousine, to the office of the crisis management team out in Queensbridge.

"We talked about our families," Adams said. "The importance of why we're doing what we're doing. The importance of really focusing on crime and the proliferation of guns." For Adams, who'd been beaten by a cop in his youth, this was heady stuff. He made a point of telling people that federal funds and moral support weren't the only things the president offered. "In the back of the presidential limousine, he pulled out his peanut butter and jelly sandwich and said, 'Hey, Eric. You want a piece?'"

Back at the White House that night, Biden called Ron Klain. "He said first of all how much he enjoyed it, how much chemistry he has with Adams," Klain said, "but also how impressed he was by how thoughtful this joint federal/local task force was, and by the presentation ATF did that day. He likes what Adams is doing."

Adams was more than just a political ally. Biden liked cops, enjoyed being around them, and he desperately wanted their support. It all went back to his frustration that so many police organizations had supported Trump. The National Association of Police Organizations, which had previously backed Obama, dumped Biden in the 2020 election. The Police Benevolent Association and the National Fraternal Order of Police (FOP) also backed Trump. What did Biden have to do to prove his bona fides? He'd done more than Trump ever had to support police unions. And as a senator, Biden had written the tough 1994 crime bill. Many progressives blamed that law for causing the mass incarceration of young Black men. (Biden didn't buy that argument but admitted that the law was flawed.)

Still, the protests over George Floyd's killing in the summer of 2020 had changed him. Biden believed in police reform—ending chokeholds, no-knock warrants, and impunity for rogue cops, who often escaped accountability due to a legal provision called qualified immunity. Jim Pasco, seventy-five, head of the FOP and an old friend of Biden, said both the president and the police had changed. "For people of my era, we still feel an affection for Biden," he said. "That said, today we're far more likely to disagree with him on his approach to public safety than we might have been in the past." Biden had moved to the left and cops, who tended to be young, to the right.

But Biden still believed he could win them over. It was common sense: Bad cops ruined everything for good cops. He was sure he could talk police organizations into agreeing with him—if he could just get everybody in the same room.

Unfortunately, Biden's attempts at federal police reform had stalled. Senator Cory Booker (D-NJ) led an effort to try to forge bipartisan criminal justice and police reform. A former mayor of Newark, New Jersey, Booker brought his trademark passion to the subject. Teaming with Karen Bass (D-CA), Booker spent months trying to cobble together a bill with Senator Tim Scott (R-SC). They made real progress and won significant concessions from police organization leaders, including the FOP's Jim Pasco. But in sensitive negotiations, timing is everything. Details of the talks were leaked to the media while the bill was still half-baked, torpedoing any possibility of compromise. In August, Scott walked away from the negotiations, accusing Democrats of wanting to reduce funding for police. Booker countered that Scott wouldn't even agree to a Trump-era executive order that required police to meet minimum standards. The talks collapsed.

In March 2022, Booker told me he was working to restart negotiations over police reform.

Meanwhile the crime wave continued. Democrats, eyeing the midterm elections, were worried. "There's a level of discomfort for Democrats when we talk about real crime issues," said Adams. "And let's say it takes six months to a year to roll out a program and see results. We don't have six months to a year to deal with the shooters we're seeing across our country. We need to stop the shooters right now."

On April 12, in Brooklyn, Mayor Adams's backyard, a man set off smoke bombs and then opened fire on a subway car, hitting ten people and injuring twenty-nine others. Miraculously, no one was killed.

For Biden, time was running out to show that he had a plan to make the country safe.

TWENTY-TWO

A HAND WORSE THAN FDR'S

By Thanksgiving of 2021, it seemed that the U.S. might soon return to its pre-pandemic normalcy. But like the illusory hopes of the previous July Fourth weekend, that wishful thinking was dashed. Jeff Zients thought he and his pandemic team would finally get a well-deserved rest on Thanksgiving Day. "We'd been going twenty-four-seven for a year at that point, including the transition," he recalled. Zients had invited his extended family to his home for a holiday feast. He woke up early and opened his email. "There were multiple messages about a new variant," he said. "It seemed to be very transmissible, according to the South African experts who'd started to study it. And that was trouble."

Zients had a sinking feeling. But he and his team had been through this drill before. "We knew what to do, which was to get the team together, brief the president, get his direction, and move forward—and execute, execute, execute."

Zients called Joe Biden, who was spending the holiday with his family on Nantucket Island, off the coast of Massachusetts. "We interrupted the president's Thanksgiving, but that's exactly what he expected of us," Zients said. "It quickly boiled down to three key questions: Was the new variant more transmissible? Was it more severe? And how did our vaccines perform against it—how much protection did they provide?"

Dr. Anthony Fauci gathered data from South Africa, and Zients worked the phone with HHS, the CDC, the FDA, and FEMA, trying to figure out "how do we deal with the fact that there's a new variant that appears to be more transmissible?" By the end of the next day, Friday, travel restrictions had been put in place, barring entry into the U.S. of foreign nationals who'd recently been in eight African countries. The new variant, known as Omicron, was wildly contagious, but no one yet knew how lethal it might be.

The answer came within a few days. "The doctors determined that the most important thing was to get more and more Americans boosted," said Zients, "that the vaccine would likely hold up against Omicron and the boosting would provide the highest level of protection. And that ended up being absolutely the right call."

Fortunately, Omicron was less severe than Delta and the prior variants. "Thankfully, the vaccines worked, particularly with the booster shot," said Zients. "So the doctors were proven to be absolutely correct—and jumping into action quickly Thanksgiving morning prevented hundreds of thousands of deaths. It reinforced our mantra that we'd be prepared for every scenario and that we'd act with a sense of urgency guided by the science and the doctors."

Since joining the administration, Zients and his team had made impressive progress—200 million people had been vaccinated; hospitalizations and deaths had been dramatically reduced. But polls showed that Biden wasn't getting much credit for his handling of the pandemic. And though Americans were much less likely to be hospitalized and die from COVID, thanks to widespread vaccination, Omicron wouldn't be the last variant to strike on Biden's watch.

———————

Looking back on 2021, Ron Klain was ebullient. "We had the most successful first year of any president ever," he told me. "We passed more legislation than any president in his first year. We brought the unemployment rate down more than any president has in history. We created more jobs than any president in his first year. Economic growth is soaring, the highest it's been since Reagan. We got more federal judges confirmed than any president since Nixon. Of our three major pieces of legislation, we got two done [the ARP and BIF] and signed into law. The third [BBB] has passed one of the two chambers."

It was all true—yet by the spring of 2022 barely forty percent of Americans approved of Joe Biden's performance and fifty-five percent disapproved. Something was going on that had less to do with metrics than an underlying truth: A majority of Americans thought the country was headed in the wrong direction.

The national mood was sour. It was reminiscent of 1979, when President Jimmy Carter delivered a famous speech that became known by a word he never used: "malaise." Like Biden, Carter had been battered by a tsunami of crises—a spike in oil prices by the Organization of the Petroleum Exporting Countries (OPEC), a border inundated by Cuban refugees, galloping inflation, sky-high interest rates—even a Soviet invasion of Afghanistan. All this before Iranian militants in Tehran seized Americans at the U.S. embassy and held fifty-two of them hostage for 444 days. "I think the parallels with the Biden administration are there," said Jack Watson, who became Carter's chief of staff in

June 1980. "We were dealing with inflation. We were dealing with the supply chain. We were dealing with oil supply issues and the increasing cost of imported petroleum and all its effects across the economy."

The spiraling cost of oil affects much more than prices at the pump. "It touches everything," said Watson. "When we were experiencing a ten percent increase every month in the price of imported oil over the twelve-month period from December '79 to '80, the whole economy was affected. It touched automobile interiors and plastics and everything. Interest rates and inflation were affected." Carter, like Biden decades later, could do little to reduce inflation in the short term; over the long term, Carter's appointment of a fiscal hawk named Paul Volcker to head the Federal Reserve turned out to be transformational. Volcker's hiking of interest rates eventually tamed inflation for decades to follow. But it came too late to help Carter in the 1980 election against Ronald Reagan. And when Iranian militants seized the U.S. embassy in Tehran and took sixty-six Americans hostage, Carter's reelection prospects were doomed. He'd passed almost as much legislation as LBJ. But Carter was turned out of office after a single term.

Even without a hostage crisis, Biden had been dealt a more daunting hand.

I asked Ron Klain if Biden felt that way. "I think there are times when he feels that God dealt him a terrible hand—worse than FDR's," he said. "But I think he also appreciates that there's a big opportunity to beat these challenges and move forward." What Biden *didn't* appreciate was the press's harping on phony crises. "What frustrates him is the media going into a frenzy about whether or not anyone will be able to buy a turkey for Thanksgiving and whether everyone's Christmas presents will show up," said Klain. "Everyone did get a turkey, and all the Christmas presents did arrive on time. If there isn't a real panic, it seems like the media *invents* the panic." Indeed, Biden and his team had managed to ease supply chain bottlenecks so that plenty of turkeys and presents arrived in time for the holidays. But the press barely reported that.

———

Yet Biden's problems were real. The country was roiled by the highest inflation in forty years, turmoil at the southern border, and culture wars over transgender students and critical race theory. Action to stem global warming was more urgent than ever but stalled.

After the pandemic, Biden's biggest immediate problem was inflation. It still bedeviled the economy—and Biden seemed helpless to ameliorate it. He'd tapped the Strategic Petroleum Reserve and badgered oil-rich countries to step up their production. But on May 10, 2022, the price of gas at the pump spiked to its highest level yet: $4.37.

That same day, Biden announced a number of other measures to bring down costs: lowering the price of internet access; expanding access to ethanol-based gasoline; freezing student debt payments until August. But economists predicted there'd be no letup in inflation anytime soon.

And there was more trouble at the southern border. In March, border patrol agents had encountered 221,000 illegal immigrants, the highest total since Biden took office. With the pandemic health crisis receding, Biden had announced that immigration authorities would no longer enforce Title 42, the HHS provision that allowed the deportation of immigrants for health reasons. That was a relief to the progressive wing of the Democratic Party; Title 42 had long been their bête noir. But lifting the provision threatened to trigger another surge of immigrants. Alejandro Mayorkas, head of the Department of Homeland Security, said he was preparing for as many as eighteen thousand immigrants a day.

Meanwhile, Joe Manchin and Kyrsten Sinema were still balking at Biden's efforts to renegotiate a scaled-back BBB bill.

And sometimes it seemed that even Biden's most powerful friends couldn't help him.

———

On April 5, 2022, Barack Obama paid a visit to the White House. It was the first time the former president had set foot in the West Wing since Donald Trump's inaugural five years earlier. Obama had come to help Biden unveil a proposed expansion of the ACA, the forty-fourth president's signature achievement. A glitch in the ACA prevented millions of families from qualifying for health insurance subsidies. Fixing it could give 200,000 uninsured people access to coverage and reduce premiums for nearly a million more.

Stepping up to the podium in the East Room, flanked by Joe Biden and Kamala Harris, Obama was greeted by enthusiastic applause. He waited for a beat, and then began: "*Vice* President Biden . . ." The room erupted in laughter. "That was a *joke*," Obama said, flashing his trademark grin. He stepped over to Biden and gave him a half hug. "That was all set up," Obama said, returning to the microphone. He dutifully thanked the White House staff and his former colleagues and then got down to business:

> *. . . most of all coming back here gives me a chance to say thank you and spend some time with an extraordinary friend and partner who was by my side for eight years. Joe Biden and I did a lot together. We helped save the global economy, made record*

investments in clean energy, put guardrails on our financial sys-
tem, helped turn the auto industry around, repealed "don't ask,
don't tell." But nothing made me prouder than providing better
health care and more protections to millions of people across this
country.

The rest of Obama's remarks were devoted to the fix for his beloved ACA. Except for a fleeting reference to the ARP, the former
president made no mention of Biden's first-year accomplishments—
from tackling COVID-19 to revitalizing infrastructure to facing
down a tyrant in Europe. Obama said nothing about BBB, still languishing in Congress. Biden's White House advisers insisted that
the forty-fourth president had delivered exactly what they asked of
him. Still, Obama's omissions seemed odd; after all, a little praise for
Biden's agenda from America's most popular Democrat might have
given the president a much-needed political boost.

Afterward the former president was mobbed by ex-colleagues and
admirers, all reaching for his hand. Obama was in his element, a political rock star. In the crush of people, Biden looked a little lost.

They were an odd couple: the cerebral, reserved mentor and his
earnest, outgoing protégé. According to friends, Obama's aloofness toward Biden was partly his natural reserve but also driven by perceived
slights. Obama was competitive, prideful about his legacy, sensitive
to any suggestion that his presidency had been small-bore instead of
transformational. So it didn't go over well with him when Biden's staff
boasted that *their* agenda was bigger and bolder. Obama had also been
irked by media coverage comparing Biden to FDR and LBJ and gush-
ing about his former vice president's bold legislative plans. And he was
annoyed when White House staffers, in their zeal to promote Biden's

trillion-dollar-plus ARP, criticized Obama's 2009 stimulus as small potatoes.

Not only was Biden not getting much love from Obama; the awkward reunion was also a reminder that compared to his predecessor, he was, well, *old*. Fox News and Republican critics were constantly banging this drum. "Let's be honest here," said Senator Rick Scott (R-FL). "Joe Biden is unwell. He's unfit for office. He's incoherent, incapacitated, and confused. He doesn't know where he is half the time."

This was, of course, false. Biden was mentally sharp, even if he appeared physically frail. But it wasn't just MAGA people who wondered about Biden's stamina as he approached the midpoint of his first term. It was the same question that Jim Jones, LBJ's former chief, had posed back in December 2020: Could a soon-to-be-eighty-two-year-old man, battered by four years of stress and crisis, serve effectively for another full term as president? When I spoke to Jones again in late April 2022, he was still worried about Biden's gait, and the toll the presidency might be taking on him.

Biden's close aides batted these concerns away. Bruce Reed, sixty-two, Biden's deputy chief, who accompanied the president on most of his trips, still marveled at his boss's energy. He recalled the time they were flying home from Geneva after a grueling European trip in June 2021. In eight days, Biden and his team had conducted four summits—with the G7 countries, the European Union, NATO, and Russian president Vladimir Putin. Dragging themselves onto Air Force One, Reed recalled, "We had this reverse red-eye, seven- or eight-hour flight back to Joint Base Andrews. And everybody was absolutely exhausted."

Everybody except Biden. Reed and three colleagues were trying to doze off in the senior staff cabin when the boss walked in: "The president sat down and told stories most of the way home—easily four, maybe five hours of stories." Reed had heard some of these tales before—like "the first time I met Putin" encounter, when then vice president Biden told the Russian autocrat that he had no soul.

Biden's deputy chief and his jet-lagged colleagues pried their eyes open and listened as the boss kept talking—all the way home.

"It was a vivid demonstration of unbelievable stamina," Reed told me.

Biden would need all the stamina he could muster to keep the NATO alliance intact in the months ahead.

TWENTY-THREE

THE WAY THE STORY ENDS

For Joe Biden, arming Ukraine while avoiding escalation into World War III had been like walking a geopolitical tightrope. So far, he'd kept his balance. But in March 2022, Biden and his team were blindsided; the Polish government announced, out of the blue, that it planned to supply Soviet-era Russian MiG fighter jets to Ukraine. To make matters worse, rather than send the MiGs directly, Poland would deliver them to Ramstein Air Base, the U.S. Air Force installation in Germany. From there, Ukrainian pilots would fly the fighter jets into the war zone.

This was exactly the kind of tactical landmine Biden had been trying to avoid. MiGs were high-profile weapons that Vladimir Putin might perceive as game changers when flown by Ukraine's pilots. It was one thing for the Poles to offer Zelensky MiGs, another for the U.S. to provide them directly; Putin might consider that an unacceptable provocation, tantamount to America getting directly involved in the war.

In the Oval Office, the president met with his chief military advisers, Mark Milley and Lloyd Austin. Milley explained that Ukrainian pilots hadn't been trained to fly MiGs, so they wouldn't be useful and posed a risk of escalation. The Pentagon could block the jets' transfer to Ramstein, but Poland had already made a public announcement—it was imperative that they walk it back. The prospect of the U.S. and a NATO ally at loggerheads over weapons Zelensky said he needed was a story the media would pounce on. Luckily, there was someone en route to Poland who might be able to defuse the crisis: Vice President Kamala Harris.

Harris had come a long way since her awkward visit to Guatemala in the summer of 2021. In public she remained a work in progress, and was still taking a beating in the polls. But behind the scenes Harris was more assertive and confident. Not only had she carried off successful diplomatic forays in Paris and Munich, but she'd also shown a growing command of national security issues. She'd spent hours with the president in PDB briefings every week. (While the printed PDB was circulated every day, in-person Oval Office briefings took place two to three times a week.) During these sessions, Harris sat in the big yellow chair under the FDR painting and Biden took the chair next to it; seated on the couches were Jake Sullivan and his deputy, Jonathan Finer; DNI Avril Haines; and Harris's national security adviser, Philip Gordon. CIA director Burns came twice a week. Tony Blinken, General Milley, and Lloyd Austin dropped in sporadically.

Biden's PDB sessions were scheduled for a half hour but always went longer—often *much* longer, given the president's predilection for deep dives into world affairs. "People think that the PDB is just a briefing, but it's much more than that," said a senior White House adviser. "This is the place, with the smallest possible group, where their understanding of foreign policy is shaped and often decisions are made." A briefer from the DNI's office kicked things off, but then Biden would jump in and Harris would follow. She brought her prosecutor's chops to the briefings. "You've probably seen her playing this role in other contexts, where she's a very rigorous cross-examiner," said Gordon. "That's the role she plays in the PDB, making sure every argument is airtight and all the questions are answered." Biden seemed to genuinely appreciate her input.

As the MiGs story broke, the vice president was coincidentally on Air Force Two, flying to Poland for a meeting with President Andrzej Duda. From the Oval Office Biden reached her somewhere over the Atlantic. Tell Duda to put the MiGs plan on ice, he told her. Call a press conference and show we're in lockstep on this. It's important not to jeopardize allied unity against Putin. "Tell Duda it's my policy and that you're speaking for me," Biden said. The U.S. and Poland would be doing a lot of other things militarily in support of Ukraine, but this was the last thing they needed.

On March 10, Harris met with Duda at Belweder Palace in Warsaw. She didn't beat around the bush. "Look, we're not going to support the transfer of these planes for the reasons we've stated, but let's focus on what we *are* doing," she told him. The U.S. was sending Poland two Patriot missile batteries and 4,700 American troops. Poland and the U.S. would cooperate on deploying missile defenses and combat brigades to Romania and other Eastern European countries. It was important that they put the MiGs issue behind them.

Duda pressed the vice president for help resettling Ukrainian refugees with American relatives in the U.S. Harris promised to look into that and pledged an additional $53 million in new humanitarian aid. Afterward, at a press conference, a reporter asked about the snafu over the MiGs. "I want to be very clear," Harris replied. "The United States and Poland are united in what we have done and are prepared to help Ukraine and the people of Ukraine." She called for an international probe of Russian war crimes, the first U.S. official to do so. "When it comes to crimes and violations of international norms and rules, we are also very clear that any intentional attack on innocent civilians is a violation," she declared. "Absolutely there should be an investigation and we should all be watching."

The MiGs controversy blew over.

The MiGs episode was practically the only crack in the wall of NATO unity. On April 28, Biden asked Congress for $33 billion in additional arms and humanitarian assistance for Ukraine, a dramatic escalation in U.S. support; Congress would later raise the amount to $54 billion. Collectively, G7 and European Union countries had kicked in pledges of $29 billion.

On May 9, Biden signed into law the Ukraine Democracy Defense Lend-Lease Act of 2022. Passed the previous month by the House in a 417-to-10 vote and by the Senate unanimously, the act would enable the U.S. to send weapons to Ukraine without having to pass spending measures through Congress, cutting red tape and speeding up the process. (Technically, Ukraine would be expected to pay the U.S. back, but the act left that process open-ended.) Lend-lease was a throwback to March 1941, the darkest days of World War II, when Great Britain desperately needed planes, tanks, and ships to defend itself against Hitler's Germany, but Franklin Roosevelt needed to maintain U.S. neutrality. He did so by creating the program, sending destroyers to the U.K. in return for IOUs.

More than eighty years later, the U.S. was once again the arsenal of democracy.

Leon Panetta, who'd been so critical of Biden's handling of the Afghanistan withdrawal, saluted his leadership on Ukraine. "Forty years of experience in foreign affairs is paying off for this guy right now," he told me. "Joe Biden's ability to unify NATO is a real reflection of his understanding of how alliances have to work. Not every president understands that big-picture approach, but he's been there. He knows it." But Panetta had a caveat. "The bottom line is that Putin has to fail. Ukraine has to succeed—it has to get rid of the Russians and reestablish its sovereignty and independence. That has to be the way the story ends."

Biden and his team seemed to have reached the same conclusion: Helping Ukraine fight Putin to a draw was not enough; Ukraine needed to win.

Until now, Biden and his team had been reluctant to say so publicly. Two weeks after my call with Panetta, I spoke with Secretary of State Tony Blinken. He called me from his plane, returning from a visit to Panama. I asked him if he and Joe Biden shared Panetta's view that Ukraine had to win the war. "I don't have any doubt that when it comes to the fundamentals, Ukraine is going to prevail," Blinken replied. "Putin's objective is literally to end the existence of Ukraine as an independent, sovereign country and, in one way or another, to subsume it back into Russia. And that's already failed. It's inconceivable now to imagine that that could happen. There's going to be a sovereign, independent Ukraine a lot longer than Vladimir Putin's going to be on the scene."

On April 24, Blinken and Defense Secretary Lloyd Austin traveled by train from southeastern Poland to Kyiv. The trip, the first by high-ranking American officials since the invasion, was kept secret for security reasons; they traveled in a railroad car with black shades drawn. But word of the visit was announced by President Zelensky before they arrived. The U.S. team met with Ukraine's president in his office, taking notes as Zelensky rattled off a list of weapons he needed. Blinken and Austin pledged millions more in security assistance and increased training for Ukrainian troops and announced the restoration of an American embassy in Kyiv, with a newly appointed U.S. ambassador.

After crossing the border back into Poland, the American officials gave a press conference in an airplane hangar. Ukraine should "remain a sovereign country, a democratic country, able to protect its sovereign territory," General Austin said. Then he added, "We want to see Russia weakened to the degree that it can't do the kinds of things that it has done in invading Ukraine."

This was new territory. "Weakening Russia" went beyond driving its troops out of Ukraine; it suggested hastening the demise of Putin. Underscoring the defense secretary's point, Blinken told reporters: "We don't know how the rest of this war will unfold, but we do know that a sovereign, independent Ukraine will be around a lot longer than Vladimir Putin is on the scene."

There it was: the idea that the U.S. wanted Putin gone. It was the most definitive statement Blinken had made in public—a diplomatic version of what Biden had said in his famous ad lib in Warsaw: This man cannot remain in power. The only questions seemed to be how and when the Russian leader would be removed.

The administration's new assertiveness reflected a stark reality: The war had made Putin a pariah. Given the horrific atrocities committed by Russian troops on Ukrainian civilians, it was hard to imagine the Russian autocrat being invited back into the community of civilized nations. The horrors discovered in the town of Bucha—civilians executed with their hands tied behind their backs, women raped and killed in front of their families, bodies thrown into mass graves—were only part of it. The Russian military had bombed train stations and maternity hospitals and shelters. Russian planes had targeted a theater where hundreds of families had taken shelter, with the word "children" painted on the ground outside. Though the administration hadn't said so publicly, the CIA had collected evidence linking war crimes to the Russian high command.

And Putin wasn't done yet. It wasn't hard to imagine him using unconventional weapons.

From the beginning of the war, Russian officials had threatened to use nuclear weapons. Speaking in St. Petersburg on April 27, Putin did so again, warning: "If someone intends to interfere in what is going on from the outside they must know that constitutes an unacceptable strategic threat to Russia. They must know that our response to counterstrikes will be lightning fast." Commentators on Russia's state-controlled television speculated that in the event of a strategic nuclear exchange between the U.S. and Russia, at least *they* would go to Heaven.

During our conversation at CIA headquarters, I asked Bill Burns, "Has the CIA done an assessment of how likely Putin might be to order a nuclear strike—to do the unthinkable?"

"We've done a variety of assessments on that issue, because it's obviously of foremost concern," Burns replied. "Given the kind of saber rattling that we've heard from the Russian leadership, we can't take lightly those possibilities." Russian military doctrine reserved the right to use tactical nuclear weapons in the event that NATO was going to intervene militarily on the ground in Ukraine, or the Russian leadership believed it was going to lose the war.

The prospect of Putin using such weapons was chilling; no one knew where that might lead. Hence Joe Biden's repeated vows never to send American troops into Ukraine and thereby invite such a possibility. Burns credited the president with skillfully navigating this dangerous terrain. "It's been a mark of strong leadership for him to see clearly the risks of a World War Three," he told me, "and the risks of escalation with another nuclear superpower—and yet be very clear on what we're about in terms of Article Five and defending every inch of NATO territory and doing literally everything humanly possible to support the Ukrainians."

Doing everything humanly possible included some things the public wasn't supposed to see. In early May, relying on anonymous sources, *The New York Times* reported that the U.S. had shared intelligence with the Ukrainians that enabled them to track and kill Russian generals. Indeed, Russia's military had suffered astonishing losses in their highest ranks. A dozen generals were thought to have died in Ukrainian bombings or missile strikes. Soon after this disclosure, another media report claimed that Ukraine's sinking of the Russian flagship the *Moskva* had also been a direct result of U.S.-supplied intelligence.

Joe Biden was furious. The stories, based on unauthorized leaks, were dangerous. "He didn't like what he considered to be publicly taunting the Russians, potentially exposing sources and methods, possibly exposing operational details," said Klain. "That's the exact opposite of what we're supposed to be doing." Biden called CIA director Burns and demanded that he get control of the people in his building. DNI Avril Haines and Lloyd Austin also got presidential tongue-lashings.

With Putin painted into a corner, the danger of a Russian strike on NATO soil couldn't be discounted. If the Russian autocrat believed that defeat in Ukraine would mean his removal from power—or worse, an ignominious death like Saddam Hussein's or Muammar Gaddafi's—then he might resort to anything to prevail.

In late April 2022, humiliated by their aborted attempt to conquer Kyiv, the Russian military regrouped in the east, in the Donbas region. How would Putin's calculus be affected if Russian troops were stymied here? During his conversation with me at CIA headquarters, Bill Burns posed the question himself: "Does Putin then decide it's time to cut his losses and negotiate more seriously?"

"How likely do you think that is?" I asked.

"I don't know," Burns replied. "I think Putin sees this as existential now. I think he believes he can't afford a loss. And so he can keep this up for a while if he's convinced that he's not going to easily recover from this. On the other hand, he could make an argument that this was all about protecting the Donbas and that he's succeeded in doing that. See if he can extract something from Zelensky in terms of Ukraine's long-term neutrality. But I honestly don't know."

"But could Putin really reach a modus vivendi with Zelensky?"

"No, I think it'd be a pause and something that he would then try to come back to." In other words, Putin wouldn't give up until he conquered all of Ukraine.

On top of these stark possibilities, there was the risk of miscalculation or an accidental Russian strike—nuclear or conventional. The best way for the U.S. to avoid a disastrous escalation was to communicate clearly and directly with Russian leadership. But as of April 2020, the two superpowers were barely communicating with each other.

Tony Blinken hadn't spoken to Lavrov, his Russian counterpart, since the invasion began (and would not do so until July 30, 2022). In fact, there was virtually no communication between the U.S. and Russia at the highest levels. While there was still an American ambas-

sador in Moscow, his conversations with the Kremlin were limited to embassy housekeeping. And the State Department's Special Envoy for Hostage Affairs, who would organize the swap of an imprisoned Russian pilot for a former U.S. Marine, stayed in that narrow lane.

As of late April, two months after the invasion, only Jake Sullivan had communicated with his counterpart, Nikolai Patrushev; they'd spoken just twice—to no avail. In late May, Defense Secretary Austin finally connected with Sergei Shoigu, the Russian Federation's minister of defense. Austin urged him to accept a cease-fire—but was rebuffed. "One of the Achilles' heels of autocracies," Blinken said, "is that there is no one to speak truth to power, and power has a very close circle of people."

Meanwhile, the First Lady, Jill Biden, was restless. Profoundly moved by the images of suffering women and children in Ukraine, she wanted to do something.

TWENTY-FOUR

MOTHER'S DAY IN UKRAINE

The president constantly complained that he missed Jill Biden. He saw less of her now than he ever had in the course of their marriage; not only was *he* busy all day long, but the First Lady was also in constant motion; she was the first presidential spouse ever to hold down another full-time job, teaching English at Northern Virginia Community College. First Lady Michelle Obama had been astounded by the then Second Lady's discipline in juggling affairs of state and schoolwork; while riding with the First Lady in limos to events, Dr. Biden would grade papers. And now, as if she weren't busy enough, Jill Biden had something else on her plate: a possible meeting in a war zone with an intriguing stranger: Olena Zelenska, the First Lady of Ukraine.

Months before the Russian invasion, Volodymyr Zelensky's wife had written to Dr. Biden, suggesting a conference of First Spouses from countries in the region. They'd struck up a correspondence, but at the time Dr. Biden's teaching schedule had made a trip impossible. The invasion had changed everything.

Jill Biden had been horrified by the war and the heartbreaking exodus of Ukrainian refugees—scenes right out of World War II newsreels, desperate women and children boarding trains, leaving sons and husbands behind. She and the president talked about the war every night. Appalled by the bombing of maternity hospitals and kindergartens, she approved when Joe publicly labeled Putin a "war criminal" on March 16. This burst of Bidenesque candor triggered another attempt by White House staffers to walk it back; Jen Psaki explained that the president was just "speaking from his heart"; actual war crimes could only be established by a legal review. It was the Warsaw ad lib all over again.

The First Lady was eager to show her solidarity with the women and children of Ukraine. She discussed it with her senior adviser, Anthony Bernal. "Well, really, this is about moms," she told him. "So can we do something around Mother's Day to show our support of these Ukrainian mothers?" He replied, "Well, what about travel?" "I was thinking the same thing," Dr. Biden replied. "Like maybe this is the time to go stand with the mothers." Bernal ran the idea by Jake Sullivan and his NSC staff; they suggested a visit to refugee centers in Slovakia and Romania. Bernal started working on a plan with the White House Military Office and the Secret Service.

As the trip came together, an audacious idea surfaced. "As we looked at the geography in Slovakia, we realized that the community we were going to was right on the border with Ukraine," recalled Bernal. "Ten minutes and you're inside the country. So I off-the-cuff asked a question: 'Could we go to Ukraine?' At first everybody thought I was crazy, and they said, 'Are you being serious?'"

He was. But would such a trip be safe? Unlike Iraq and Afghanistan, where presidents had made visits over the years, Ukraine's territory was controlled not by the U.S. military but by its own beleaguered armed forces, who were busy fighting the Russian invaders. On the plus side, the First Lady traveled with a lighter footprint than the president; she could get in and out of the country without the traveling circus that accompanied the commander in chief. Bernal spoke on a secure line to U.S. diplomats rebased in Poland from Ukraine; they loved the idea. There was a school fifteen miles inside the border, they said, where the First Lady could visit with mothers and children and learn about their experiences. It wouldn't be much more dangerous than going to the border area. "If you think they're going to bomb her there, they're going to bomb her where we are," they said. The bottom line, according to Bernal: "Could we do it safely? They felt like we could."

And, the diplomats added, "it was possible that a high-level Ukrainian would come to see her." Until the very last minute, no one knew that Ukrainian would be Ms. Zelenska.

The excursion to the war zone was far from a sure thing. An advance team would have to scout the site. And if word of the First Lady's visit leaked, the consequences could be dire. "It was dangerous," said a senior White House adviser. "It was dangerous to have conversations even over hard lines at this point. We didn't want to talk to our advance teams over phones. We sent out a team that we knew could go do it. They made only one advance to the space." The decision to actually cross the border into Ukraine would be made at the last minute. Only Bernal and a few others knew about the plan.

Just as Jill Biden and her team were boarding their plane for Europe, Bernal got word that Ukraine's First Lady would indeed meet with her. He waited until they were airborne to tell Dr. Biden. "Oh my God, really?" the First Lady said. "Do you think we can do this safely?" Ukraine's First Lady was a prime target for assassination by Russian hit teams. Bernal assured Dr. Biden that both the Secret Service and the Regional Security Office (of the U.S. embassy in Kyiv, now relocated in Warsaw) had okayed the plan, but he added, "Look, we haven't told anybody because if that day it's unsafe, we're not going to go."

On May 6, Jill Biden and her party landed in Otopeni, Romania. She paid a visit to U.S. service members at a military base and, to cheers and applause, presented them with five gallons of Heinz ketchup (she'd heard the base was running low). Later she visited refugee shelters and comforted desperate mothers and children as they staggered in from the Ukraine border. "They wear brave faces, but their emotion is portrayed in the slope of their shoulders, the nervousness in their bodies," Dr. Biden wrote later. "Something is missing—laughter, a common language among women." Afterward the First Lady and her entourage traveled to Slovakia. In the city of Kosice, she met a frightened little girl named Yulie and her mother. "How can I explain this to my child?" the mother asked Dr. Biden. "It's senseless," she replied.

Olena Zelenska, forty-four, Ukraine's First Lady, had been in hiding since the Russian invasion began; she and her children, Oleksandra, seventeen, and Kyrylo, nine, had been living in an undisclosed location. But on Mother's Day, Olena traveled to Uzhhorod, a town near the Slovakia border. There she awaited Jill Biden's arrival.

Dr. Biden and her team didn't know the trip was a "go" until they climbed into their vehicles after their last scheduled meeting with Slovakia's prime minister, Eduard Heger. A handful of reporters were now informed of the visit and told they could accompany the First Lady as a pool. But they were forbidden to transmit stories until the motorcade crossed back into Slovakia.

The ride into Ukraine's war zone felt surreal. "It was oddly silent," said a senior official. "It looked like a normal Sunday, with people going about their business, coming out of churches or going to the bakery. And, of course, we're in this large convoy of black cars. People were turning around and trying to figure out what the hell was going on." Jill Biden's seven-car motorcade pulled into the parking lot of a school. A black SUV idled nearby. Four large, heavily armored men brandishing automatic weapons surrounded it. Finally, Olena Zelenska stepped out and came over to greet her distinguished visitor. The First Ladies embraced, and Dr. Biden gave her new friend a bouquet of flowers.

Inside the school, converted to a refugee center, they sat across a table from each other as the pool cameras rolled. "I thought it was important to show the Ukrainian people that this war has to stop and this war has been brutal and that the people of the United States stand with the people of Ukraine," said Dr. Biden. "Do you feel it?" "Yes, I feel it," replied Zelenska with a smile. "I would like to thank you for a very courageous act. Because we understand what it takes for the U.S. First Lady to come here during a war."

When the reporters departed, the First Ladies spoke privately. Zelenska told her American guest that Ukraine desperately needed U.S. help providing mental health treatment for women and children who'd witnessed unspeakable horrors: killings, torture, and rape. Dr. Biden agreed to do whatever she could. But Zelenska was also just curious: How, with a full-time teaching job, did she find time to visit a war zone? Jill explained that she'd just finished grading end-of-semester final exams.

The visit, scheduled to last seventy-five minutes, had gone on for two hours. It was time to depart; Jill Biden's security detail would breathe easier when she was safely back across the border. The First Ladies hugged and said goodbyes. As her motorcade rolled west toward Slovakia, Jill Biden called the president on her secure phone to tell him she was safe. The convoy rode in silence the rest of the way to the border.

On the flight home, the First Lady jotted down her impressions of the trip on a legal pad and handed it to Bernal. "Maybe there's an op-ed," she said. Indeed, there was—and it was published on CNN's website that week.

Coverage of the meeting, a daring and heartfelt display of motherly solidarity and U.S. support for Ukraine, led most of the American TV news programs that weekend.

————

Jill Biden had been a traveling ambassador for her husband for decades, though it took a while for her to feel comfortable in the role. She'd been a political wife since 1977, when she married the then Delaware senator—a widower and single father of two boys as the result of a terrible car accident four and a half years earlier. Jill became a doting mother to Biden's sons, Beau and Hunter, who'd survived the crash that killed Joe's wife and infant daughter. And in 1981 she and Joe had a daughter, Ashley. Jill had campaigned at Joe's side through six winning Senate races, two losing presidential campaigns, and finally the 2020 victory over Trump.

Eight years as Second Lady had prepared Dr. Biden for the First Lady's role. On Inauguration Day, she knew exactly what she wanted to do; upon arriving with Joe at the White House, without even changing out of her inaugural outfit, she headed for the Eisenhower Executive Office Building (EEOB), where she videotaped a message thanking the National Guard and others who'd made the day's ceremonies possible. The next day she led a Zoom call with eleven thousand teachers and the presidents of the National Education Association (NEA) and

American Federation of Teachers (AFT). At the height of the COVID pandemic, half the nation's teachers were conducting their classes virtually. Dr. Biden wanted to show them that she understood (she'd been teaching virtually too), and that she had their backs.

The president joked that if he hadn't pushed for tuition-free community colleges, he'd be sleeping in the Lincoln Bedroom. (The original BBB provided for free tuition, but that feature had been removed when Joe Manchin balked.) Along with education, Jill Biden cared especially deeply about two other issues: military families and cancer. She called herself a National Guard mom; her beloved late son, Beau, had been a member. And, of course, Beau had tragically succumbed to brain cancer.

Amid the pandemic, it was challenging for the First Lady to travel. But not impossible. When the Olympics were held in Beijing in July 2021, spouses, parents, and relatives of U.S. athletes were barred from attending because of COVID. The U.S. had withdrawn its diplomatic contingent in protest over Chinese human rights abuses. But Dr. Biden was determined to attend, to show support for U.S. Olympians. "She had to fight and we had to fight too," said her communications director, Elizabeth Alexander. "She said, 'Look, I want to go. I want to represent the United States and make sure our athletes know that we're with them.'" In the end, the First Lady prevailed. And though COVID protocols prevented her from greeting the athletes in person, they appreciated her presence in the bleachers.

As COVID loosened its grip, the First Lady's travel picked up. During Biden's first year, she visited thirty-five states. "She believes that showing up matters," said Alexander. "Part of her role is to meet people where they are." She went to more tribal nations than any other First Lady during her first year—and to Alabama, Mississippi, Tennessee, North Carolina, and the red parts of Florida. At many of these stops she preached the safety and efficacy of COVID vaccines. In the aftermath of natural or man-made disasters, she and Joe were consolers in chief; her common touch was as finely honed as her husband's. "You saw that when she went to Kentucky after the big tornado," said Alexander. "You saw that when she went to Surfside [Florida, where a condominium collapsed, killing ninety-nine people]. You saw that over and over again."

In late August 2021, the First Lady's empathy and poise were sorely tested after the dignified transfer ceremony for the thirteen service members killed in the suicide bombing in Kabul. When the president was excoriated by a few of the grieving relatives, it was a triple blow to Jill Biden—she was not only the president's wife but also a National Guard mother and champion of military families. "It was hard to see the president criticized, because she knows his heart and knows that all he was trying to do was comfort others," said one of her advisers.

Ron Klain, who knew something about putting in long hours, was impressed by the First Lady's work ethic. "She's going from early in the morning until late at night," he told me in May 2022. "She's down in South America right now. She's in Ecuador on her way to Costa Rica. She's just incredibly, incredibly hardworking." When the president wasn't complaining about how much he missed the First Lady, he bragged about her. "Almost every week he'll take a minute or two and say, with enormous pride, what a great job she's doing, how hard she's working," said Klain. "He always comes back to her having a full-time job and a full agenda as First Lady."

Jill Biden understood political stagecraft. At the 2022 State of the Union speech, the First Lady wore a dress with one sleeve embroidered with a sunflower, Ukraine's national flower, and sat with the country's ambassador to the U.S. And she barnstormed for Joe whenever her teaching schedule permitted—usually Tuesdays and Thursdays between classes, now that she was physically back at the college. Jen O'Malley Dillon, Biden's former campaign manager, planned her domestic trips for maximum political advantage. After the State of the Union, Dr. Biden had gone to Arizona, Nevada, and Kentucky to promote the president's BBB and "unity" agenda. She led fundraisers for the Democratic National Committee and spoke to community college students.

Klain thought her most valuable gift was injecting the outside world into the president's bubble. She and Joe Biden rarely talked policy. "Their conversations," he said, "are more of her saying, 'Hey, this is what people are saying. After school I talked to some teachers or I went to this event—and people were saying this, people were saying that.'" She was also a shrewd judge of people around her husband. Like Nancy Reagan, she could detect those who were pursuing their own agendas at the president's expense. Dr. Biden was always looking ahead and around corners: "She's a teacher at her core," said Alexander. "So she wants to understand, what's the plan, what's the strategy, what's the long-term goal of what we're trying to accomplish?"

In early May, an unprecedented leak from the Supreme Court served as a reminder that elections have consequences. In a blockbuster report, *Politico* published an early draft of a majority opinion, written by Justice Samuel Alito, signaling that the court would overturn the landmark decision in *Roe v. Wade*, which upheld a constitutional right for women to have abortions. As *Politico* put it:

> *The draft opinion is a full-throated, unflinching repudiation of the 1973 decision which guaranteed federal constitutional pro-*

tections of abortion rights and a subsequent 1992 decision—Planned Parenthood v. Casey—that largely maintained the right. "Roe was egregiously wrong from the start," Alito writes. . . .

Jill Biden, now seventy, had been twenty-one when *Roe* was decided and was appalled by the prospect of seeing it overturned. Yet that reversal was almost certain to happen—because Trump had appointed three Supreme Court justices. This was after Barack Obama, in 2015, had been refused so much as a hearing for his own top court pick, Merrick Garland. Mitch McConnell, then the Senate Majority Leader, was accused by many Democrats of rigging the political process, using as a pretext for not letting the Senate consider Garland's nomination the fact that it came too close to the next presidential election.

The evening after the *Politico* disclosure, Kamala Harris spoke at a gala dinner for EMILY's List, the organization dedicated to electing pro-choice political candidates. When she took the stage, the vice president pulled no punches:

> *Those Republican leaders who are trying to weaponize the use of the law against women—well, we say, "How dare they?" How dare they tell a woman what she can do and cannot do with her own body? How dare they? How dare they try to stop her from determining her own future? How dare they try to deny women their rights and their freedoms? . . .*

The prospect of being denied a right taken for granted for half a century resonated powerfully with women, especially Democrats. As Jennifer Rubin wrote in *The Washington Post*:

The court leak rocked millions of Americans, especially women, in what felt like the closest thing to election night 2016 . . . the sense of desperation, vulnerability, anger and fear then did not drive women to hide under their beds. Donald Trump's election spurred a period of remarkable civic engagement, organizing, fundraising and network-building (across the aisle in some cases).

Appearing on Symone Sanders's MSNBC show, Jill Biden weighed in. Whereas Harris had gone for the jugular, talking about women's right to make decisions about their bodies, the First Lady cast the issue as a political imperative. Protesting was fine, she said, "but we have to take actions. And this is when elections really matter. So if it matters . . . to your viewers, they have to elect people that think the way that they do."

The First Lady continued, "Of the five conservative justices who would likely rule to overturn *Roe*, four of them were appointed by presidents who didn't win the popular vote." Indeed, Joe Biden's recently confirmed Supreme Court justice, Ketanji Brown Jackson, had been the first in recent memory chosen by a popularly elected president. But Jackson, the first Black female Supreme Court justice, had yet to be seated. "So people have to get involved," Dr. Biden continued. "That's the only way that this is going to change."

It was a preview of the role Jill Biden would play in the 2022 elections and beyond, when women's rights wouldn't be the only thing at stake.

TWENTY-FIVE

THE MAGA CROWD

Tyranny was threatening NATO and Eastern Europe, but dark, authoritarian forces were also on the march at home. In the late spring of 2022, the Trumpian lie of a stolen 2020 election was alive and well, and its believers seemed to be gaining strength. Many subscribed to a creed known as "replacement theory," which posited that Jews were recruiting Blacks and other minorities in a campaign to replace whites and eradicate Western civilization. This conspiratorial claptrap was amplified by Tucker Carlson of Fox News.

On April 22, Earth Day, Joe Biden traveled to Seattle to announce the signing of an executive order protecting forests. In the spectacular outdoor setting of Seward Park, he tried to sound an optimistic note: "I think that we're in one of those moments in world history and in American history, where . . . we really have an opportunity to do things we couldn't have done two, five, ten years ago." The trouble was, virtually no Republicans would support anything he proposed. He continued:

> *This ain't your father's Republican Party. Not—not a joke . . . this is the MAGA party now. . . . These guys are a different breed of cat. They're not like what I served with for so many years.*

For Biden this had been the biggest shock of his presidency; the Republican Party bore no resemblance to the one he'd known for decades as senator and vice president. He wasn't naive; he didn't think he could turn back the clock and get Mitch McConnell to play Tip O'Neill to his Ronald Reagan, striking legislative deals over whiskey in the White House residence. But Biden was surprised by the extent of the GOP's scorched-earth nihilism, its blind obedience to a man who'd lost the presidency and the House and Senate along with it (a feat not accomplished since Herbert Hoover). It wasn't just Biden's policies that this MAGA-beholden GOP opposed; it was the idea that Biden, or any other Democrat, could be considered legitimate. To this crowd, elections counted only when Republicans won. The rules of democratic governance no longer applied.

Biden continued:

And the people who know better are afraid to act correctly, because they know they'll be primaried. I've had—I won't mention any of them; I promised I never would, and I won't—but up to six come to me and say, "Joe, I want to be with you on such and such, but I can't. I'll be primaried. I'll lose my race. I'll lose my race."

So, folks, we got to—this is going to start to change.

But it hadn't changed.

MAGA was on the move. Ohio was a case in point. J. D. Vance, the once staunch anti-Trump author of *Hillbilly Elegy*, had suddenly become a MAGA disciple—just in time to run in the Republican primary for U.S. senator. The gambit worked: With Trump's blessing, and Vance's full-throated endorsement of the 2020 election lie, he won the nomination overwhelmingly. Meanwhile, back in Washington, Ginni Thomas, wife of Supreme Court Justice Clarence Thomas, was unmasked as a cheerleader for the January 6 MAGA insurrection; she'd badgered both Trump's chief Mark Meadows and Arizona state election officials, unsuccessfully, to overturn Biden's legitimate election. Despite her activism for the MAGA cause, Justice Thomas had not only *not* recused himself from Supreme Court decisions involving January 6; he'd also been the lone dissenter in a case in which the court rejected Trump's attempt to withhold documents from the January 6 committee.

It wasn't just MAGA writ large that bothered Biden; he felt its influence all too close to home—in his Secret Service detail. Lately, the Secret Service had looked both incompetent and politicized. In an embarrassing episode, four employees—two agents and two officers— had allegedly been duped by con men posing as agents of the DHS; they'd befriended the employees, offering gifts such as iPhones, a flat-screen television, and free rent in apartments they controlled.

But far more troubling was the scandal involving the Secret Service and the January 6 attack on the Capitol, which came to light in July 2022. The DHS inspector general, Joseph V. Cuffari, who had asked the Secret Service to turn over all its text messages from January 5 and January 6, 2021, revealed that all but one of those messages had been erased. The Secret Service claimed, unconvincingly, that this was the inadvertent result of an agencywide "migration" of data that occurred while upgrading its phones.

And that was just the half of it. Members of Trump's Secret Service detail had reportedly cheered on the Capitol assault. Moreover, it turned out that Cuffari had known about the agency's erasure of the texts for months but failed to report it, which triggered a clamor for his resignation. Fueling suspicion, the Secret Service, renowned for its prowess at retrieving lost electronic data, claimed that when it came to finding its own, nothing could be done.

At best this was incompetence; at worst, something much more alarming. After all, on January 6, 2021, hiding in a loading dock below the Capitol from a mob that wanted to hang him, Vice President Mike Pence had refused a request from his Secret Service detail to get into his vehicle. "I'm not getting in the car," he said emphatically. Representative Jamie Raskin (D-MD), a member of the congressional January 6 committee, said of Pence: "He knew exactly what this inside coup they had planned for was going to do." God only knew where Pence's agents might have taken him.

By now, Biden wasn't taking any chances either. Wary of his own Secret Service agents, the president no longer spoke freely in their presence.

The MAGA movement was unique. Polarization wasn't new in American politics, but this was something different—a major political party in thrall to a cult of personality. As Mike Donilon, the keeper of Biden's message, put it, "Here's something that we're living with that no one in the history of this country's ever lived with. Which is not only a defeated presidential candidate of a major party refusing to accept an election but *a former president* refusing to accept an election. No president, other than Joe Biden, has ever had to deal with that. It's different. It's a problem. So we fight through that every day. Look, the Republican Party and the country could have made a different choice a year ago than it did. But it didn't."

For all that, there were signs that Trump's spell on the electorate was slipping. In late May 2022, in the race for the Republican nomination as Georgia's governor, the candidate Trump endorsed, David Perdue, was routed by Brian Kemp, the man the former president had vilified for certifying Joe Biden's electors in 2020. And in Alabama, the forty-fifth president's favored candidate for Senate, Mo Brooks, ran so poorly in the polls that Trump withdrew his endorsement, denouncing the state's primary process as "cockamamie."

Leon Panetta thought the Trump phenomenon was fizzling. "I think the Trump act is almost over," he told me. "You can only bullshit people so long. It finally catches up with you. And it's beginning to happen to Trump. I mean, the comments he made about Putin being a genius and playing the same old cards that he played when he was the president. I just think the American people basically know this guy for what he is, and it's beginning to impact on him and his influence as a political person in this country."

Biden was convinced he could beat "the former guy" in a rematch, if it came to that, in 2024. It was the broader MAGA movement that worried him. It seemed more dangerous than any one person because it was built around an insidious but contagious idea: that truth and facts and science—and votes—didn't matter unless they served to keep your people in power.

And even if Trump's star was fading, the MAGA movement seemed indestructible. Biden found its staying power unfathomable. "I think he thought that Trumpism would kind of fade after Trump's presidency," said Ron Klain. "We won by more than seven million votes. It was a clear national mandate for Biden. We won with over three hundred electoral votes. And yet we were fighting over whether people should be vaccinated. And fighting about whether people should use medicines that are fake. It really surprises the president."

————

In the late spring of 2022, the door that had been opened at Charlottesville, the one Biden had been determined to shut, was flung wide open again.

On May 14, in Buffalo, New York, an eighteen-year-old carrying a Bushmaster XM-15 semiautomatic rifle opened fire on shoppers at a Tops grocery store. Ten people, all of them Black, were killed and three injured. The shooter had driven across New York State and murdered them because of their race. It soon became clear that he'd been driven by the same "replacement theory" that animated Tucker Carlson and many MAGA true believers.

When asked about the massacre, Trump declined to condemn it, launching instead into an irrelevant riff about American soldiers who didn't die on his watch in Afghanistan.

On May 17, in Buffalo, Joe Biden addressed a crowd of mourners:

In America, evil will not win. I promise you. Hate will not prevail and white supremacy will not have the last word. . . . What happened here is simple and straightforward: terrorism. Terrorism. Domestic terrorism. Violence inflicted in the service of hate and a vicious thirst for power that defines one group of people being inherently inferior to any other group. A hate that, through the media and politics, the internet, has radicalized angry, alienated, lost, and isolated individuals into falsely believing that they will be replaced. That's the word. "Replaced" by the other. By people who don't look like them. I and all of you reject the lie. I call on all Americans to reject the lie, and I condemn those who spread the lie for power, political gain, and for profit.

He went on:

That's what it is. We've now seen too many times the deadly and destructive violence this ideology unleashes. We heard the chants— "you will not replace us"—in Charlottesville, Virginia. . . . Look, the American experiment in democracy is in a danger like it hasn't been in my lifetime. It's in danger this hour.

It was still true, as it had been on Inauguration Day, that the country's greatest national security threat came not from foreign terrorist groups like Al Qaeda or ISIS but from Americans who rejected democracy and the rule of law.

And it was still unclear whether Joe Biden could do anything to turn those forces back.

TWENTY-SIX

THE FIGHT OF HIS LIFE

What were the lessons of Joe Biden's presidency at the two-year mark? During his campaign he'd promised an ambitious agenda—from defeating the COVID pandemic to jump-starting the economy to ending racial injustice to reforming the police to rescuing the planet from global warming. And, of course, unifying the country, restoring civility, and winning the battle for the soul of the nation. All presidents promise more than they can deliver, and voters deserved to know where Biden stood on all of these urgent issues.

History shows that presidents often stumble when they try to do too many things. Bill Clinton learned this the hard way. "One day the president came out of the Oval Office and he had another one of his great ideas," recalled Erskine Bowles, Clinton's third White House chief of staff. "And believe me, they were unbelievably great ideas. And I turned to him and said, 'Mr. President, you've got to go back into that Oval Office right now! You've got to look at this list of things that you and I agreed you wanted to get done. If you'll stay focused on those three or four things, I can set up the organization and structure and focus to make 'em real. But you can't do a thousand things.'"

Ultimately, Clinton realized that Bowles was right. By narrowing his priorities, he was able to block Republican Speaker Newt Gingrich's attempt to gut the social safety net; he balanced the federal budget—and coasted to reelection.

Joe Biden came into office with legislative goals that rivaled LBJ's Great Society or FDR's New Deal but lacked the solid Democratic majorities many thought were needed to achieve them. With a small margin in the House and an evenly split Senate, enacting the ARP, BIF, and BBB bills, voting rights, police reform, gun control, and everything else he'd promised was going to be a tall order. Tricks of the legislative trade like reconciliation weren't magic wands. The times and the circumstances called for focusing on a few achievable things.

Instead, Biden and his team pursued almost all their priorities simultaneously; the BIF and BBB bills became linked, stuck in legislative purgatory for months, while moderates and liberals bashed each other and while the president appeared indecisive about how to proceed. The sausage-making spectacle, as Ron Klain called it, damaged the most valuable commodity Biden had: his reputation for competence.

And yet Biden's ambitious approach to legislating ultimately paid off. Indeed, in late July 2022, after secret negotiations with Majority Leader Chuck Schumer, Senator Joe Manchin agreed to support a pared-down version of Build Back Better. The new bill was stripped of its social safety net provisions—universal prekindergarten, free community college, expanded childcare, and parental leave. But the legislation, called the Inflation Reduction Act, was transformative nonetheless: it provided $369 billion in tax credits and grants for solar and wind power, electric vehicles, and efficient home heating, and billions more for subsidized healthcare. Further, it lowered prescription drug costs by permitting Medicare to negotiate the prices of high-cost drugs with pharmaceutical companies, which had been an aim of Democratic legislators for some thirty years. And, by raising taxes on corporations, the bill would also reduce the federal deficit by $300 billion.

The president's approval rating remained low, and he still struggled with inflation, crime, and the southern border. But Joe Biden was enjoying a reversal of fortune—with strong jobs reports; falling gas prices; a lethal drone strike on Al Qaeda's leader, Ayman al-Zawahiri; Ukraine's continued resistance against the Russian invasion; and the imminent admission of Finland and Sweden into NATO. He'd also notched bipartisan legislative victories—a modest gun safety measure, and the CHIPs and Science Act, investing in the semiconductor industry. Along with the American Rescue Plan and infrastructure bills, this represented, as *The New York Times* put it, "one of the most expansive assertions of government in the modern age." It was a legislative record that rivaled LBJ's. It was also a vindication of chief of staff Ron Klain's patient, nose-to-the-grindstone stewardship.

Joe Biden rejected the notion that a president should focus on achieving a few things. "I'm proud to say that we've had a lot of big days," he told me. "That includes the biggest economic recovery package since FDR. The biggest infrastructure investment since Eisenhower. The second-biggest health-care reform since LBJ. The most substantive gun safety bill since Clinton. The most important investment in climate, ever. Meanwhile, we've led the greatest jobs recovery in history, appointed a record number of federal judges, and put the first Black woman on the Supreme Court. We've even seen Sweden and Finland join NATO."

Biden's worst day as president had been the terrible ISIS-K suicide bombing that killed thirteen service members in Kabul in August 2021. But what was his best day? When I interviewed the president in the fall of 2022, I asked him: "Was it signing the Inflation Reduction

Act? Taking Al Qaeda's leader Ayman al-Zawahiri off the battlefield?" Biden's answer was surprising. "The most emotional moment for me may have been when I signed the Sergeant First Class Heath Robinson PACT Act into law and got to hand my pen over to his little girl, Brielle," Biden said.

The PACT Act, passed in July 2022, provided healthcare benefits to millions of veterans sickened by toxic exposure to burn pits and other hazards. "Heath was a decorated combat medic in the Army National Guard, stationed near Baghdad, just yards from burn pits the size of football fields," Biden explained. "Cancer ravaged his body. He fought it to the end—and his wife Danielle kept fighting. Heath was just thirty-nine years old when she and Brielle held his hand for the last time."

Although he couldn't prove it, Biden was convinced that burn pit toxins like those that caused Sergeant Robinson's cancer had also killed his son Beau.

Biden's COVID-19 response team, led by Jeff Zients, largely fulfilled the president's promise to follow facts and science and let doctors call the shots while being transparent with the public. Its messaging was sometimes inconsistent—on-and-off masking recommendations, for example—but that was the price of transparency. Biden's approach was a stark and welcome contrast to Trump's carnival barking and snake oil medicine. By getting shots into arms, Zients and his team saved more than two million American lives. By May 2022, two hundred twenty million people had been vaccinated and the economy had rebounded—with unprecedented job growth and low unemployment. And, unfortunately, inflation—triggered in part by an economy roaring back from the dead.

True, at one point Biden got ahead of himself; his promise of "independence from a deadly virus" over the July 4, 2021, weekend was dashed by the emergence of the Delta variant. It wasn't as bad as George W. Bush standing on an aircraft carrier in front of a banner marked "Mission Accomplished." But Biden paid a price for seeming to declare victory prematurely.

Yet there was little he or anyone else could do about a cult of vaccine resistance that cost American lives and hampered the country's economic recovery. Biden underestimated the misinformation surrounding the efficacy of vaccines, and the willingness of people in red states to put their anti-government ideology ahead of their own health and the public good.

Republicans complained that Biden tried to govern from the far left, but the complaint was specious. The idea that the president was a socialist would come as a surprise to Senators Bernie Sanders and Elizabeth Warren and the so-called Squad. In fact, while Trump had exploded the deficit with a $1.5 trillion tax cut for the wealthy, Biden was on track to reduce it by the same amount.

It was true that culture war controversies—over critical race theory, transgender rights, and defunding the police—had worked against Democrats in certain gubernatorial and Senate races. But it was hard to blame Biden for the excesses of his progressive wing—and on the issue of crime, he'd tacked hard to the center with his support for New York mayor Eric Adams.

When it came to communicating, Biden tried to do two things that were contradictory: unify the country and call out the Big Lie of a stolen 2020 election. His desire to do both was understandable and even laudable. After all, the president believed that Americans were fundamentally reasonable and educable. "Our principle has always been that we want to unify the country around shared values," said Ron Klain. "And we'll continue to do that. But there are people in this country that don't share those values—people who stand for white supremacy or for votes not counting in an election. That's what the battle for the soul of the nation is all about."

The trouble was, those people were abundant in vast swaths of the country and they controlled the Republican Party. Joe Biden came from a different time and place. Shaped by the collegial culture of a bygone Senate, he believed in bipartisanship as an article of faith. He had a twentieth-century notion that he could speak to people's common sense. Given half a chance, Biden thought he could persuade most Americans to treat one another with respect, to compromise, and to respect the truth—and, faced with a lethal pandemic, to wear masks and take vaccines.

But nearly forty percent of the country wasn't listening.

Biden's reputation for competence had been damaged by the bungled U.S. withdrawal from Afghanistan, which was hastily planned and poorly executed. His damn-the-torpedoes determination to end the war trumped a careful plan to do so safely and competently. The episode accelerated a slide in his approval rating in the summer of 2021.

Yet Biden recovered on the world stage. At least as much as his handling of the pandemic, Biden's conduct of the Ukraine war would ultimately define his presidency. Putin's invasion was a seismic, history-altering event. And long before the first missile was fired in the battle for Kyiv, Biden had been prescient about the coming conflict—accurately calling it a contest between democracy and autocracy.

Events vindicated his words. "We all kind of assumed it was just kind of a broad-brush, big picture of democracy versus autocracy," said Leon Panetta. "But now you have it in spades with the war in Ukraine. Without question, the United States and our allies are confronting the highest-profile tyrant of the twenty-first century up to this point. The war's obviously very dangerous. But I have to think it's very pivotal. Just as World War One defined the struggle for power in the twentieth century, what happens with Putin and Ukraine and Russia is going to tell us an awful lot about what's going to happen in the twenty-first century."

The stakes were immense, Panetta believed, for both the world and Joe Biden: "This war in Ukraine has really strengthened Joe Biden's image as a world leader. His confrontation with Putin is going to determine what the hell his legacy is going to be as president. I think it's that big a deal."

———

At the outset of his presidency, given his far-reaching agenda, some observers compared Biden to FDR. A year and a half later, with Biden beset by crises, others likened him to Jimmy Carter. Representative Jim Clyburn (D-SC) thought Biden was more like Harry Truman—and it was true that Scranton Joe not only shared Truman's flair for plain speaking; he also was rebuilding and strengthening the architecture of the postwar world that Truman had created. But there was another historical figure that Biden resembled.

Volodymyr Zelensky was constantly being compared to Winston Churchill. Ukraine's charismatic leader certainly shared the British prime minister's courage and eloquence. (And his determination to drag the U.S. into war.) But Biden had a few things in common with Churchill as well.

At first glance, the two leaders were utterly dissimilar. Churchill was a hidebound aristocrat with a silver tongue. Biden was a blue-collar Democrat who mangled his words. But they'd both spent their careers close to power without quite grasping the brass ring. Both had been defeated politically, considered washed-up, and mocked for their loquaciousness. And yet they'd both prepared themselves for a moment when their countries would need them.

Churchill's moment came when Adolf Hitler tried to conquer England. Biden's came when Vladimir Putin invaded Ukraine and threatened the survival of Western democracy. The historian William Manchester, in the first volume of his trilogy on Churchill, *The Last Lion*, wrote about the leader England needed in 1940:

> *[He] would have to be a passionate Manichaean who saw the world as a medieval struggle to the death between the powers of good and the powers of evil, who held that individuals are responsible for their actions and that the . . . dictator was therefore wicked. . . .*
>
> *Now at last, at last, his hour had struck. He had been waiting in Parliament for forty years, had grown bald and gray in his nation's service, had endured slander and calumny only to be summoned when the situation seemed hopeless. . . .*

Substitute the Senate for Parliament and Manchester could have been describing Joe Biden. He'd been summoned in 2020 to replace an authoritarian president who'd threatened to end democracy. But that wouldn't be the only thing Biden would be remembered for. His place in history would depend on how well he stood up to a foreign dictator who threatened democracy not only in Europe but also in the West. Joe Biden was uniquely qualified to rally the U.S. and NATO to restore the international order that had prevented a world war for eight decades. And so he did.

In his interview with me in September 2022, Biden portrayed the war in Ukraine in almost apocalyptic terms. "President Putin thought his invasion would be over in days," he said. "It's now lasted more than six months, because the Ukrainian people aren't giving up. They know that their right to exist as a democratic, independent, sovereign nation is at stake. President Putin didn't just attack Ukraine on February 24, 2022. He attacked the fundamental principles of sovereignty and independence that protect peace and stability everywhere."

"What would victory for Ukraine look like?" I asked him.

"America's goal here is straightforward," Biden replied. "We want to see a democratic, independent, sovereign, and prosperous Ukraine, with the means to deter and defend itself against further aggression. We'll continue cooperating with our allies and partners on Russian sanctions, the toughest ever imposed on a major economy. We'll keep providing Ukraine with advanced weaponry, including Javelin antitank missiles, Stinger antiaircraft missiles, powerful artillery and precision rocket systems, radars, unmanned aerial vehicles, Mi-17 helicopters, and ammunition. We'll also send billions more in financial assistance, as authorized by Congress. We'll work with our allies and partners to address the global food crisis that Russia's aggression is making worse. We'll help our European allies and others reduce their dependence on Russian fossil fuels, and speed our transition to a clean energy future. And we'll continue reinforcing NATO's eastern flank with forces and capabilities from the United States and other allies."

Barring a catastrophic escalation into nuclear war, or a collapse of U.S. resolve and NATO unity, Ukraine seemed almost certain to prevail in the end; its borders might have to be negotiated, but Russia stood almost no chance of achieving Putin's goal of conquering the country. If so, Biden, along with Zelensky, would deserve the lion's share of credit. But that wouldn't necessarily cure Biden's political woes. His predecessors had learned painfully that domestic problems could trump international successes. Churchill had been thrown out of office in 1945 after leading Great Britain to victory over Hitler. George H. W. Bush had been defeated in the 1992 presidential election after routing Saddam Hussein's armies in Kuwait. No one could be sure if Biden would suffer the same political fate, or even if he would run for reelection in 2024.

Presidents do not give up power lightly. Andy Card, George W. Bush's chief, once said, "If anybody tells you they're leaving the White House voluntarily, they're probably lying." This applies to presidents, of any age, who are driven by vast reserves of ego and ambition. But how old is too old to run for reelection? It wasn't just right-wing news outlets that were questioning Biden's mental acuity. Card favored a Constitutional amendment forbidding presidents from running after the age of seventy-five. "I'm seventy-five and I can't do things I used to do," he said.

But Jimmy Carter's former chief, Jack Watson, disagreed. "Aging is such an extremely individual thing," he observed. "Some people are physically, mentally, emotionally, and energetically 'older' at sixty-five than other people are in their eighties." Watson, now eighty-three, noted that the investor Warren Buffett was still going strong at the age of ninety-two. The last years of Picasso's life (he died at the age of ninety-one) were among his most creative and prolific. And U.S. Supreme Court justices John Marshall, Oliver Wendell Holmes, Louis Brandeis, and Ruth Bader Ginsburg, to name just a few, all served with distinction into their eighties. "Let the voters observe, assess, and evaluate the candidates for the presidency," Watson argued, "and let them, not the calendar, decide. That's what democracy is all about."

In September 2022, asked by correspondent Scott Pelley on *60 Minutes* if he was still up to the job, Biden replied, "Watch me."

The president would soon have to make a decision about running.

But Joe Biden had endured too much to take anything for granted. Who knew what might lie ahead—what vicissitudes of health or history might change his calculation? Lyndon Johnson had bowed out of his reelection race in 1968 when his challenger for the nomination, the anti–Vietnam War candidate Eugene McCarthy, placed a strong second in the New Hampshire primary. Unlike LBJ, Biden had ended an unpopular war and had no serious challenger for the nomination. Still, as Admiral Stavridis had once said, predicting trouble during the withdrawal from Afghanistan, the world will ultimately have its way with you.

In our virtual interview, in the fall of 2022, Joe Biden sounded like a president intent on running for reelection—but aware that nothing in life is certain. "I intend to run," he insisted, "but it's much too early to make that kind of decision. I'm a great respecter of fate."

There were at least two, and perhaps six, years to go before Joe Biden's fight would be over.

GET UP!

Even after two years as president, Joe Biden could still hear his father's voice every time he'd been knocked down by one of life's cruel punches: "Get up!" It was the foundational principle of his personal and political life, and he heard it whenever fate tried to pummel him. "The newspapers are calling you a plagiarist, Biden? *Get up!* Your wife and daughter—I'm sorry, Joe, there was nothing we could do to save them? *Get up!* . . . The kids make fun of you because you stutter . . . ? *Get up!* . . . That was his phrase," Biden wrote in his book, *Promises to Keep*, "and it has echoed through my life."

In the summer of 2022, with gas prices rising, his approval numbers sinking, and his prized Build Back Better (BBB) bill all but dead, Joe Biden appeared to be, politically, flat on his back. Then the president suddenly picked himself up. The trajectory of his presidency changed in late July, when Chuck Schumer and Joe Manchin emerged from a series of secret meetings with an ambitious agreement that would revive Biden's presidency. Known as the Inflation Reduction Act, it would breathe new life into major planks of BBB.

But how had this stunning resurrection come about?

The deal was portrayed as a breakthrough by two senators who'd managed to cut a deal by leaving the Biden White House in the dark. In truth, the secret talks were abetted if not orchestrated by Biden's team; Ron Klain and his colleagues were consulted every step of the way.

Back in December, negotiations over BBB between the West Virginia senator and the White House had devolved into acrimony after Biden put out a statement that Manchin thought singled him out as an obstacle. Manchin had promised Biden he'd support a scaled-back, $1.75-trillion version of his most ambitious legislative proposal. But days later, on *FOX News Sunday*, Manchin announced that he was done with BBB. In response, White House press secretary Jen Psaki put out a second statement calling out the senator's "sudden and inexplicable reversal in his position."

Furious, Biden called the West Virginia senator's cell phone—but Manchin had turned it off; the call went to voicemail. He and the president didn't speak for weeks.

Manchin would later downplay his spats with the White House as "rough spots," but his pride was wounded. He blamed Biden's team for turning him into a pariah. Harassed by environmental protesters paddling kayaks and shouting through bullhorns outside his houseboat, he said he feared for his safety and his family's.

Still, Manchin knew he was losing in the court of public opinion. He'd become, in the eyes of many Americans, a science-denying, coal-loving plutocrat—the man who was dooming the planet. Even more disturbing to Manchin, he was being shunned by his colleagues on Capitol Hill. "Joe Manchin is a pack animal," said one senior White House adviser, trying to explain why the senator was looking for a way to be re-embraced. "I mean that not in a pejorative way—but some people don't mind being isolated from their colleagues and peers; Senator Manchin isn't one of them."

Klain and his team saw an opening.

In February, over dinner with Manchin and Secretary of Commerce Gina Raimondo, Biden's White House chief apologized to the senator on his team's behalf; if he'd been offended by anything they'd said, Klain told him, he was sorry; that hadn't been their intent.

Manchin was ready to forgive and forge ahead. But he'd painted himself into a political corner. He'd branded himself among conservative West Virginians as the man who'd killed Biden's top legislative priority. "Build Back Better had to be dead and he couldn't give Biden a win," explained a White House adviser. "His whole thing was that he was the guy who stopped the Biden plan. And so he needed a different way to get to yes."

Klain realized the White House needed to change its approach. "I think everyone likes to have as their model Lyndon Johnson," he told me. "A president gets senators or representatives in a room and leans his body into them, and yells at them until they say yes. And maybe that works sometimes, but it works less often in real life than it does on TV shows, and it didn't work with Joe Manchin." To the West Virginia senator, the House version of BBB was unacceptable, but so was the process. "I think we came off to him like a used car salesman," explained Klain. "We had him in the showroom and we were saying, 'You need to buy this car today!' And, 'Oh, well! You really do want windshield wipers on the car too!'" Ultimately, Klain realized, it was Manchin who had to make the sale. The key was to "let him have the time and the space where he didn't feel pressured, where he put the parameters around how far he would go, to let him come to it."

In late March, Klain reached out to both Manchin and Schumer. "You guys should just go settle this," he told them. The veteran New York senator, Schumer, told his West Virginia counterpart that he wasn't beholden to the progressives or the White House; they could start from square one. But, in fact, Klain and his team were consulted at every step. "Manchin and Schumer needed to know that we would provide cover with the progressive groups," said a White House adviser. "That a lot of stuff that mattered to a lot of people wasn't going to be in the bill." As the talks progressed, Joe Biden personally called "green" senators like Ed Markey (D-MA) and Ben Sasse (R-NE) to prepare them for bitter pills they'd have to swallow.

Secrecy was essential lest the infant agreement be smothered in its crib. But Klain and a handful of White House staffers were in the loop: Steve Ricchetti, Susan Rice, Louisa Terrell, and Brian Deese. Deese crunched the numbers and details. Klain and Ricchetti briefed Joe Biden regularly on the talks' progress.

Manchin now had a license to kill what he considered to be government handouts in the original bill. Though there was no evidence for it, Manchin told friends that some families were using child tax credit checks, granted under the American Rescue Plan, to buy illegal drugs. This tax credit was to be extended under BBB. Klain's team was under no illusions about the hard bargain Manchin would drive. "The care stuff was going to go away," explained a White House adviser. "And there would be just basically prescription drugs and climate and taxes. And we also understood that Manchin's price would be some kind of pipeline, and we made it clear that we would support that."

Afterward, in a private meeting with donors, Manchin bragged about his authorship of Biden's most important legislative achievement; he'd axed the bill's social safety net components. And while he'd signed on to sweeping climate provisions, Manchin had preserved his favorite, emissions-spewing shale pipeline in West Virginia. The talks with Schumer were "straightforward and easy," Manchin boasted. "Chuck let me write the bill," he said.

But Klain and his team had been coauthors. Biden's chief explained the political choreography: "It was slow. It was painful. But we were never going to get a deal with Joe Manchin where we put the thing on the table and he said yes. Manchin had to put the thing on the table and we had to say yes. That is the part of this whole process that no one can understand: passing bills in an evenly divided Congress came down to understanding people and personalities."

The deal was a boon for Biden and a gut punch to Republicans. Mitch McConnell, widely regarded as the Hill's master strategist, was blindsided and outmaneuvered. He'd agreed to support Biden's CHIPS and Science Act only because he thought the Democrats' dream of a big-spending reconciliation bill was dead. Just after the deal was announced, in what looked like spiteful payback by McConnell, Senate Republicans blocked the PACT Act, Biden's cherished health care bill for veterans sickened by exposure to burn pits. It would take an aggressive lobbying campaign by the entertainer/activist Jon Stewart to get that bill back onto the Senate floor and voted into law.

Just how significant the Inflation Reduction Act was—and how demoralizing to the GOP—became clear two months later. Never mind that the bill had passed through the budget reconciliation process and that neither McConnell nor any other Republican had actually voted for it. On September 30, 2022, Donald Trump blasted McConnell for its passage on his social media site *Truth Social*:

Is McConnell approving all of these Trillions of Dollars worth of Democrat sponsored Bills, without even the slightest bit of nego-

tiation, because he hates Donald J. Trump, and he knows I am strongly opposed to them, or is he doing it because he believes in the Fake and Highly Destructive Green New Deal, and is willing to take the Country down with him? In any event, either reason is unacceptable. He has a DEATH WISH. Must immediately seek help and advise from his China loving wife, Coco Chow!

The former president didn't always write his own posts, but this one—with the veiled threat of violence, the racist allusion to his target's wife, and the mangled spelling—left little doubt who the author was.

Mired in a new scandal over top-secret documents that he'd absconded with to Mar-a-Lago, and facing potential criminal prosecution in Georgia and Washington, D.C., Trump could do little but howl from the sidelines. Meanwhile, Biden was notching victories. In addition to a string of legislative successes, the president had managed to defuse several crises-in-the-making.

Competence, it seemed, had been restored as the administration's brand: Labor Secretary Marty Walsh led round-the-clock negotiations that resulted in a tentative deal with the nation's railroad workers, averting a strike that would have tanked the economy. In late September, Biden quickly mobilized a federal response to the devastation in Florida caused by Hurricane Ian. His actions reinforced the impression that government could respond effectively to crises. Even Biden's bitter political foe, Florida governor Ron DeSantis, seemed impressed; he temporarily called off his feud with the president. By October, Biden's approval rating had climbed as high as 48 percent, according to a CBS poll.

Yet, as Biden's fortunes improved, the country seemed more polarized than ever. The extremist elements within the MAGA movement had many foot soldiers, and their defeated but unrepentant leader, Donald Trump, was preparing to launch another presidential campaign.

Just how volatile the political climate had become was driven home dramatically on October 28, 2022. Early that morning, an intruder broke into Nancy Pelosi's house in San Francisco. Hoping to take the Democratic Speaker hostage, he instead encountered her husband Paul Pelosi and attacked him with a hammer, fracturing his skull, before police subdued him. Judging from his online screeds, David DePape, the alleged assailant, subscribed to QAnon conspiracies and the Big Lie that the 2020 election had been stolen.

The reaction of Republican leaders to Pelosi's assault spoke volumes about the decline of decency in the Trump era. Virginia governor Glenn Youngkin, after professing that "there's no room for violence anywhere," declared "we're going to send her [Nancy Pelosi] back to be with him in California." Kari Lake, running for governor of Arizona, joked about the lack of security at the Pelosi residence. Not to be outdone, Trump first broached the idea that the attack was suspicious; then, tossing red meat to a riled-up crowd, he called Nancy Pelosi an "animal." Trump's unabashed amorality had always been a national disgrace; now it was, if any more proof were needed after January 6, something more dangerous. Not only politicians but their families too seemed vulnerable to fanatical acolytes of a former president who glorified political violence.

As the midterm elections approached, many Democrats wondered: Where was Kamala Harris? Since her appearance at the EMILY's List dinner, where she'd blasted the Supreme Court's imminent overturning of *Roe v Wade*, the vice president seemed to have gone radio silent. Democrats who expected her to lead the charge publicly against the GOP's assault on women's rights were perplexed.

When Harris did get noticed, it was often for the wrong reason. At the DNC's Women's Leadership Forum in late September, a statement by the VP about the importance of equity in addressing climate change was pounced upon by Republicans as evidence that she was proposing to dole out hurricane relief on the basis of race rather than need. She'd said no such thing, but it became another Republican cudgel.

In late September 2022, the vice president offered to provide me written answers to questions I sent her by email.

"How different is the role of vice president from senator?" I asked her. "Have you been surprised by the level and intensity of scrutiny?"

"I have served in elected office for almost two decades," she replied, "—as district attorney of San Francisco, as attorney general of California, and as a United States senator. Each of those roles has come with scrutiny. Understanding the significant responsibility and impact of public office, the American people hold the leaders they elect to a high standard—as they should."

Harris declined to answer a question I sent her about "turmoil and morale problems among your staff going back to your time as California attorney general." And she also wouldn't say what her worst day had been as vice president. One of her best days, she said, was presiding over the confirmation of Ketanji Brown Jackson as associate justice of the Supreme Court. "Justice Jackson has spent her career fighting for equal justice and equal rights. Her experience, judgment, and wisdom will make our Court and our country stronger for decades to come. And, for decades to come, Judge Jackson will inspire the young leaders of our nation."

On the day of Justice Jackson's confirmation, Harris wrote a note to her teenage goddaughter Helena. "I told her about the profound sense of hope I felt that day—for her future and for our future as a nation. I also gave stationery to Senator Booker and Senator Warner— encouraging them to write their own letter to a young woman in their lives. These moments reinforce the belief that we must remind young people in our nation to dream with ambition, lead with conviction, and know that our nation needs their leadership."

But, of course, Justice Jackson had been seated too late to affect the Court's decision in *Dobbs v Jackson Women's Health Organization*, which overturned *Roe v Wade*, the ruling that had riled Harris and energized the Democratic base. "Now that the Court has followed through and abolished women's Constitutional right to an abortion," I asked her, "how critical will this issue be to the upcoming midterm elections? And how important is it for you to lead the administration's charge?"

The vice president replied, "Since the *Dobbs* decision, I have convened state legislators from across the country to discuss how we can work together to protect women's freedom to make decisions about their own bodies—without government interference. I have convened health care providers, constitutional law experts, faith leaders, state attorneys general, disability rights leaders, higher education leaders, advocates, students, and civil rights and reproductive rights leaders. You do not have to abandon your faith or your beliefs to agree that the government should not be making these most personal decisions for a woman."

She continued, "And the President and I are clear: This is part of a larger fight. The same extremist so-called leaders who are fighting to restrict a woman's right to make decisions about her own body are also fighting to restrict the freedom to vote, and to restrict LGBTQ+

rights. In this moment, fundamental principles of freedom and liberty are under assault. And all Americans must come together to defend those principles."

It was a rousing battle cry for Democrats as they prepared for the midterm elections—but it wasn't one they'd been hearing very often from Harris in public.

With the midterm elections looming, the conventional wisdom was that Biden's accomplishments and the fraught issue of abortion mattered far less to voters than the twin scourges of record inflation and rising crime. Moreover, history suggested an almost inevitable Democratic rout. First-term presidents were almost always punished at the midterm polls; in 1994, under Bill Clinton, the Democrats had lost 52 seats in the House and eight in the Senate; in 2010, under Barack Obama, they lost 63 and six, respectively. The imminent prospect of a "red wave" swamping Democrats had become a near certainty according to most pundits and reporters.

On the eve of the elections, *The New York Times* reported on Joe Biden's "faith" that he and the Democrats would do better than predicted:

It is not a faith shared by everyone, not even among Democrats, not even among his own advisers and allies, some of whom view the coming days with dread. After turning to Mr. Biden for a sense of normalcy two years ago following the turmoil of Mr. Trump, voters now appear poised to register discontent that he has not delivered it the way they expected . . .

The next day, *Politico* published a critical assessment of Ron Klain, suggesting that it was time for Biden's chief to move on. "Over the last two years," it reported, "some have come to view Klain as a micro-manager and grown frustrated with his certainty about his own political instincts. . . ."

———————

The early evening of November 8, 2022, election day, betrayed no hint of the unexpected political earthquake to come. In Florida, Republican governor Ron DeSantis routed his opponent, former Democratic governor Charlie Crist. Marco Rubio, the incumbent Republican senator, handily defeated his Democratic challenger, Val Demings. But as the night wore on, the narrative of a red wave quickly ebbed.

A sign that the tide was turning came in New Hampshire, where Democratic senator Maggie Hassan, thought to be in a dead heat with a Trump-backed challenger, Republican Ron Bolduc, won by nine points. A string of Democratic victories followed: Michigan's Democratic governor, Gretchen Whitmer, beat her Republican opponent, Tudor Dixon, by the same margin. New York governor Kathy Hochul, predicted to be in danger of losing to Republican Lee Zeldin, won by five points. Just after 1:00 a.m., networks projected that in the fiercely fought contest for Pennsylvania's U.S. Senate seat Lieutenant Governor John Fetterman had defeated Republican Dr. Mehmet Oz.

Biden had defied the axiom that first-term presidents get trounced in the midterms. Against the fierce headwinds of inflation and a low approval rating, Biden and the Democrats had turned in a historically strong performance. For forty years, in midterm elections, incumbent presidents had lost, on average, 28 seats in the House and four in the Senate. And yet Biden's party had succeeded in preserving a 50-50 split in the Senate by winning close races in Arizona and Nevada. Moreover, the Democrats could take control of the Senate (no longer needing Kamala Harris to break tie votes)—if Raphael Warnock defeated Republican Herschel Walker in a run-off election scheduled for December 6, 2022. Democrats even had an outside chance of keeping their House majority. More likely, Republicans would eke out a narrow advantage in that chamber.

At 1:16 a.m., late on election night, Ron Klain sent me an email. "Maybe we don't suck as much as people thought," he wrote. "Like maybe the nattering negatives who dumped to *Politico* were wrong!"

Klain and his team felt triumphant. A year earlier, Biden's White House chief had been on the verge of quitting; he'd stayed because he didn't want to leave Biden in the lurch as the 2022 midterms approached. Despite second-guessing from critics, Klain and his team had stubbornly stuck to their game plan; Biden's November 2 speech at Union Station, a full-throated defense of democracy, had been ridiculed by some pundits; CNN called Biden's remarks "head scratching." Voters, the pundits said, wanted Biden to focus on inflation. Likewise, Biden had been lambasted for talking about women's reproductive rights on the stump. And yet election exit polls showed that both concern for democracy and a backlash against the Supreme Court's *Dobbs* decision had been winning issues for Democrats.

In an email to me on November 9, Klain wrote: "Very proud. Proud of our team and the smart choices we made about where to fight and where to focus."

Election day had been a thorough repudiation of Trump. It was true that J. D. Vance, a Trump defender, had won a Senate seat in Ohio. But he was the exception to the rule; most Trump disciples in competitive races were crushed. Doug Mastriano, Pennsylvania's election-denying Republican candidate for governor, was trounced by Democrat Josh Shapiro, and even Republican Brian Kemp's return to office as Georgia's governor amounted to a rejection of Trump, since Kemp had resisted Trump's meddling and insults in the 2020 election. Nationwide, twelve election-denying candidates for governor were defeated; as of this writing, four days after the elections, a thirteenth, Arizona's Kari Lake, was locked in a race that was still too close to call. However that might turn out, Americans had overwhelmingly rejected candidates who stoked conspiracies about stolen elections. As Mike Barnicle put it on *Morning Joe*, voters chose "normal" over "crazy."

What would the midterm results mean for the rest of Joe Biden's first-term agenda?

Just before the elections, a White House adviser had told me: "We still have a big childcare problem in America. We still need to have universal pre-kindergarten. We still need to take care of seniors and disabled people and home care. And those three big parts of the president's agenda remain undone."

Given the new math in Congress, with Republicans likely to control the House, albeit narrowly, those parts of Biden's agenda would almost certainly remain undone. "Biden's ability, for the balance of his term, to get anything really big done is virtually nil," said Jack Watson, Jimmy Carter's former chief of staff. The president's child tax credit, passed as part of the American Rescue Plan, had reduced child poverty by 40 percent. But any hope of extending it was gone. "That was epochal," said Watson. "It was a New Deal–level achievement. And we're not going to get that. We're not going to get that kind of thing."

And yet, for Biden, divided government might have some advantages. In his first two years, the president had come under fire from progressive Democrats for falling short on their priorities, from childcare to voting rights. A robust Republican opposition might give Biden a useful foil, someone to point to if he failed to deliver on progressive priorities. In effect, Republican opposition could be a license to govern from the center, Biden's comfort zone.

Elections have consequences. A Republican House, likely under a new Speaker Kevin McCarthy, would end the work of the January 6 Committee—and in all probability launch investigations into the GOP's favorite bogeymen: Hunter Biden, Dr. Anthony Fauci, and perhaps even President Biden himself, with a partisan (and almost certainly futile) impeachment inquiry. Biden would have to guard against GOP attempts to hold raising the debt ceiling hostage to draconian cuts in Medicare, Social Security, and other Democratic priorities. Still, Democrats had dodged a bullet. A Republican takeover of the Senate could have made confirming judicial and high-level appointments almost impossible.

Given the GOP's disarray and the looming battle for control of the party between a wounded Donald Trump and an ascendant Ron DeSantis, Biden might well succeed in getting a few stray Republicans to sign on to some bipartisan legislation.

Like President Obama during his second term, Biden would have to rely heavily on executive orders to get things done. To do so, he'd need a strong new chief of staff to replace Ron Klain, who was preparing to depart after nearly two years in the most grueling and thankless job in government. Whoever his successor might be—Klain predicted the next chief could be a woman—he or she would have to help Biden govern in a more partisan climate than ever.

First on the new chief's to-do list would be executing the legislative accomplishments of the first two years. Those landmark achievements wouldn't really count until Americans felt the practical results in their lives, as when paying less for prescription drugs or buying an electric car. "We can have a big debate about whether or not what we've done in these two years is the most progressive agenda of any president or second most or whatever," said Klain. "But the ultimate measure of that is whether or not these things work."

In the remaining years of his first term, Joe Biden faced other daunting tests.

First, he would have to avoid a recession and bring inflation under control.

Second, he'd have to hold the U.S.-NATO alliance together, not only to ensure Ukraine's victory and Putin's defeat, but for the long run. As Ukraine's armed forces pushed Russian troops out of the eastern provinces they'd occupied since 2014, there was a real possibility that Russia's army would collapse. Putin was turning increasingly desperate. His war could end the way the Soviet occupation of Afghanistan had concluded in 1989, with ignominious retreat. But it was also possible that Putin would lash out recklessly with nuclear or unconventional weapons. Biden shared his CIA director Bill Burns's belief that, in the Russian autocrat's calculus, the stakes in Ukraine were existential. In early October 2022, Biden told a gathering of donors, "We have not faced the prospect of Armageddon since Kennedy and the Cuban Missile Crisis. We are trying to figure out: What is Putin's off-ramp?"

Biden was preoccupied with the possibility that Putin might use a nuclear weapon. Said Klain, "He's very focused on being prepared in case Putin does it, and trying to figure out what we can do to deter him from doing it." Putin seemed to be preparing world opinion for the unthinkable; he'd publicly declared that America's detonation of atomic bombs over Hiroshima and Nagasaki in 1945 had set a precedent that he had every right to follow. According to Klain, Biden was preparing for the worst: "We're on a path that could lead to that outcome. We don't know what Putin will do, but tragically, it's not impossible to imagine."

In its last televised hearing before the midterms, the House Select Committee on the January 6 Attack unveiled startling new evidence that the Secret Service had been aware of specific and credible threats to Vice President Mike Pence and others. One tipster had warned of lethal plots: "They think they will have a large enough group to march into DC armed and will outnumber the police so they can't be stopped. Their plan is to literally kill people." Trump's security detail knew that many in the crowd were armed—with weapons that included a Glock, a pistol, and a rifle. One message was especially chilling: "With so many weapons found so far, you wonder how many are unknown," one Secret Service employee wrote. "Could be sporty after dark."

And yet, armed with this intelligence, the Secret Service had done little or nothing to avert the violence of January 6. This fueled the perception that the agency required a thorough overhaul.

The committee also revealed new evidence that Trump had known full well that he'd lost the 2020 election. Trump himself had privately acknowledged his defeat. His communications director spoke of encountering the dejected president watching TV: "Can you believe I lost to this f—ing guy?" Trump said, referring to Biden.

"He had all of this information," concluded Liz Cheney, the Republican congresswoman from Wyoming and deputy chair of the committee, "but still he made the conscious choice to claim fraudulently that the election was stolen."

Biden's presidency would soon confront a momentous test. Presented with an overwhelming case by the January 6 House committee, and evidence gathered by his own investigators, Biden's attorney general, Merrick Garland, faced a decision. If he failed to indict Trump, millions of Americans would conclude that the American justice system was hollow, despite Garland's vow that no man was above the law. And if Garland chose to prosecute the former president, potentially triggering violent protests by his followers, Biden would have to find a way to prevent the country from being torn apart.

Ultimately, Biden's presidency would be defined not only by how he managed a worldwide pandemic, a war in Ukraine, rising inflation, and the storms of global warming; it would be judged by whether his attorney general chose to prosecute a former U.S. president who'd tried to strangle democracy.

Biden had won the first battle by defeating Trump in the 2020 presidential election. But victory wouldn't be complete, according to Klain, until "the candidate who gets the most votes in 2024 is inaugurated as president, which Joe Biden hopes and expects will be him."

Democracy had held by a thread in 2020. But there were no guarantees that it would hold again. It was all too possible that the actual winner in 2024 could be denied office by partisan extremists who refused to accept the result. Although at least twelve election-denying gubernatorial candidates were defeated in the midterms, some 160 believers in the Big Lie were elected to other state offices.

The peaceful transfer of power in 2020 had been in doubt until 11:59 a.m. on January 20, 2021, when Trump's deputy chief of staff Chris Liddell drove through the Southwest Gate, tipped his fedora to the Secret Service, and roared off. A minute later, control of the nuclear football and the military had passed to Trump's successor. Against considerable odds, Joe Biden had become president.

When I asked Klain to pick the best day of the last two years, he chose that one. "The fundamental challenge was: Was there going to be a Biden presidency?" he said. "We're proud of all the things we've done. But none of those things would have happened if we hadn't had the first day."

Chris Whipple
November 12, 2022
New York City

AUTHOR'S NOTE

Donald Rumsfeld, Gerald Ford's chief of staff, once told me that running the White House was like climbing into the cockpit of a disabled airplane and trying to land it safely. Now I know what he meant; chronicling a White House in real time is a lot like that. My destination was uncertain, the news cycle dizzying, and every time I set a flight path, unforeseen events would intrude—a COVID variant or a Russian invasion—and knock the plane off course. I was battling wind shear, wrestling with the controls, and just hoping to land safely.

My first challenge was persuading people in Joe Biden's White House to talk. Unlike the principals in my previous books, *The Gatekeepers* and *The Spymasters*, these officials weren't looking back on their careers from the safe haven of retirement. They were in the thick of political combat, loath to reveal secrets or stray off message. This made on-the-record conversations almost impossible. As a result, most of the interviews for this book were conducted on "deep background." That meant that I could use the information but agreed not to quote my sources directly without going back to them for permission.

Yet Biden's closest advisers were remarkably generous with me, on and off the record. I'm especially grateful to Ron Klain. He sat for regular interviews, despite the merciless demands of the chief of staff's job. Steve Ricchetti and Mike Donilon shared their experiences working with the president. So did Anita Dunn, Jen O'Malley Dillon, Bruce Reed, Cedric Richmond, Jen Psaki, Gina McCarthy, and Louisa Terrell. Jeff Zients and Andy Slavitt walked me through the challenges of tackling the most lethal public health crisis in a century. Labor Secretary Marty Walsh explained the politics of bipartisan infrastructure. General Mark Milley, chairman of the Joint Chiefs of Staff, gave me a master class on both the chaotic withdrawal from Afghanistan and the staunch resistance, aided by U.S.-supplied weapons and intelligence, of Ukraine's troops against Russian invaders.

For their riveting, previously untold stories about the fraught 2020 presidential transition, I'm indebted to Chris Liddell, former deputy chief of staff in the Trump White House; Ted Kaufman, Joe Biden's transition director and close friend; Bob Bauer, the Biden campaign's senior legal counsel; Mary Gibert, the GSA transition coordinator; Josh Bolten, George W. Bush's White House chief of staff; David Marchick, director of the Center for Presidential Transition at the Partnership for Public Service; Max Stier, CEO of the Partnership for Public Service; Robert O'Brien, Trump's national security adviser; his deputy, Mark Pottinger; and Martha Kumar, director of the White House Transition Project. The writer Michael Lewis, author of the superb *The Fifth Risk*, shared his insights into the federal agencies under Trump.

Not all power resides in the White House. Antony Blinken told me how he and his State Department colleagues worked tirelessly to rally NATO allies long before the invasion of Ukraine. Blinken also told me how, in his view, the Afghanistan evacuation was derailed by flawed intelligence. Speaking with me in his office high above Langley, Virginia, CIA director Bill Burns pushed back on this narrative, directly contradicting his longtime friend and colleague, insisting that the CIA had been clear-eyed about the fragility of the Afghan armed forces. Burns also gave me vivid accounts of his dramatic visits with Putin and Zelensky in the months before the Ukraine invasion. On a Zoom call from the American embassy in Paris, John Kerry, the SPEC, told me about the challenge of battling global warming during a time of war and upheaval in the energy markets.

The Fight of His Life wouldn't have been possible without help from key staffers at the White House and NSC. I'm especially grateful to Remi Yamamoto, senior adviser for communications in the office of the White House chief of staff. Thanks also to Rachel Palermo, Jasmine Williams, Adrienne Watson, Bill Rosa, Samantha Reposa, and Subhan Cheema.

I relied heavily on the wisdom of former White House chiefs of staff: Lyndon Johnson's Jim Jones; Gerald Ford's Dick Cheney; Jimmy Carter's Jack Watson; Ronald Reagan's James A. Baker III; Bill Clinton's Thomas H. "Mack" McLarty, Leon Panetta, Erskine Bowles, and John Podesta; George W. Bush's Andrew Card and Joshua Bolten; and Barack Obama's Rahm Emanuel, Bill Daley, Jack Lew, and Denis McDonough; and Donald Trump's Reince Priebus. I'll always treasure my friendship with the late Kenneth Duberstein, Reagan's final chief of staff. Sadly, Ken died of a rare kidney disease in 2022.

While writing about the U.S. withdrawal from Afghanistan and the Ukraine invasion, I called on some giants in the world of national security: the aforementioned Leon Panetta, the former CIA director and defense secretary; Fiona Hill, the renowned Putin expert; James Clapper and John Negroponte, former DNIs; Admiral James Stavridis, the former NATO Supreme Allied Commander; Richard Clarke, counterterrorism adviser to Bill Clinton and George W. Bush; Richard Armitage, deputy to Secretary of State Colin Powell; Frank Wisner Jr., the veteran diplomat; Anthony "Tony" Lake, Bill Clinton's national security adviser; Jeremy Bash, former chief of staff at the CIA and Pentagon; Ronald Neumann, former U.S. ambassador to Afghanistan; Paul Pillar, former National Intelligence Officer for the Near East and South Asia at the CIA; Vali Nasr, the Majid Khadduri Professor of International Affairs and Middle East Studies at the Johns Hopkins School of Advanced International Studies; and Ted Wittenstein, Executive Director, International Security Studies, at Yale's Jackson Institute for Global Affairs.

For their insights into Joe Biden, I'm indebted to his friends and colleagues: Christopher Dodd, the former senator from Connecticut; Representative James Clyburn (D-SC); New Jersey senator Cory Booker; Connecticut senator Richard Blumenthal; New Hampshire senator Jeanne Shaheen; Virginia senator Mark Warner; Eric Adams, mayor of New York City. I also want to thank Jay Carney, Obama's White House press secretary; Tom Brokaw, former anchor of NBC's *Nightly News*; Bob Schieffer, former anchor of CBS News's *Face the Nation*; political historian Jonathan Alter; John Dickerson of CBS's *60 Minutes*; and Mary Hager, executive producer of CBS's *Face the Nation*.

At the State Department, Ned Price, Bill Russo, and Megan Apper were indispensable, as was Whitney Smith in the office of the SPEC. I leaned heavily on the expertise of Michael Carpenter, U.S. ambassador to the OSCE; Karen Donfried, assistant secretary of state for European and Eurasian affairs; Derek Chollet, State Department counselor; Julianne Smith, U.S. permanent representative to NATO; Jonathan Pershing, deputy climate envoy; Sue Biniaz, deputy legal adviser; and

Tom Sullivan, deputy chief of staff for policy. Todd Stern, Obama's former climate envoy, gave me a crash course on climate policy. At the NSC, I learned a great deal from Yohannes Abraham, chief of staff, and Emily Horne, the spokesperson.

In the vice president's office, I'm grateful to Chief of Staff Tina Flournoy, Communications Director Jamal Simmons, Deputy Director Herbie Ziskend, National Security Adviser Philip Gordon, Dean Lieberman, Josh Hsu, and Rohini Kosoglu.

In the First Lady's office, I am indebted to communications director Elizabeth Alexander, press secretary Michael LaRosa, and senior adviser Anthony Bernal.

At the CIA, Susan Buikema-Miller and Tammy Thorp were invaluable. Dr. Marcella Nunez-Smith and Luciana Borio shared their experiences on the White House pandemic response teams of both Donald Trump and Joe Biden.

Congress has a Gang of Eight; while writing this book, I had my own superb "Gang of Seven"—friends and shrewd political observers who read chapters-in-progress and gave me notes. They included the aforementioned Jack Watson; David Hume Kennerly, the Pulitzer Prize–winning photographer (who also contributed two superb photographs to this book); David Martin, Pentagon correspondent for CBS News; Bruce Riedel, former CIA Middle East analyst; Greg Zorthian, former president of the *Financial Times* in America and Worldwide General Manager of *Time*, and my friend since freshman year at Yale; Nancy Collins, interviewer extraordinaire for *Vanity Fair* and ABC News *PrimeTime Live*; and Michael Jacobson, former senior vice president of Lazard Frères and my first editor at Yale's *New Journal*.

As she always does, Lisa Queen wore four hats—as my literary agent, early chapter reader, reality therapist, and good friend. My editor at Scribner, Rick Horgan, was a superb editor and air traffic controller, talking me in for a landing as I careened toward the runway. Nan Graham, Scribner's publisher, and Colin Harrison, the editor-in-chief, never lost faith despite a white-knuckle schedule. Copy editor Barbara Wild and proofreaders Lisa Nicholas and Kristen Strange saved me from countless embarrassments. Lisa Rivlin, the legal vetter, was a pleasure to work with. Brian Belfiglio, Scribner's publicist, will undoubtedly spread the word far and wide. Chatwalee Phoungbut took beautiful care of my website, chriswhipple.net. Scribner's Olivia Bernhard, Mark LaFlaur, and Beckett Rueda made sure the book came together despite the chaos inflicted on the publishing business by the pandemic.

A tip of my hat goes to good friends who supplied wisdom and encouragement along the way: Jules and Jacqueline Naudet; Gedeon Naudet and Aude Coquatrix; Josh Getlin and Heidi Evans; Alex Getlin; David and Liz Chidekel; Trip McCrossin; Donna Parsons; Susan Zirinsky and Joe Peyronnin; Peter Baker and Susan Glasser; David and Rachel Turnley; Peter Turnley; Tom Powers; Jonathan Alter; Harry and Gigi Benson; Don Dahler; Charles Tremayne and Caroline Grist; Ward and Susan Pennebaker; Jonathan Larsen; Caroline Borge Keenan; Bruce McIntosh; David Friend and Nancy Paulsen; Christopher Buckley; Milt and Judy Kass; John Hutchins; KC Ramsay; and Jeff VanNest.

The Fight of His Life was a family affair. My brother-in-law Terry Marr, nieces Abby and Melissa, and their significant others, David and Gary, endured endless Trump and Biden war stories. My son, Sam Whipple, consumed by his own project—producing the documentary film *January 6*—never complained about all the tennis matches we missed. Finally, as with my previous books, *The Gatekeepers* and

The Spymasters, two people above all were indispensable. My sister Ann Marr provided brilliant copyediting, editorial wisdom, love, and encouragement. And my wife, Cary, to whom this book is dedicated, made everything possible: as editor, researcher, transcriber, photo editor, fact-checker—and, more important, loving companion.

NOTES

INTRODUCTION

2 *"red lights flashing"*: Author interview with William Burns, April 8, 2022.

3 *"edgy, measured way"*: Author interview with William Burns, April 8, 2022.

4 *"what will stop it from invading another country?"*: Author's written interview with President Joe Biden, September 19, 2022.

4 *"Blood and Soil"*: Claudia Rankine, "Was Charlottesville the Exception or the Rule?," *New York Times*, September 13, 2017.

4 *"very fine people on both sides"*: Inae Oh, "Trump Defends Claim That There Were 'Very Fine People on Both Sides' of White Supremacist Rally," *Mother Jones*, April 26, 2019.

5 *"This was dangerous"*: Author interview with Mike Donilon, June 29, 2021.

5 *"battle for the soul of the nation"*: Joe Biden, "We Are Living through a Battle for the Soul of This Nation," *The Atlantic*, August 27, 2017.

5 *"Get up"*: John M. Broder, "Father's Tough Life an Inspiration for Biden," *New York Times*, October 23, 2008.

CHAPTER ONE: WHAT WILL YOU DO IF HE LOSES?

7 *"Want to go for a walk?"*: Author interview with Ted Kaufman, July 27, 2021.

8 *"We were back and forth":* Author interview with Ted Kaufman, July 27, 2021.

8 *"If you went to a corporate CEO":* Author interview with Ted Kaufman, August 10, 2021.

9 *"in suspense":* Donald Trump, Presidential Debate, University of Nevada, October 19, 2016.

10 *"the most beautiful ark that never sailed":* Author interview with Christopher "Chris" Liddell, November 14, 2021.

10 *"I thought they'd never cooperate":* Author interview with Ted Kaufman, July 27, 2021.

11 *"what are your plans":* Author interview with David Marchick, August 15, 2021.

11 *"I guess we've got to figure that out":* Author interview with David Marchick, August 15, 2021.

11 *"you need to land this plane":* Author interview with David Marchick, August 15, 2021.

11 *"We had a plan":* Author interview with Ted Kaufman, July 27, 2021.

11 *"Big Fucking Deal":* Andrew Prokop, "Biden's Reconciliation Bill Would Be a Big Fucking Deal," *Vox*, August 9, 2021.

12 *"the greatest public health crisis in a hundred years":* Author interview with Jeffrey Zients, July 2, 2021.

12 *"I'm too old for this":* Author interview with Ted Kaufman, July 27, 2021.

13 *"deadly stuff":* Quint Forgey and Matthew Choi, "'This Is Deadly Stuff': Tapes Show Trump Acknowledging Virus Threat in February," *Politico*, September 9, 2020.

14 *"slim suit crowd":* Maureen Dowd, "Opinion: He Went to Jared," *New York Times*, April 4, 2020.

15 *"We had to be ready":* Author interview with Jeffrey Zients, July 2, 2021.

15 *"Talk to CDC":* Author interview with Marcella Nunez-Smith, August 5, 2021.

15 *"I think you will see by June":* Brett Samuels, "Kushner Predicts Much

of the Country Will Be 'Back to Normal' in June," *The Hill*, April 29, 2020.

CHAPTER TWO: YOU NEED TO LAND THIS PLANE

16 *"I could just get on with doing my job"*: Author interview with Christopher Liddell, November 14, 2021.

16 *"It was incredibly complicated"*: Author interview with Ted Kaufman, August 10, 2021.

17 *"I heard that you guys were having problems"*: Author interview with Ron Klain, March 6, 2021.

17 *"Let's make sure that we play this by the book"*: Author interview with Christopher Liddell, August 6, 2021.

18 *"Liddell was our conduit"*: Author interview with Mary Gibert, September 9, 2021.

18 *"Chris would have been shot"*: Author interview with David Marchick, August 15, 2021.

18 *"responsibility caucus"*: Author interview with David Marchick, August 15, 2021.

18 *"unconventional challenges"*: Author interview with Ted Kaufman, July 27, 2021.

18 *"we stopped at seventy"*: Author interview with Ted Kaufman, July 27, 2021.

18 *"Recession turns into a Depression"*: Author interview with Ted Kaufman, July 27, 2021.

18 *"government response"*: Author interview with Ted Kaufman, July 27, 2021.

19 *"Is it something we were concerned about"*: Author interview with Ted Kaufman, July 27, 2021.

19 *"I'll have to see"*: Donald Trump, *FOX News Sunday*, Fox News, July 19, 2020.

19 *"There won't be a transfer"*: Tommy Beer, "Here's Everything Trump

Has Said about Refusing to Give Up Power," *Forbes*, September 24, 2020.

19 *"Memorandum of Understanding":* Author interview with Mary Gibert, September 9, 2021.

19 *"I figured* that's *never going to happen":* Author interview with Ted Kaufman, August 20, 2021.

20 *"one of my prized possessions":* Author interview with Ted Kaufman, July 27, 2021.

20 *"Ascertainment is not a ceremonial process":* Author interview with Mary Gibert, August 9, 2021.

21 *"We had six hundred lawyers":* Author interview with Bob Bauer, December 17, 2021.

21 *"Remember that dinner we had":* Author interview with David Marchick, August 15, 2021.

21 *"Liddell was in meetings":* Author interview with David Marchick, August 15, 2021.

22 *"You could see the talent":* Author interview with Thomas F. "Mack" McLarty, February 26, 2021.

22 *an overgrown Model U.N. student:* Mark Leibovich, "The Ascension of Ron Klain," *New York Times*, July 18, 2021.

22 *"Ebola czar":* Jennifer Epstein, "Obama Selects Klain as Ebola Czar," *Politico*, October 17, 2014.

22 *"Look, we've got to decide":* Author interview with Ron Klain, March 16, 2021.

23 *carried them for him:* Edward-Isaac Dovere, "The Mastermind behind Biden's No-Drama Approach to Trump," *The Atlantic*, November 30, 2020.

24 *"It's been a little hard":* Leibovich, "The Ascension of Ron Klain."

24 *"shadow agency":* Author interview with David Marchick, August 15, 2021.

24 *"Biden transition's innovation":* Author interview with David Marchick, August 15, 2021.

25 *"surge":* Peter Weber, "Joe Biden said he consistently opposed Obama's

Afghanistan surge. Obama alumni says he's right," *yahoo!news*, December 19, 2019.

25 *"jammed"*: Kevin Liptak, Jeff Zeleny, and Betsy Klein, "The Presidents' Club Returns with Biden Restoring Consultations That Trump Dismissed," CNNPolitics, April 29, 2021.

26 *"This was no accident"*: George Packer, "Joe Biden's Saigon," *The Atlantic*, January 31, 2022.

27 *"Oh, sure"*: Author interview with Ted Kaufman, September 16, 2021.

27 *"Our whole thing was basically a legal strategy"*: Author interview with Ron Klain, March 16, 2021.

CHAPTER THREE: WE'LL ALWAYS HAVE YOUR BACK

29 *"A lot of people said Ronald Reagan was an idiot"*: Author interview with Joshua Bolten, February 19, 2021.

29 *"This is one of those moments"*: Author interview with James Jones, April 2, 2021.

30 *"I see in him some of the things that I couldn't do"*: Author interview with James Jones, April 2, 2021.

30 *"I can tell when he's tired"*: Author interview with James Jones, April 2, 2021.

30 *"Everyone's going to want Biden to do this"*: Author interview with James Jones, April 2, 2021.

30 *"I am not going to exploit"*: Ronald Reagan, Presidential Debate, Kansas City Municipal Auditorium, October 21, 1984.

31 *"he doesn't have any discipline"*: Author interview with Mike Donilon, June 29, 2021.

31 *"You got on an elevator with him"*: Author interview with Bob Schieffer, July 14, 2021.

31 *"Go back and look at his speeches"*: Author interview with Ted Kaufman, July 27, 2021.

32 *"The role of team leader"*: Author interview with Jack Watson, February 16, 2021.

32 *"personnel director"*: Elaine Woo, "Nancy Reagan Dies in Los Angeles at 94: Former First Lady was President Reagan's Closest Advisor," *Los Angeles Times*, March 6, 2016.

34 *"That is the day he became president"*: Andrew Card, *Your World with Neil Cavuto*, Fox News, September 11, 2020.

34 *"institutions of our democracy"*: Author interview with Andrew Card, March 24, 2021.

34 *"What gets to the president"*: Author interview with Joshua Bolten, February 19, 2021.

36 *"It's now or never"*: Author interview with Jack Watson, February 16, 2021.

37 *"Be there, will be wild!"*: Donald Trump, Twitter, December 19, 2020, 1:42 a.m.

CHAPTER FOUR: OUR OWN VERSION OF HELL

38 *"I woke up in the morning"*: Author interview with Christopher Liddell, August 6, 2021.

39 *"If Pence had gone completely rogue"*: Author interview with Bob Bauer, December 17, 2021.

39 *"We were watching the riot build"*: Author interview with Bruce Reed, July 3, 2021.

40 *"an attack on the place he loved"*: Author interview with Bruce Reed, July 3, 2021.

40 *"Camp Auschwitz"*: Melissa Eddy, "Amid the Rampage at the U.S. Capitol, a Sweatshirt Stirs Troubling Memories," *New York Times*, January 8, 2021.

40 *"We were really sick at heart"*: Author interview with Ron Klain, March 16, 2021.

40 *"And the next thing I knew"*: Author interview with Christopher Liddell, August 6, 2021.

40 *"Oh my God"*: Author interview with Christopher Liddell, August 6, 2021.

41 *"'Holy Hell'"*: Author interview with Christopher Liddell, August 6, 2021.

41 *"Mike Pence didn't have the courage"*: Donald Trump, Twitter, January 6, 2021, 2:24 p.m.

41 *"stolen election"*: Hayley Miller, "Trump Claims Election 'Rigged' or 'Stolen' over 100 Times Ahead of Capitol Riot," *HuffPost*, February 9, 2021.

42 *"At this hour, our democracy is under unprecedented assault"*: Joe Biden, Remarks at the Queen Theater, Wilmington, DE, January 6, 2021.

42 *"I know your pain"*: Donald Trump, Remarks at the White House, January 6, 2021.

43 *"My biggest fear"*: Author interview with Mary Gibert, September 9, 2021.

43 *"And he's not a weepy kind of guy"*: Author interview with Joshua Bolten, November 11, 2021.

43 *"'Look, if you leave'"*: Author interview with Joshua Bolten, November 11, 2021.

43 *"I have enormous sympathy for your situation"*: Author interview with Joshua Bolten, November 11, 2021.

44 *"I have disagreed with many things"*: Author interview with Joshua Bolten, November 11, 2021.

44 *"it's even more critical that we stay"*: Author interview with Christopher Liddell, August 6, 2021.

44 *"I'm going to do what you suggest"*: Author interview with Joshua Bolten, November 11, 2021.

45 *"I thought there would be a lot of noise"*: Author interview with Christopher Liddell, August 6, 2021.

45 *"Who knows what he might do?"*: Bob Woodward and Robert Costa, *Peril* (New York: Simon & Schuster, 2021), xxii.

45 *"This is deep"*: Woodward and Costa, *Peril*, xxiii.

46 *"deplorables"*: Katelyn Newman, "Trump Tweets Thanks to 'Deplorables,'" *US News & World Report*, November 8, 2017.

46 *"Knock the crap out of them"*: Donald Trump, Campaign rally in Cedar Rapids, IA, February 1, 2016.

46 *"patriots"*: Heather Digby Parton, "Trump's Signal to His Followers Is Clear: Violence and Chaos Are My Only Hope," *Salon*, August 31, 2020.

48 *"potato"*: Erika Neddenien, "We Tracked Down the Kid Vice President Quayle Made Misspell 'Potato,'" *BuzzFeed News*, September 11, 2019.

48 *"political pundits have made fun of Dan Quayle"*: Author interview with Bob Bauer, December 17, 2021.

49 *"football"*: David E. Sanger and William J. Broad, "Who's Got the Nuclear Football? Actually, the Question Is When Biden Gets 'the Biscuit,'" *New York Times*, January 19, 2021.

50 *"There were just all kinds of efforts"*: Author interview with David Marchick, August 15, 2021.

50 *"It's hard to imagine it could get much nastier"*: Author interview with Mary Gibert, September 9, 2021.

50 *"The entire White House staff turns over"*: Author interview with Joshua Bolten, November 11, 2021.

50 *"We all went through our own version of hell"*: Author interview with Christopher Liddell, August 6, 2021.

CHAPTER FIVE: LET'S GET TO WORK

52 *"to absorb pain and suffering"*: Joe Biden, "Joe Biden Remembers Where He Was the Day John Kennedy Was Assassinated," *Esquire*, November 18, 2013.

53 "Shockingly *gracious*": Author interview with Ron Klain, June 12, 2021.

53 *"It's from him to me"*: Author interview with Ron Klain, June 12, 2021.

54 *"he's got many different layers":* Author phone call with Jared Kushner, July 18, 2021.

54 *"America is at an inflection point":* Author interview with President Joe Biden, September 19, 2022.

56 *"We can withstand the assault":* Author interview with President Joe Biden, September 19, 2022.

57 *"Our democracy isn't perfect":* Author interview with President Joe Biden, September 19, 2022.

57 *"What's happening in our country today is not normal":* Author interview with President Joe Biden, September 19, 2022.

58 *"the most experienced collective team":* Author interview with James Stavridis, August 9, 2021.

59 *"Let's get to work":* Author interview with Ron Klain, June 12, 2021.

CHAPTER SIX: WHEN IS THIS GOING TO CREST?

61 *"Ron is his strategic supergenius":* Author interview with Jen Psaki, September 24, 2021.

62 *"We have more women in the West Wing":* Author interview with Jen O'Malley Dillon, May 13, 2022.

63 *"He is completely comfortable with women":* Author interview with Jen Psaki, September 24, 2021.

63 *"have a seat":* Author interview with Jen Psaki, September 24, 2021.

63 *"I want you to feel":* Author interview with Jen Psaki, September 24, 2021.

63 *"There are strong women leaders here":* Author interview with Jen O'Malley Dillon, May 13, 2022.

64 *"the bubble":* David Jackson, "Book: Isolated Obama Tries to Break White House 'Bubble,'" *USA Today*, May 1, 2013.

64 *"the tomb":* Bob Woodward and Robert Costa, *Peril* (New York: Simon & Schuster, 2021), 407.

64 *"former guy":* Oma Seddiq, "Biden Says He's 'Tired of Talking' about

'Former Guy' Trump in First Town Hall as President," *Business Insider*, February 16, 2021.

67 *"It was like building a house":* Author interview with Jeffrey Zients, July 2, 2021.

67 *"a lot of time, energy, and creativity":* Author interview with Jeffrey Zients, July 2, 2021.

68 *"to act with urgency":* Author interview with Jeffrey Zients, July 2, 2021.

68 *"whatever we can to overwhelm this problem":* Author interview with Jeffrey Zients, July 2, 2021.

68 *"I know this is going to be hard":* Author interview with Jeffrey Zients, April 14, 2022.

68 *"What Jeff brings to the table":* Author interview with Ron Klain, June 12, 2021.

69 *"equity":* Executive Order on Ensuring an Equitable Pandemic Response and Recovery, January 21, 2021.

69 *"We were talking about masking":* Author interview with Marcella Nunez-Smith, August 5, 2021.

69 *"We were racing against the variant":* Author interview with Andy Slavitt, October 14, 2021.

70 *"we discovered that there really was no plan":* Author interview with Jeffrey Zients, April 14, 2022.

70 *"The rest of the world":* Author interview with Andy Slavitt, October 14, 2021.

70 *"We're going to order everything of everything":* Author interview with Ron Klain, July 18, 2021.

71 *"They were shipping doses":* Author interview with Jeffrey Zients, July 2, 2021.

71 *"It wasn't surprising to me at all":* Author interview with Andy Slavitt, October 14, 2021.

71 *"spent a lot of time thinking about getting vaccines":* Author interview with Marcella Nunez-Smith, August 5, 2021.

71 *"It was about ensuring enough supply"*: Author interview with Jeffrey Zients, July 2, 2021.

71 *"Our daily rhythm was defined by two reports"*: Author interview with Andy Slavitt, October 14, 2021.

72 *"There was a woman who posted a picture"*: Author interview with Andy Slavitt, October 14, 2021.

72 *"It was a very big deal"*: Author interview with Ron Klain, March 16, 2021.

73 *"There were several gut-check moments"*: Author interview with Ron Klain, March 16, 2021.

73 *"There was an off-ramp"*: Author interview with Ron Klain, March 16, 2021.

74 *"It was very clear"*: Author interview with Andy Slavitt, October 14, 2021.

74 *"that's a double-edged sword"*: Author interview with Andy Slavitt, October 14, 2021.

74 *"He was just thrilled"*: Author interview with Ron Klain, July 18, 2021.

75 *"Biden and his advisers have proven"*: Susan B. Glasser, "It's Morning (and Mourning) in Biden's America," *The New Yorker*, March 12, 2021.

75 *"we are beating the virus"*: Joe Biden, Remarks at the White House, July 4, 2021.

75 *"On July 2 we had a good jobs report"*: Author interview with Ron Klain, July 18, 2021.

76 *"We were getting data"*: Author interview with Jeffrey Zients, April 14, 2022.

76 *"fastest-growing respiratory illness of all time"*: Author interview with Andy Slavitt, October 14, 2021.

CHAPTER SEVEN: IT'S GOING TO BE AWFUL TO WATCH

77 *"I have to go now"*: Joe Biden, *Promises to Keep* (New York: Random House, 2007), Kindle location 5706.

78 *"he reached the conclusion"*: Author interview with Ron Klain, September 11, 2021.

78 *"surge"*: Peter Baker, "How Obama Came to Plan for 'Surge' in Afghanistan," *New York Times*, December 5, 2009.

78 *"once-in-a-generation intellect"*: Mark Leibovich, "Jake Sullivan, Biden's Adviser, a Figure of Fascination and Schadenfreude," *New York Times*, December 1, 2021.

79 *"potential future president"*: Leibovich, "Jake Sullivan, Biden's Adviser," *New York Times*, December 1, 2021.

79 *"midwestern wholesomeness"*: Author interview with Tali Farhadian Weinstein, December 23, 2021.

79 *"his sense of responsibility"*: Author interview with Tali Farhadian Weinstein, December 23, 2021.

80 *"If Dean Acheson came back to life"*: Author interview with James Stavridis, August 9, 2021.

80 *"Ideas are great"*: Author interview with Richard Armitage, December 6, 2021.

81 *"he or she is accountable for everything"*: Author interview with Richard Clarke, December 13, 2021.

82 *"pull the plug"*: Author interview with James Stavridis, August 9, 2021.

82 *"Leave them there"*: Author interview with James Stavridis, August 9, 2021.

82 *"We didn't pull them out"*: Author interview with James Stavridis, August 9, 2021.

82 *"I think it's strategically important"*: Author interview with James Stavridis, August 9, 2021.

83 *"It's time to go home"*: Author interview with James Stavridis, August 9, 2021.

83 *"very fair in airing all the views"*: Author interview with Mark Milley, May 27, 2022.

84 *"it's cost, benefit, risk"*: Author interview with Mark Milley, May 27, 2021.

84 *"We can't beat the Taliban"*: Author interview with Bruce Riedel, September 14, 2021.

85 *"we train foreign armies on the American plan"*: Author interview with Anthony Lake, March 14, 2022.

86 *"Did they not see it?"*: Author interview with Ronald Neumann, December 6, 2021.

86 *"'what are you doing?'"*: Author interview with Andrew Card, August 19, 2021.

86 *"in quadraphonic sound"*: Bob Woodward and Robert Costa, *Peril* (New York: Simon & Schuster, 2021), 376.

86 *"Biden just wanted to get out"*: Author interview with Bruce Riedel, September 14, 2021.

87 *"the oxygen for international policy debates"*: Author interview with James Stavridis, August 9, 2021.

CHAPTER EIGHT: THE HARDEST OF HARD DAYS

88 *"I have concluded that it's time"*: Joe Biden, Remarks at the White House, April 14, 2021.

89 *"the enemy of the American people"*: Donald Trump, Twitter, April 5, 2019.

89 *"confident"*: Katie Shepherd, "Biden Apologizes for Snapping at CNN Reporter over Putin Questions: 'I Shouldn't Have Been Such a Wise Guy,'" *Washington Post*, June 17, 2021.

89 *"He's always very connected"*: Author interview with Ron Klain, September 11, 2021.

90 *"The weight of it"*: Author interview with Ron Klain, September 11, 2021.

90 *"The drawdown is proceeding":* Joe Biden, Remarks at the White House, July 8, 2021.

90 *"Zero":* Joe Biden, Remarks at the White House, July 8, 2021.

91 *"worst-case prediction":* Author interview with Antony Blinken, April 20, 2022.

92 *"I asked one of the Green Berets":* Email from David Martin to the author, September 13, 2021.

93 *"We're going to fight to the death":* Zachary Basu, "Blinken on Afghanistan: 'We Inherited a Deadline. We Did Not Inherit a Plan,'" Axios, September 13, 2021.

93 *"Absolutely, totally":* Author interview with Mark Milley, May 27, 2022.

95 *"I had the same feeling":* Author interview with Leon Panetta, August 19, 2021.

95 *Bay of Pigs:* Leon Panetta, *Inside Politics*, CNN, August 16, 2021.

96 *"as intense as anything I've seen":* Author interview with William Burns, April 8, 2022.

97 *"We held our breath every day":* Author interview with Ron Klain, September 11, 2021.

97 *"the crowds weren't quite as numerous":* Author interview with William Burns, April 8, 2022.

97 *"We just got a report":* Author interview with Ron Klain, October 30, 2021.

98 *"The worst that can happen":* Mark Leibovich, "Jake Sullivan, Biden's Adviser, a Figure of Fascination and Schadenfreude," *New York Times*, December 1, 2021.

98 *"It was awful":* Author interview with William Burns, April 8, 2022.

98 *"It wasn't that people were crying":* Author interview with Jen Psaki, September 24, 2021.

98 *"I've had some horrible days":* Author interview with Mark Milley, May 27, 2022.

99 *"You could just feel the weight":* Author interview with Jen Psaki, September 24, 2021.

99 *"Tough week":* Email from Ron Klain to the author, August 29, 2021.

99 *"There are a lot of hard days on this job"*: Author interview with President Joe Biden, September 19, 2022.

100 *"righteous"*: Eric Schmitt, "Military Analysis Raises Questions about Deadly Drone Strike in Kabul," *New York Times*, September 5, 2021.

100 *"dignified transfer"*: Jackie Salo and Jorge Fitz-Gibbon, "Biden Attends Ceremony for Fallen 13 Troops Killed in Afghanistan," *New York Post*, August 29, 2021.

101 *"You cannot kneel on our flag"*: Matt Viser, "'Don't You Ever Forget That Name': Biden's Tough Meeting with Grieving Relatives," *Washington Post*, August 30, 2021.

101 *"I hope you burn in hell"*: Viser, "'Don't You Ever Forget That Name.'"

101 *"a deep, misunderstood sadness"*: Author interview with Jen Psaki, September 24, 2021.

101 *"That's deeply personal"*: Author interview with Jen Psaki, September 24, 2021.

101 *"This is what being president is"*: Author interview with Ron Klain, September 11, 2021.

CHAPTER NINE: ELEVEN DAYS IN AUGUST

102 *"We were genuinely surprised"*: Author interview with Ron Klain, September 11, 2021.

102 *"the game may be over"*: Ronald E. Neumann, James Cunningham, Hugo Llorens, Richard Olson, and Earl Anthony Wayne, "Afghanistan: What Now to Avoid Disaster?," *New Atlanticist/Atlantic Council*, May 11, 2021.

102 *"whether it was eleven days or a month and a half"*: Author interview with Richard Armitage, December 6, 2021.

103 *"we had NATO fighting with us"*: Author interview with Leon Panetta, August 19, 2021.

103 *"The status quo of April, May 2021"*: Author interview with Bruce Riedel, September 14, 2021.

104 *"We began pulling out the troops"*: Author interview with Mark Milley, May 27, 2022.

104 *"The contractors weren't going to stay"*: Author interview with Mark Milley, May 27, 2022.

104 *"We did our best"*: Author interview with Richard Clarke, December 13, 2021.

104 *"people were telling the president what he wanted to hear"*: Author interview with Leon Panetta, August 19, 2021.

105 *"it was Leon's army"*: Author interview with Ron Klain, September 11, 2021.

105 *"never gotten a bad grade"*: David Ignatius, *Morning Joe*, MSNBC, August 19, 2021.

106 *"That Sullivan may be too nice a guy"*: Author interview with Richard Armitage, December 6, 2021.

106 *"what I see in Jake is sadness"*: Author interview with Ron Klain, December 18, 2021.

107 *"I don't believe it was"*: Author interview with William Burns, April 8, 2022.

107 *"it was a pretty sober analysis"*: Author interview with William Burns, April 8, 2022.

108 *"there was an intelligence assessment that proved to be wrong"*: Author interview with Antony Blinken, April 20, 2022.

108 *"The intelligence I saw predicted months"*: Author interview with Mark Milley, May 27, 2022.

110 *"The larger point is this"*: Author interview with Antony Blinken, April 20, 2022.

110 *"There's a lack of appreciation"*: Author interview with John Negroponte, December 1, 2021.

110 *"lily pads"*: Lara Jakes, "At Every Step, Afghans Coming to America Encounter Stumbling Blocks," *New York Times*, December 21, 2021.

111 *"the buck stops with me"*: Aaron Blake, "Biden Says the 'Buck Stops with Me'—While Pinning Blame on Trump and Many Afghans," *Washington Post*, August 16, 2021.

111 *"an extraordinary success"*: Joe Biden, Remarks at the White House, August 31, 2021.

111 *"Mission: Very, Very Hard"*: Email from James Stavridis to the author, August 19, 2021.

112 *"he just wasn't going to do that"*: Author interview with Ron Klain, September 11, 2021.

112 *"It's the clearest and most painful reminder"*: Author interview with President Joe Biden, September 19, 2022.

CHAPTER TEN: A WORK IN PROGRESS

113 *"different background and experience"*: Author interview with Anita Dunn, March 19, 2021.

114 *"a deepening of the relationship"*: Author interview with Tina Flournoy, April 12, 2021.

114 *"the synergy between the president and the vice president"*: Johnnetta Cole, *The Last Word with Lawrence O'Donnell*, MSNBC, July 8, 2021.

114 *"it always surprises me"*: Author interview with Ron Klain, July 18, 2021.

115 *"And that little girl was me"*: Kamala Harris, Presidential Debate, Adrienne Arsht Center for the Performing Arts, Miami, June 27, 2019.

115 *"but she wasn't wrong"*: Author interview with Jonathan Alter, September 2, 2021.

116 *"the most insignificant office"*: Eugene J. McCarthy, "The Crown Prince," *New York Times*, August 17, 1972.

116 *"You die, I'll fly"*: Steve Hendrix, "Why Bush and Obama's Eulogies of John McCain Were Historic," *Washington Post*, September 1, 2018.

119 *"it's sick"*: Joe Biden, Remarks at the White House, March 25, 2021.

122 *"It is obvious"*: Ed O'Keefe, "Guatemala President Says Kamala Harris 'Doesn't Hold Back' Ahead of Immigration Talks," cbsnews.com, June 6, 2021.

122 *"You haven't been to the border"*: Lester Holt interview with Kamala Harris, *NBC Nightly News*, NBC, June 8, 2021.

123 *"my focus is dealing with the root causes":* Lester Holt interview with Kamala Harris, *NBC Nightly News*, NBC, June 8, 2021.

124 *"sometimes you will strike out":* Author interview with Ron Klain, December 18, 2021.

124 *"Biden is a good guy":* Joe Biden, Remarks at the White House, March 25, 2021.

125 *"an abusive environment":* Christopher Cadelago, Daniel Lippman, and Eugene Daniels, "'Not a Healthy Environment': Kamala Harris' Office Rife with Dissent," *Politico*, June 30, 2021.

126 *"Staff Exodus Reignites Questions":* Cleve R. Wootson Jr. and Tyler Pager, "A Kamala Harris Staff Exodus Reignites Questions about Her Leadership Style—and Her Future Ambitions," *Washington Post*, December 4, 2021.

126 *"Certainly, that's happened":* Author interview with Tina Flournoy, January 14, 2022.

127 *"dealing with her dysfunction":* Author interview with Gil Duran, January 7, 2022.

129 *"Her portfolio is trash":* Eugene Daniels, Alex Thompson, and Tina Sfondeles, "Major Harris Surrogate Goes Full DGAF," *Politico*, October 8, 2021.

CHAPTER ELEVEN: IT'S A WHOLE NEW BALL GAME

130 *"If I told you":* Author interview with Ron Klain, December 18, 2021.

131 *"a whole new ball game":* Author interview with Andy Slavitt, February 1, 2022.

131 *"That's what led to the decision":* Author interview with Jeffrey Zients, April 14, 2022.

131 *"We've got to be vigilant":* Author interview with Andy Slavitt, October 14, 2021.

133 *"He would bring these stories back":* Author interview with Jeffrey Zients, April 14, 2022.

133 *"That was a really important meeting"*: Author interview with Jeffrey Zients, April 14, 2022.

134 *"have we done everything we can?"*: Author interview with Jeffrey Zients, April 14, 2022.

134 *"He signed off on vaccination requirements"*: Author interview with Jeffrey Zients, April 14, 2022.

134 *"our patience is wearing thin"*: Joe Biden, Remarks at the White House, September 9, 2021.

134 *"People don't like mandates"*: Author interview with Ron Klain, October 30, 2021.

135 *"It's unpleasant"*: Author interview with Ron Klain, October 30, 2021.

136 *"It's a huge psychological thing"*: Author interview with Ron Klain, October 30, 2021.

137 *"Summer from Hell"*: Adam Wren, "Inside Ron Klain's Summer from Hell—and How He Got Here," *Business Insider*, September 12, 2021.

137 *"Hurricane Katrina"*: Author interview with Joshua Bolten, January 22, 2022.

137 *"messaging"*: Paul Waldman, "Opinion: Biden Does Not Have a Messaging Problem. And There's No Messaging Solution," *Washington Post*, November 23, 2021.

137 *"Scranton Joe"*: Tina Sfondeles and Alex Thompson, "Why 'Scranton Joe' Loves Nantucket," *Politico*, November 24, 2021.

138 *"the best prepared person"*: Author interview with Christopher Dodd, November 4, 2021.

138 *"I just need a little breathing room"*: Joe Biden, Remarks at the National League of Cities Congressional City Conference, Marriott Marquis, Washington, D.C., March 14, 2022.

138 *"somewhere out there"*: Waldman, "Opinion: Biden Does Not Have a Messaging Problem."

139 *"a pandemic of the unvaccinated"*: Joe Biden, Remarks at the White House, September 24, 2021.

139 *"we had one hundred million people who were not vaccinated"*: Author interview with Ron Klain, October 30, 2021.

139 *"It's no longer about Delta"*: Author interview with Andy Slavitt, February 1, 2022.

CHAPTER TWELVE: I'M NOT FEARED

140 *"Johnson treatment"*: John Coleman, "The Johnson Treatment: Pushing and Persuading like LBJ," Forbes, June 30, 2018.

140 *"it's personal relationships"*: Author interview with Steve Ricchetti, July 2, 2021.

141 *"American Jobs Plan"*: White House Fact Sheet: The American Jobs Plan, March 31, 2021.

141 *"human infrastructure"*: Susan Milligan, "Biden Sells 'Human Infrastructure' Plan despite Imperiled Bipartisan Package," *US News & World Report*, June 29, 2021.

142 *"he was neither Bernie Sanders nor Elizabeth Warren"*: Author interview with Joshua Bolten, July 20, 2021.

142 *"a working-class populist"*: Author interview with Joshua Bolten, July 20, 2021.

142 *"'Take over the banks!'"*: Author interview with Jonathan Alter, September 2, 2021.

143 *"Roosevelt had polio"*: Author interview with Jonathan Alter, September 2, 2021.

143 *"Not a whit"*: Author interview with Ted Kaufman, July 27, 2021.

143 *"You've gotta be kidding me"*: Author interview with Ted Kaufman, July 27, 2021.

143 *"it's an effort to be like FDR"*: Author interview with Mike Donilon, January 28, 2022.

144 *"FDR was not that good"*: Author interview with James Clyburn, March 4, 2022.

144 *"I need to see more Harry"*: Author interview with James Clyburn, March 4, 2022.

144 "his *strategy and his personality*": Author interview with Steve Ricchetti, July 2, 2021.

145 *"they will not be viewed as unreasonable"*: Author interview with Joshua Bolten, July 20, 2021.

145 *"his ability to get things done"*: Author interview with Ron Klain, March 16, 2021.

145 *"I like Joe"*: Author interview with Marty Walsh, January 25, 2022.

146 *"you're really fucking me"*: Bob Woodward and Robert Costa, *Peril* (New York: Simon & Schuster, 2021), 359.

146 *"bomb thrower"*: Lizzie Widdicombe, "What Does Kyrsten Sinema Really Want?," *The New Yorker*, October 20, 2021.

147 *"Fuck off"*: James Walker, "Kyrsten Sinema Wears 'F*** Off' Ring after Controversial $15 Minimum Wage Vote," *Newsweek*, April 19, 2021.

147 *"could we do infrastructure?"*: Author interview with Mark Warner, January 21, 2022.

147 *"very, very detail focused"*: Author interview with Mark Warner, January 21, 2022.

147 *"Gang of Ten"*: Myah Ward, "GOP Senators See Path to Narrower Infrastructure Deal," *Politico*, May 2, 2021.

148 *"the president was just a master"*: Author interview with Marty Walsh, January 25, 2022.

148 *"we have a deal"*: Joe Biden, Remarks at the White House, June 24, 2021.

149 *"I'm not signing"*: Joe Biden, Remarks at the White House, June 24, 2021.

149 *"No deal by extortion"*: Lindsey Graham, Twitter, June 25, 2021, 10:33 a.m. EST.

149 *"That came very close"*: Author interview with Joshua Bolten, January 22, 2022.

150 *"human infrastructure"*: Milligan, "Biden Sells 'Human Infrastructure' Plan."

150 *"I refuse to choose"*: Ayelet Sheffey, "AOC Slams Biden for Prematurely

Celebrating His Infrastructure Win: 'Messaging It as a Solution Alone Is Going to Get Us in Trouble,'" Yahoo News, November 8, 2021.

150 *"You don't want to get on their bad side"*: Author interview with Peter Baker, November 9, 2021.

151 *"center of energy"*: Author interview with Peter Baker, November 9, 2021.

151 *"you are either getting both bills or neither"*: Jim Tankersley, "Podesta Warns Democrats: Scale Back the $3.5 Trillion Social Policy Bill or Lose Congress," *New York Times*, September 22, 2021.

151 *"part of the sausage making"*: Author interview with Ron Klain, February 6, 2022.

152 *"our majorities are so narrow"*: Author interview with Ron Klain, February 6, 2022.

152 *"Joe Biden is president"*: Morgan Chalfant, "Biden Visits Capitol with Agenda in the Balance," *The Hill*, October 1, 2021.

153 *"we're going to get it done"*: Jonathan Weisman and Emily Cochrane, "Biden Pulls Back on Infrastructure Bill, Tying It to Social Policy Measure," *New York Times*, October 1, 2021.

153 *"We just don't operate that way"*: Author interview with Steve Ricchetti, February 11, 2022.

153 *"the prime minister"*: Mark Leibovich, "The Ascension of Ron Klain," *New York Times*, July 18, 2021.

153 *"I want Ron to succeed"*: Author interview with Andrew Card, January 20, 2022.

154 *"a target on his front and on his back"*: Chris Whipple, Jules Naudet, Gedeon Naudet, and David Hume Kennerly, *The Presidents' Gatekeepers*, Discovery.

154 *"Those aren't the only parts"*: Whipple, Naudet, Naudet, and Kennerly, *The Presidents' Gatekeepers*.

154 *"he's passionate about both"*: Author interview with Marty Walsh, January 25, 2022.

154 *"the White House changed tactics"*: Author interview with Peter Baker, November 9, 2021.

155 *"how do you get this done?"*: Author interview with James Clyburn, March 4, 2022.

155 *"I don't think it's hyperbole"*: Joe Biden, Remarks at the U.S. Capitol, October 28, 2021.

156 *"an incredibly successful visit"*: Author interview with Ron Klain, February 6, 2022.

156 *"in my almost forty years in the Congress"*: Author interview with Christopher Dodd, November 4, 2021.

CHAPTER THIRTEEN: IT'S FIFTY-FIFTY

157 *"last call at night"*: Author interview with Ron Klain, October 30, 2021.

158 *"makes or breaks the presidency"*: Author interview with Ron Klain, October 30, 2021.

158 *"It wasn't our plan"*: Author interview with Ron Klain, October 30, 2021.

158 *"it could still blow up"*: Author interview with Ron Klain, October 30, 2021.

159 *"I think it's fifty-fifty"*: Author interview with Ron Klain, October 30, 2021.

159 *"any one senator could say no"*: Author interview with Ron Klain, October 30, 2021.

160 *"you don't need every single thing"*: Author interview with Ron Klain, October 30, 2021.

160 *"handouts"*: Philip Elliott, "Nobody Should Be Surprised Joe Manchin Killed Biden's Agenda," *Time*, December 20, 2021.

160 *"we are in this morass on Capitol Hill"*: Author interview with Ron Klain, October 30, 2021.

161 *"every week we're on the ten-yard line"*: Author interview with Ron Klain, October 30, 2021.

161 *"that'll be a momentum blow"*: Author interview with Ron Klain, October 30, 2021.

161 *"'The Afghan army is great!'"*: Author interview with Ron Klain, October 30, 2021.

162 *"I love Leon"*: Author interview with Ron Klain, October 30, 2021.

163 *"menacing thunder"*: Lisa Lerer, "Rough Night for Democrats Exposes the Party's Weakness," *New York Times*, November 3, 2021.

163 *"party's motivation has been replaced"*: Lerer, "Rough Night for Democrats."

163 *"this past fall has been a wake-up call"*: Author interview with Christopher Dodd, November 4, 2021.

CHAPTER FOURTEEN: CODE RED

165 *"resort"*: Author interview with John Kerry, February 16, 2022.

165 *"moon suits"*: Author interview with John Kerry, February 16, 2022.

166 *"strategic miscalculation"*: Robin Brant, "Climate-above-All Plea by US Fails to Stir China," BBC News, September 2, 2021.

166 *"I want you to do something"*: Interview with John Kerry, February 16, 2022.

166 *"near and dear to my heart"*: Interview with John Kerry, February 16, 2022.

166 *"revved up and ready to go"*: Author interview with Todd Stern, December 23, 2021.

167 *"code red for humanity"*: Tim Dickinson, "'Code Red for Humanity': New U.N. Climate Report Raises Alarm on Warming," *Rolling Stone*, August 9, 2021.

168 *"nationally determined contributions"*: Author interview with Gina McCarthy, December 10, 2021.

168 *"don't know how this man actually does"*: Author interview with Gina McCarthy, December 10, 2021.

168 *"you gorgeous preppy"*: Kurt Anderson, "'Doonesbury' at War," *New York Times*, June 19, 2005.

169 *"first goal was to show"*: Author interview with Gina McCarthy, December 10, 2021.

169 *"if you can't get them on board"*: Author interview with John Kerry, February 16, 2022.

169 *"Major Emitters Forum"*: Author interview with John Kerry, February 16, 2022.

169 *"we had the EU"*: Author interview with John Kerry, February 16, 2022.

170 *"a person of the big gesture"*: Author interview with Todd Stern, December 23, 2021.

170 *"this isn't going to work"*: Author interview with John Kerry, February 16, 2022.

171 *"He's not going to wear them down"*: Author interview with Todd Stern, December 23, 2021.

171 *"That's not Chinese"*: Author interview with John Kerry, February 16, 2022.

171 *"Xi is making these decisions"*: Author interview with John Kerry, February 16, 2022.

172 *"we're the best"*: Author interview with Gina McCarthy, December 10, 2021.

172 *"horrible four years"*: Author interview with John Kerry, February 16, 2022.

172 *"the single biggest thing we could do to deal with China"*: Author interview with John Kerry, February 16, 2022.

173 *"there's a terrible situation in Washington right now"*: Author interview with John Kerry, February 16, 2022.

173 *"guy jumps off a 100-story building"*: Fatma Khaled, "Joe Biden's Remarkable Week May Just Rescue His Presidency," *Newsweek*, November 7, 2021.

173 *"hot to trot"*: Author interview with John Kerry, February 16, 2022.

173 *"the eyes of history upon us"*: Joe Biden, Remarks at the COP26, Glasgow, Scotland, November 1, 2021.

174 *"you're sitting down":* Author interview with Gina McCarthy, December 10, 2021.

174 *"It took until three in the morning":* Author interview with John Kerry, February 16, 2022.

174 *"And that kills us":* Author interview with John Kerry, February 16, 2022.

175 *"Glasgow was disappointing in a lot of important ways":* Author interview with Todd Stern, December 23, 2021.

CHAPTER FIFTEEN: INFRASTRUCTURE WEEK

177 *"we went upstairs to the residence":* Author interview with Ron Klain, December 18, 2021.

177 *"we were stuck":* Author interview with Ron Klain, December 18, 2021.

178 *"I will get this done":* Author interview with Ron Klain, December 18, 2021.

178 *"to get this across the finish line":* Author interview with Steve Ricchetti, February 11, 2022.

179 *"Time's up":* Author interview with Peter Baker, November 9, 2021.

179 *"Gang of Ten":* Burgess Everett and Marianne Levine, "The Power of 10: Inside the 'Unlikely Partnership' That Sealed an Infrastructure Win," *Politico*, August 10, 2021.

180 *"Hello, Kristen!":* Author interview with Joshua Bolten, January 22, 2022.

180 *"He really should know the first name":* Author interview with Joshua Bolten, January 22, 2022.

180 *"we just kept our heads down":* Author interview with Steve Ricchetti, February 11, 2022.

180 *"one president got it done":* Author interview with Ron Klain, February 6, 2022.

180 *"stop referring to the BBB as huge"*: David Axelrod, Twitter, November 22, 2021, 12:54 p.m. EST.

181 *"I'll put BBB at sixty percent"*: Author interview with Ron Klain, December 18, 2021.

181 *"We've got to get back to one-point-seven-five"*: Author interview with Ron Klain, December 18, 2021.

181 *"I can't get there"*: Joe Manchin, *FOX News Sunday*, Fox News, December 19, 2021.

182 *"Senator Manchin promised to continue"*: Statement from White House Press Secretary Jen Psaki, December 19, 2021.

182 *"I think they overreached"*: Author interview with Joshua Bolten, January 22, 2022.

CHAPTER SIXTEEN: THEY WANT ME TO BE PRESIDENT

184 *"very fine people on both sides"*: Inae Oh, "Trump Defends Claim That There Were 'Very Fine People on Both Sides' of White Supremacist Rally," *Mother Jones*, April 26, 2019.

184 *"I have to speak out"*: Author interview with Mike Donilon, June 29, 2021.

185 *"that long trail emerged"*: Joe Biden, "We Are Living through a Battle for the Soul of this Nation," *The Atlantic*, August 27, 2017.

185 *"the oldest and darkest forces in America"*: Biden, "We Are Living through a Battle."

185 *"battle for the soul of this nation"*: Biden, "We Are Living through a Battle."

185 *"It's nonsense"*: Author interview with Mike Donilon, June 29, 2021.

186 *"I think it's one of the reasons he won"*: Author interview with Mike Donilon, June 29, 2021.

186 *"really doubled down on the Big Lie"*: Author interview with Mike Donilon, January 28, 2022.

186 *"there's truth and there's lies"*: Author interview with Mike Donilon, January 28, 2022.

186 *"I'm speaking to you today"*: Joe Biden, Remarks at the South Court Auditorium, Eisenhower Executive Office Building, January 6, 2022.

187 *"And here is the truth"*: Joe Biden, Remarks at the South Court Auditorium, Eisenhower Executive Office Building, January 6, 2022.

188 *"It was the best speech of his presidency"*: Author interview with Leon Panetta, February 2, 2022.

188 *"Contract with America"*: Newt Gingrich, "A New Contract with America," *Newsweek*, October 1, 2021.

188 *"the president is relevant"*: Peter Keating, "Remembering Oklahoma City, and How Bill Clinton Saved His Presidency," *New York*, April 19, 2010.

188 *"you have not lost everything"*: Bill Clinton, Oklahoma Bombing Memorial Prayer Service Address, Oklahoma City, April 23, 1995.

189 *"everything was going to hell"*: Author interview with Leon Panetta, February 2, 2022.

190 *"carve-out"*: Steve Benen, "To Protect Voting Rights, Dems Eye Carve-Out to Filibuster Rules," *The Maddowblog*, November 4, 2021.

190 *"special rule"*: Congressional Institute, "IX. Special Rules for Major Bills."

191 *"even if you lose, it's okay"*: Author interview with Leon Panetta, February 2, 2022.

191 *"made the extra effort to go and vote on election day"*: Author interview with Ron Klain, February 6, 2022.

191 *"the cradle of civil rights"*: Joe Biden, Remarks at Atlanta University Center Consortium, Atlanta, GA, January 11, 2022.

192 *"I ask every elected official in America"*: Joe Biden, Remarks at Atlanta University Center Consortium, Atlanta, GA, January 11, 2022.

192 *"profoundly unpresidential"*: Mike DeBonis, "Schumer Sets Up Final Senate Confrontation on Voting Rights and the Filibuster," *Washington Post*, January 12, 2022.

192 *"It was an exclusive speech"*: Author interview with Andrew Card, January 20, 2022.

192 *"Give 'em hell, Harry"*: Henry Olsen, "Opinion: Give 'Em Hell, Donald!," *Washington Post*, February 3, 2020.

193 *"the underlying disease of division"*: Ivana Saric, "Sinema Cites 'Disease of Division,' Says She Won't Support Changing Filibuster Rules," Axios, January 13, 2022.

194 *"we can come back and try it a second time"*: Joe Biden, Remarks at the U.S. Capitol, January 13, 2022.

194 *"We knew we didn't have the votes"*: Author interview with Ron Klain, February 6, 2022.

195 *"Russia will be held accountable"*: Joe Biden, Press Conference at the White House, January 19, 2022.

195 *"that's a renewed invasion"*: Jen Psaki, Statement on Russian Aggression toward Ukraine, January 19, 2022.

196 *"I actually like Mitch McConnell"*: Joe Biden, Press Conference at the White House, January 19, 2022.

196 *"Are you kidding me?"*: Joe Biden, Press Conference at the White House, January 19, 2022.

197 *"there's no need to"*: Joe Biden, Press Conference at the White House, January 19, 2022.

198 *"It's going to be hard"*: Joe Biden, Press Conference at the White House, January 19, 2022.

199 *"I think he continued to* think *as a senator"*: Author interview with Leon Panetta, February 2, 2022.

CHAPTER SEVENTEEN: EVERYONE'S GOT A PLAN

200 *"It's a puzzle"*: Author interview with William Burns, April 8, 2022.

201 *"This is much bigger than normal"*: Author interview with Mark Milley, May 27, 2022.

201 *"warning indications"*: Author interview with Mark Milley, May 27, 2022.

201 *"pull-aside"*: Author interview with Antony Blinken, April 20, 2022.

202 *"It was an eye-opener"*: Author interview with Antony Blinken, April 20, 2022.

202 *"honest brokers"*: Chris Whipple, "Op-Ed: Can a New Spymaster Turn Around the Embattled CIA?," *Los Angeles Times*, January 13, 2021.

204 *"I didn't want to risk World War Three"*: Author interview with William Burns, April 8, 2022.

204 *"he was very tempered"*: Author interview with William Burns, April 8, 2022.

204 *"I just came away convinced"*: Author interview with William Burns, April 8, 2022.

204 *"Was that really what this was about"*: Author interview with Antony Blinken, April 20, 2022.

205 *"Can I ask you a question?"*: Author interview with Andrew Card, March 11, 2022.

206 *"trustworthy"*: Sam Levine, "George W. Bush Warns That Putin Won't Stop Unless Someone Stands Up to Him," *HuffPost*, March 2, 2017.

206 *"a sense of his soul"*: Levine, "George W. Bush Warns."

206 *"Every dictator knows the game"*: Author interview with Garry Kasparov, January 18, 2018.

206 *"reset"*: Patrick Healy and Jonathan Martin, "At Republican Gathering, All Talk Is of Hillary Clinton (None of It Is Good)," *New York Times*, April 18, 2015.

207 *"whether Putin was Putin all along"*: Author interview with Anthony Lake, March 14, 2022.

207 *"instead of standing on principles"*: Garry Kasparov, *Winter Is Coming* (New York: Public Affairs, 2015), xii.

208 *"Putin fomented a war"*: Kasparov, *Winter Is Coming*, x.

208 *"I don't think you have a soul"*: Evan Osnos, "The Biden Agenda," *The New Yorker*, July 20, 2014.

208 *"I do"*: Philip Bump, "On the Novelty of Calling a Killer a Killer," *Washington Post*, March 18, 2021.

209 *"stable and predictable"*: Jim Risch, "Opinion: Biden Wants Russia's Cooperation. But Putin Thrives on Chaos," *Washington Post*, June 11, 2021.

209 *"Everyone has a plan"*: Mike Berardino, "Mike Tyson Explains One of His Most Famous Quotes," *South Florida Sun Sentinel*, November 9, 2012.

CHAPTER EIGHTEEN: CHRONICLE OF A DEATH FORETOLD

210 *"false flag"*: Davey Alba, "Russia Has Been Laying Groundwork Online for a 'False Flag' Operation, Misinformation Researchers Say," *New York Times*, February 19, 2022.

211 *"we had some extraordinary intelligence"*: Author interview with Antony Blinken, April 20, 2022.

211 *"You could see the Russians kind of floundering"*: Author interview with William Burns, April 8, 2022.

211 *"body of lies and false narratives"*: Morgan Chalfant and Rebecca Beitsch, "Biden's CIA Head Leads the Charge against Putin's Information War," *The Hill*, March 13, 2022.

212 *"looked like he hadn't slept in a week"*: Author interview with Richard Clarke, December 13, 2021.

212 *"do everything possible to reengage"*: Author interview with Antony Blinken, April 20, 2022.

213 *"a big part of this is showing up"*: Author interview with Antony Blinken, April 20, 2022.

214 *"Our teams have met"*: Author interview with Phil Gordon, April 3, 2022.

214 *"shopping spree"*: Adriana Diaz, "Kamala Harris Spends $500 on Cookware at a Store in Paris," *Daily Mail*, November 25, 2021.

215 *"engagements"*: Author interview with Ned Price, March 16, 2022.

215 *"Tiger Teams"*: Ellen Nakashima and Ashley Parker, "Inside the White House Preparations for a Russian Invasion," *Washington Post*, February 14, 2022.

215 *"massive consequences and severe cost"*: Lara Jakes, "Diplomats Warn Russia of 'Massive Consequences' If It Invades Ukraine," *New York Times*, December 12, 2021.

216 *"hybrid warfare"*: Daniel Baer, "Biden May Be Outplaying Putin in One Critical Way," *Washington Post*, February 9, 2022.

216 *"This is much bigger than what we've observed before"*: Author interview with Mark Milley, May 27, 2022.

216 *"What's driving this?"*: Author interview with Antony Blinken, April 20, 2022.

217 *"there were places where the Venn diagram overlapped"*: Author interview with Karen Donfried, March 21, 2021.

217 *"it will reshape the world"*: Author interview with Bill Russo, March 16, 2022.

218 *"creating a panic"*: Callie Patteson, "Zelensky Rebukes Western 'Panic' over Russia Invasion Fear after Biden Call," *New York Post*, January 28, 2022.

219 *"no limits"*: Alexandra Stevenson and Keith Bradsher, "China Has Tools to Help Russia's Economy. None Are Big Enough to Save It," *New York Times*, March 11, 2022.

219 *"You are not our enemy"*: Joe Biden, Remarks at the White House, February 15, 2022.

221 *"Davos for Defense"*: Reuters Staff, "No Russia at This Year's Munich Security Conference—Event Chair," Reuters, February 14, 2022.

221 *"appeasement"*: Jennifer Szalai, "In 'Appeasement,' How Peace with the Nazis Was Always an Illusion," *New York Times*, June 4, 2019.

221 *"Her political instincts have been inconsistent"*: Cleve R. Wootson, Jr., Ashley Parker, and John Hudson, "In Munich during a Tumultuous Time, Harris Faces Her Biggest International Spotlight," *Washington Post*, February 16, 2022.

221 *"the mistakes of the twentieth century"*: "Zelensky's Full Speech at Munich Security Conference," *The Kyiv Independent*, February 19, 2022.

222 *"America's commitment to Article Five is ironclad"*: Kamala Harris, Remarks at the Hotel Bayerischer Hof, Munich, Germany, February 19, 2022.

222 *"you really need to take this seriously"*: Author interview with Phil Gordon, April 3, 2022.

223 *"Modern Ukraine was entirely and fully created by Russia"*: Vladimir Putin, Remarks on RT, February 21, 2022.

223 *"No matter who tries to stand in our way"*: Vladimir Putin, Remarks on RT, February 24, 2022.

224 *"I can't believe it"*: Author interview with Ron Klain, March 26, 2022.

CHAPTER NINETEEN: NO ONE ELSE CAN DO THIS

226 *"It's been an eye-opener"*: Author interview with John Kerry, February 16, 2022.

226 *"I believe we have to change"*: Author interview with John Kerry, February 16, 2022.

226 *"He wants to try to change"*: Author interview with John Kerry, February 16, 2022.

227 *"President Xi hasn't left China"*: Author interview with Ron Klain, March 26, 2022.

227 *"we can make this happen"*: Author interview with Gina McCarthy, September 30, 2021.

227 *"he's good at that stuff"*: Author interview with John Kerry, February 16, 2022.

227 *"I think we're making some headway"*: Author interview with Ron Klain, March 26, 2022.

228 *"There will still be a planet here"*: Author interview with John Kerry, February 16, 2022.

CHAPTER TWENTY: THIS MAN CANNOT REMAIN IN POWER

229 *"Tonight is definitely the night"*: Author interview with Ron Klain, May 21, 2022.

229 *"The president was painfully aware"*: Author interview with Ron Klain, May 21, 2022.

229 *"an awful lot of destruction and death"*: Author interview with William Burns, April 8, 2022.

230 *"There's a big difference"*: Author interview with Mark Milley, May 27, 2022.

231 *"We thought their performance would be much better"*: Author interview with Mark Milley, May 27, 2022.

232 *"They didn't think they needed to"*: Author interview with William Burns, April 8, 2022.

232 *"aggressive statements"*: Vladimir Putin, Remarks on RT, February 27, 2022.

233 *"I need ammunition, not a ride"*: Patrick Reilly, "'I Need Ammunition, Not a Ride': Zelensky Declines US Evacuation Offer," *New York Post*, February 26, 2022.

233 *"a Churchillian-like figure"*: Author interview with William Burns, April 8, 2022.

233 *"You're still saying that"*: Author interview with Antony Blinken, April 20, 2022.

235 *"never sanctioned the central bank"*: Author interview with Karen Donfried, March 21, 2022.

235 *"we are doing what we can to help Ukraine"*: Author interview with Ron Klain, March 26, 2022.

236 *"no-fly zone"*: Luke Broadwater and Chris Cameron, "U.S. Lawmakers Say They Are Largely Opposed to a No-Fly Zone over Ukraine," *New York Times*, March 6, 2022.

236 *"We talked about no-fly zones"*: Author interview with Mark Milley, May 27, 2022.

236 *"World War III"*: Steve Nelson, "'That's Called World War III': Biden Defends Decision Not to Send Jets to Ukraine," *New York Post*, March 11, 2022.

236 *"defensive"*: Stephen Biddle, "Is There a Difference between 'Defensive' and 'Offensive' Weapons?," *Washington Post*, April 28, 2022.

236 *"offensive"*: Biddle, "Is There a Difference?" *Washington Post*, April 28, 2022.

237 *"strategic ambiguity"*: Andrew E. Kramer, "Ukrainian Official Outlines Intentional Ambiguity on Strikes inside Russia," *New York Times*, April 30, 2022.

237 *"Blood and Soil"*: Claudia Rankine, "Was Charlottesville the Exception or the Rule?," *New York Times*, September 13, 2017.

237 *"that's not how I think of this"*: Joe Biden, Remarks at NATO Headquarters, Brussels, Belgium, March 24, 2022.

238 *"I made a determination"*: Joe Biden, Remarks at NATO Headquarters, Brussels, Belgium, March 24, 2022.

239 *"That's not what I said"*: Joe Biden, Remarks at NATO Headquarters, Brussels, Belgium, March 24, 2022.

240 *"Be not afraid"*: Joe Biden, Remarks at the Royal Castle, Warsaw, Poland, March 26, 2022.

241 *"Russia has strangled democracy"*: Joe Biden, Remarks at the Royal Castle, Warsaw, Poland, March 26, 2022.

242 *"I'm going to leave it in"*: Chris Whipple, *The Gatekeepers: How the White House Chiefs of Staff Define Every Presidency* (New York: Crown, 2017), 156.

242 *"Mr. Gorbachev, tear down this wall!"*: James Mann, "Tear Down That Myth," *New York Times*, June 10, 2007.

242 *"this man cannot remain in power"*: Joe Biden, Remarks at the Royal Castle, Warsaw, Poland, March 26, 2022.

242 *"The president's point"*: Ashley Parker and Tyler Pager, "Biden Says Putin 'Cannot Remain in Power' in Forceful Speech in Poland," *Washington Post*, March 26, 2022.

243 *"a troubling distraction"*: Chris Megerian and Aamer Madhani, "Biden Finds No Respite at Home after Returning from Europe," apnews .com, March 27, 2022.

243 *"I continue to speak to President Putin"*: "Live Updates: Macron Cool on Biden's Comments about Putin," apnews.com, March 27, 2022.

243 *"no one will remember anything from that speech"*: George Packer, "I Worry We'll Soon Forget about Ukraine," *The Atlantic*, April 10, 2022.

243 *"I'm not walking anything back"*: Joe Biden, Remarks at the White House, March 28, 2022.

244 *"Hell, no!"*: Author interview with Leon Panetta, April 7, 2022.

244 *"the president has committed the truth"*: John Podesta, conversation with the author, Longworth House Office Building, Washington, D.C., April 26, 2022.

CHAPTER TWENTY-ONE: BIDEN OF BROOKLYN

245 *"We can't endure this anymore"*: David Leonhardt, "Nine Mass Shootings," *New York Times*, March 23, 2022.

245 *"a dark new form of American exceptionalism"*: Leonhardt, "Nine Mass Shootings."

246 *"I know what works"*: Joe Biden, State of the Union speech, March 1, 2022.

246 *"defunding the police"*: Christy E. Lopez, "Defund the Police? Here's What That Really Means," *Washington Post*, June 7, 2020.

247 *"burn, baby, burn"*: Fred P. Graham, "Law; a Look at 'Burn, Baby Burn!,'" *New York Times*, January 28, 1968.

247 *"We lost the whole civil rights movement"*: Author interview with James Clyburn, March 4, 2022.

247 *"Jaime Harrison's campaign plateaued"*: Author interview with James Clyburn, March 4, 2022.

247 *"there's nothing to talk about"*: Author interview with Cedric Richmond, March 2, 2022.

248 *"Joe brings the ordinary guy approach":* Author interview with Eric Adams, March 21, 2022.

248 *"broken windows":* Azi Paybarah, "Giuliani on Broken Windows: 'You Don't Enforce Every Rule,'" *Politico*, August 8, 2014.

248 *"stop and frisk":* David Aaro, "What Is 'Stop and Frisk'? Controversial Policing Technique Explained," foxnews.com, February 11, 2020.

249 *"Eric, I want to help you":* Author interview with Eric Adams, March 21, 2022.

249 *"let me look into it":* Author interview with Eric Adams, March 21, 2022.

249 *"they call me the Biden of Brooklyn":* Alex Thompson, Sally Goldenberg, and Tina Sfondeles, "The Biden of Brooklyn," *Politico*, July 12, 2021.

249 *"It's a good partnership":* Author interview with Ron Klain, February 6, 2022.

250 *"Enough is enough":* Joe Biden, Remarks at One Police Plaza, New York, NY, February 3, 2022.

250 *"ghost guns":* Lauren Egan and Shannon Pettypiece, "Biden Targets 'Ghost Guns' and 'Red Flag' Laws in New Gun Control Measures," NBCNews.com, April 8, 2021.

250 *"We talked about our families":* Author interview with Eric Adams, March 21, 2022.

251 *"He likes what Adams is doing":* Author interview with Ron Klain, February 6, 2022.

252 *"we still feel an affection for Biden":* Jim Pasco, *Morning Edition*, NPR, July 8, 2021.

252 *"There's a level of discomfort for Democrats":* Author interview with Eric Adams, March 21, 2022.

CHAPTER TWENTY-TWO: A HAND WORSE THAN FDR'S

254 *"We'd been going twenty-four-seven for a year":* Author interview with Jeffrey Zients, April 14, 2022.

254 *"We knew what to do"*: Author interview with Jeffrey Zients, April 14, 2022.

254 *"We interrupted the president's Thanksgiving"*: Author interview with Jeffrey Zients, April 14, 2022.

255 *"there's a new variant that appears to be more transmissible"*: Author interview with Jeffrey Zients, April 14, 2022.

255 *"the most important thing"*: Author interview with Jeffrey Zients, April 14, 2022.

255 *"the vaccines worked"*: Author interview with Jeffrey Zients, April 14, 2022.

256 *"We had the most successful first year"*: Author interview with Ron Klain, December 18, 2021.

256 *"I think the parallels with the Biden administration are there"*: Author interview with Jack Watson, April 29, 2022.

257 *"It touches everything"*: Author interview with Jack Watson, April 29, 2022.

257 *"God dealt him a terrible hand"*: Author interview with Ron Klain, December 18, 2021.

259 "Vice *President Biden"*: Barack Obama, Remarks at the White House, April 5, 2022.

259 *"That was a* joke*"*: Barack Obama, Remarks at the White House, April 5, 2022.

259 *"That was all set up"*: Barack Obama, Remarks at the White House, April 5, 2022.

259 *"coming back here gives me a chance to say thank you"*: Barack Obama, Remarks at the White House, April 5, 2022.

261 *"Joe Biden is unwell"*: Tyler Olson, "Rick Scott Says Biden Is 'Unwell' and Should Resign, As President Hammers 'Ultra-MAGA' Agenda," foxnews.com, May 10, 2022.

261 *"everybody was absolutely exhausted"*: Author interview with Bruce Reed, July 30, 2021.

CHAPTER TWENTY-THREE: THE WAY THE STORY ENDS

265 *"she's a very rigorous cross-examiner":* Author interview with Phil Gordon, April 3, 2022.

265 *"I want to be very clear":* Kamala Harris, Joint Press Conference with President Andrzej Duda of Poland, Belweder Palace, Warsaw, Poland, March 10, 2022.

266 *"paying off for this guy":* Author interview with Leon Panetta, April 7, 2022.

267 *"I don't have any doubt":* Author interview with Antony Blinken, April 20, 2022.

268 *"remain a sovereign country":* Missy Ryan and Annabelle Timsit, "U.S. Wants Russian Military 'Weakened' from Ukraine Invasion, Austin Says," *Washington Post*, April 25, 2022.

268 *"Weakening Russia":* Natasha Bertrand, Kylie Atwood, Kevin Liptak, and Alex Marquardt, "Austin's Assertion That US Wants to 'Weaken' Russia Underlines Biden Strategy Shift," CNNPolitics, April 26, 2022.

268 *"We don't know how the rest of this war will unfold":* Antony Blinken, Remarks to Traveling Press, Southeastern Poland, April 25, 2022.

269 *"children":* Meg Kelly and Karly Domb Sadof, "New Satellite Imagery Shows Bombed-Out Mariupol Theater," *Washington Post*, March 19, 2022.

269 *"our response to counterstrikes will be lightning fast":* Vladimir Putin, Meeting with Council of Lawmakers, St. Petersburg, Russia, April 27, 2022.

269 *"We've done a variety of assessments":* Author interview with William Burns, April 8, 2022.

270 *"It's been a mark of strong leadership":* Author interview with William Burns, April 8, 2022.

270 *the U.S. had shared intelligence:* Julian E. Barnes, Helene Cooper, and Eric Schmitt, "U.S. Intelligence is Helping Ukraine Kill Russian Generals, Officials Say," *New York Times*, May 4, 2022.

270 *"publicly taunting the Russians":* Author interview with Ron Klain, May 21, 2022.

271 *"he can't afford a loss"*: Author interview with William Burns, April 8, 2022.

272 *"the Achilles' heels of autocracies"*: Author interview with Antony Blinken, April 20, 2022.

CHAPTER TWENTY-FOUR: MOTHER'S DAY IN UKRAINE

274 *"war criminal"*: David E. Sanger, "By Labeling Putin a 'War Criminal,' Biden Personalizes the Conflict," *New York Times*, March 17, 2022.

274 *"speaking from his heart"*: Jen Psaki, White House Press Briefing, March 16, 2022.

274 *"this is about moms"*: Author interview with Anthony Bernal, May 24, 2022.

274 *"Ten minutes and you're inside the country"*: Author interview with Anthony Bernal, May 24, 2022.

275 *"they're going to bomb her where we are"*: Author interview with Anthony Bernal, May 24, 2022.

275 *"Could we do it safely?"*: Author interview with Anthony Bernal, May 24, 2022.

275 *"it was possible"*: Author interview with Anthony Bernal, May 24, 2022.

275 *"Oh my God"*: Author interview with Anthony Bernal, May 24, 2022.

276 *"we're not going to go"*: Author interview with Anthony Bernal, May 24, 2022.

276 *"Something is missing"*: Jill Biden, "What Ukrainian Mothers Taught Me about This War," cnn.com, May 13, 2022.

276 *"It's senseless"*: Katie Rogers, "Jill Biden's Secret Ukraine Trip," *New York Times*, May 8, 2022.

277 *"Do you feel it?"*: Ken Bredemeier, "US First Lady Jill Biden Makes Surprise Stop in Ukraine," *VOA*, May 8, 2022.

278 *"Maybe there's an op-ed"*: Author interview with Anthony Bernal, May 24, 2022.

279 *"She had to fight"*: Author interview with Elizabeth Alexander, May 23, 2022.

280 *"she went to Kentucky after the big tornado"*: Author interview with Elizabeth Alexander, May 23, 2022.

280 *"from early in the morning until late at night"*: Author interview with Ron Klain, May 21, 2022.

281 *"unity"*: Christina Wilkie, "Biden Unveils a New 'Unity Agenda' at His First State of the Union Address," cnbc.com, March 2, 2022.

281 *"this is what people are saying"*: Author interview with Ron Klain, May 21, 2022.

281 *"She's a teacher at her core"*: Author interview with Elizabeth Alexander, May 10, 2022.

281 *"a full-throated, unflinching repudiation"*: Josh Gerstein and Alexandra Ward, "Supreme Court Has Voted to Overturn Abortion Rights, Draft Opinion Shows," *Politico*, May 2, 2022.

282 *"leaders who are trying to weaponize"*: Kamala Harris, Remarks at EMILY's List National Conference and Gala, May 3, 2022.

283 *"rocked millions of Americans"*: Jennifer Rubin, "Opinion: Kamala Harris Finally Found Her Moment and Her Message," *Washington Post*, May 4, 2022.

283 *"we have to take actions"*: Jill Biden, *Symone*, MSNBC, May 8, 2022.

CHAPTER TWENTY-FIVE: THE MAGA CROWD

284 *"replacement theory"*: Dustin Jones, "What Is the 'Great Replacement' and How Is It Tied to the Buffalo Shooting Suspect?," npr.org, May 16, 2022.

284 *"we're in one of those moments"*: Joe Biden, Remarks at Seward Park, Seattle, WA, April 22, 2022.

285 *"this is going to start to change"*: Joe Biden, Remarks at Seward Park, Seattle, WA, April 22, 2022.

286 *"apartments they controlled"*: Maria Cramer and Neil Vigdor, "2 Men

Posing as Federal Agents Duped Secret Service, U.S. Says," *New York Times*, April 7, 2022.

286 *"'migration' of data"*: Luke Broadwater, "Secret Service Text Messages Around Jan. 6 Were Erased, Inspector General Says," *New York Times*, July 14, 2022.

287 *"nothing could be done"*: Carol D. Leonnig and Maria Sacchetti, "Secret Service cannot recover texts; no new details for Jan. 6 committee," *Washington Post*, July 19, 2022.

287 *"I'm not getting in the car"*: Aaron Blake, "A Top Democrat Ties Pence's 'I'm Not Getting in the Car' to Jan. 6 'Coup,'" *Washington Post*, April 26, 2022.

287 *"He knew exactly"*: Blake, "A Top Democrat."

287 *"something that we're living with"*: Author interview with Mike Donilon, January 28, 2022.

288 *"cockamamie"*: Mark Caputo, Peter Nicholas, and Allan Smith, "Trump Leaves Pa. GOP Fuming over 'Cockamamie' Primaries. Next Up: Georgia," NBCNews.com, May 19, 2022.

288 *"the Trump act is almost over"*: Author interview with Leon Panetta, April 7, 2022.

288 *"the former guy"*: Oma Seddiq, "Biden Says He's 'Tired of Talking' about 'Former Guy' Trump in First Town Hall as President," *Business Insider*, February 16, 2021.

288 *"he thought that Trumpism would kind of fade"*: Author interview with Ron Klain, May 21, 2022.

289 *"replacement theory"*: Jones, "What Is the 'Great Replacement'?," npr .org, May 16, 2022.

289 *"evil will not win"*: Joe Biden, Remarks at Delavan Grider Community Center, Buffalo, NY, May 17, 2022.

290 *"That's what it is"*: Joe Biden, Remarks at Delavan Grider Community Center, Buffalo, NY, May 17, 2022.

CHAPTER TWENTY-SIX: THE FIGHT OF HIS LIFE

291 *"the president came out of the Oval Office"*: Chris Whipple, Jules Naudet, Gedeon Naudet, and David Hume Kennerly, *The Presidents' Gatekeepers*, Discovery.

292 *"Inflation Reduction Act"*: Lisa Mascaro, "What's in, and out, of Democrats' inflation-fighting package," *Washington Post*, July 28, 2022.

293 *"we've had a lot of big days"*: Author interview with President Joe Biden, September 19, 2022.

294 *"The most emotional moment for me"*: Author interview with President Joe Biden, September 19, 2022.

294 *PACT Act:* White House Fact Sheet: PACT Act Delivers on President Biden's Promise to America's Veterans, August 2, 2022.

294 *"Biden was convinced"*: Matt Viser, "Biden wonders publicly whether burn pits caused his son's death. Activists want him to do more on the issue," *Washington Post*, November 28, 2021.

295 *"independence from a deadly virus"*: Joe Biden, Remarks at the White House, July 4, 2021.

295 *"Mission Accomplished"*: "White House Clarifies 'Mission Accomplished' Sign," *The Bryant Park Project*, NPR, May 1, 2008.

295 *"we want to unify the country"*: Author interview with Ron Klain, May 21, 2022.

296 *"big picture of democracy versus autocracy"*: Author interview with Leon Panetta, April 7, 2022.

297 *"war in Ukraine has really strengthened Joe Biden's image"*: Author interview with Leon Panetta, April 7, 2022.

298 *"would have to be a passionate Manichaean"*: William Manchester, *The Last Lion* (New York: Little, Brown, 1983), 4.

298 *"President Putin thought his invasion would be over in days"*: Author interview with President Joe Biden, September 19, 2022.

299 *"America's goal here is straightforward"*: Author interview with President Joe Biden, September 19, 2022.

300 *"they're probably lying"*: Andy Card, statement to the author, Vail Symposium, Vail, CO, September 8, 2022.

300 *"Aging is such an extremely individual thing"*: Jack Watson, statement to the author, Vail Symposium, Vail, CO, September 8, 2022.

300 *"Watch me"*: Joe Biden, *60 Minutes*, CBS, September 18, 2022.

301 *"placed a strong second in the New Hampshire primary"*: Terence McArdle, "Eugene McCarthy vs. LBJ: The New Hampshire primary showdown that changed everything 50 years ago," *Washington Post*, March 12, 2018.

301 *"I intend to run"*: Author interview with President Joe Biden, September 19, 2022.

AFTERWORD: GET UP!

303 *"Get up"*: Joe Biden, *Promises to Keep: On Life and Politics* (New York: Random House, 2007), Kindle location 237.

303 *"foundational principle"*: Biden, *Promises to Keep*, Kindle location 237.

303 *"The newspapers are calling you a plagiarist"*: Biden, *Promises to Keep*, Kindle location 252.

304 *Biden put out a statement:* Statement from President Biden on the Build Back Better Act, December 16, 2021.

304 *Manchin had announced that he was done:* Joe Manchin, *Fox News Sunday*, FOX News, December 19, 2021.

304 *"sudden and inexplicable reversal"*: Statement from Press Secretary Jen Psaki, December 19, 2021.

305 *"everyone likes to have as their model Lyndon Johnson"*: Author interview with Ron Klain, October 8, 2022.

307 *"It was slow"*: Author interview with Ron Klain, October 8, 2022.

307 *"He has a DEATH WISH"*: Donald Trump, *Truth Social*, September 30, 2022.

309 *"there's no room for violence anywhere"*: Gregory S. Schneider and Mea-

gan Flynn, "Youngkin draws ire with Pelosi comment that Democrats call insensitive," *Washington Post*, October 28, 2022.

309 *"animal":* Olivia Olander, "Trump calls Pelosi 'an animal'," *Politico*, November 7, 2022.

310 *"I have served in elected office for almost two decades":* Email from Vice President Kamala Harris to the author, October 21, 2022.

312 *"red wave":* Toluse Olorunnipa, "Democrats fear midterm drubbing as party leaders rush to defend blue seats," *Washington Post*, November 3, 2022.

312 *"It is not a faith shared by everyone":* Peter Baker, "As Midterms Near, Biden Faces a Nation as Polarized as Ever," *New York Times*, November 7, 2022.

313 *"some have come to view Klain as a micromanager":* Eli Stokols and Alex Thompson, "Staff changes are coming to the White House. Will Klain be part of them?" *Politico*, November 8, 2022.

314 *"Maybe we don't suck as much as people thought":* Email to the author from Ron Klain, November 9, 2022.

314 *"head-scratching":* Chris Cillizza, "Joe Biden's head-scratching democracy speech, *CNNpolitics.com*, November 3, 2022.

314 *"Very proud":* Email to the author from Ron Klain, November 9, 2022.

315 *"normal":* Mike Barnicle, *Morning Joe*, MSNBC, November 9, 2022.

315 *"Biden's ability":* Author interview with Jack Watson, November 9, 2022.

316 *"We can have a big debate":* Author interview with Ron Klain, October 8, 2022.

317 *"We have not faced the prospect of Armageddon":* Katie Rogers and David E. Sanger, "Biden calls the 'prospect of Armageddon' the highest since the Cuban missile crisis," *New York Times*, October 6, 2022.

317 *"He's very focused on being prepared":* Author interview with Ron Klain, October 8, 2022.

318 *"Their plan is to literally kill people":* Carol D. Leonnig, "Secret Service knew of Capitol threat more than a week before Jan. 6," *Washington Post*, October 13, 2022.

318 *"Could be sporty after dark"*: Carol D. Leonnig, "Secret Service knew of Capitol threat more than a week before Jan. 6," *Washington Post*, October 13, 2022.

318 *"Can you believe I lost to this f—ing guy?"*: Ashley Parker, "Jan. 6 hearing shows Trump knew he lost—even while claiming otherwise," *Washington Post*, October 14, 2022.

318 *"He had all of this information"*: Ashley Parker, "Jan. 6 hearing shows Trump knew he lost—even while claiming otherwise," *Washington Post*, October 14, 2022.

319 *"the candidate who gets the most votes in 2024"*: Author interview with Ron Klain, October 8, 2022.

319 *"Was there going to be a Biden presidency?"*: Author interview with Ron Klain, October 8, 2022.

INDEX

ABOUT THE AUTHOR

Chris Whipple is an author, political analyst, and Emmy Award–winning documentary filmmaker. He is a frequent guest on MSNBC, CNN, and NPR, and has contributed essays to *The New York Times*, *The Washington Post*, *Los Angeles Times*, and *Vanity Fair*. His first book, *The Gatekeepers*, an analysis of the position of White House Chief of Staff, was a *New York Times* bestseller. His critically acclaimed follow-up, *The Spymasters*, was based upon interviews with nearly every living CIA director. Whipple lives in New York City with his wife, Cary.